OLDER OFFENDERS

OLDER OFFENDERS

Perspectives in Criminology and Criminal Justice

EDITED BY Belinda McCarthy *and*
Robert Langworthy

FOREWORD BY Donald J. Newman

PRAEGER

New York
Westport, Connecticut
London

Library of Congress Cataloging-in-Publication Data

Older offenders.

Bibliography: p.
Includes index.
1. Aged offenders—United States. 2. Crime and age.
I. McCarthy, Belinda Rodgers. II. Langworthy, Robert H.
HV6791.043 1988 364.3'0880564 87-7147
ISBN 0-275-92734-2 (alk. paper)

Library of Congress Catalog Card Number: 87-7147
ISBN: 0-275-92734-2

First published in 1988

Praeger Publishers, One Madison Avenue, New York, NY 10010
A division of Greenwood Press, Inc.

Printed in the United States of America

The paper used in this book complies with the
Permanent Paper Standard issued by the National
Information Standards Organization (Z39.48-1984).

10 9 8 7 6 5 4 3 2 1

To B.B., J.H., D.S. and J.S., for their support and enthusiasm
for all aspects of scholarly endeavor.

Contents

SECTION II
PERSPECTIVES IN CRIMINOLOGY

SECTION III
PERSPECTIVES IN CRIMINAL JUSTICE

List of Figures and Tables

FIGURES

TABLES

Foreword

No matter how each term is defined, "elderly criminal" seems somehow incongruous, ludicrous, even—bringing to mind *Arsenic and Old Lace* or the over-the-hill gang—and, at best a trivial problem. "Elderly crime victim" is much more understandable, pathetic in fact. Granny-bashing is as repellent as child abuse.

Yet two major trends in American society, crime and aging, are inexorably creeping upward. Crime rates may fluctuate because of all sorts of factors from police reporting procedures to legislative "get-tough," (or, more rarely, decriminalizing) actions. But the aging of our population is certain, and, with the exception of some booms and echo booms in birth rates, nearly linear as we simultaneously move toward zero population growth and increased longevity.

Serious social science research in American criminology is really only a little over a half-century old. This can be disputed, I suppose, by naming a few studies by a few pioneers of earlier times. But major scientific attention to accurate crime measurement and the development of theories of crime measurement and the development of theories of crime causation is comparatively recent. And criminal justice, meaning the careful analysis of the processing of suspected to convicted criminals is even newer, dating, with the exception of a few early crime commisson reports, only since World War II.

One of the most interesting things about the development of criminology as an academic discipline and a basis for the testing of causal hypotheses, is that much, perhaps most, of the early work really rested on studies of juvenile delinquents, not criminals at all. From the Chicago Area Project, the *Jack Roller* and up to Ohlin and Cloward's *Delinquency and Opportunity,* kids, not adults, were used to develop theoretical models and to generalize about crime. We talked seriously of "burnout" at about age 30.

Criminal justice, on the other hand, focused mostly on the processing of adult felons, though God alone knows how many studies of the juvenile court and juvenile training schools have been made. But criminal justice, like criminology, also accepted the 30-year-old burn-out age. White-collar criminals and some gangsters were exceptions, of course, but viewed really as separate problems, both theoretically and operationally. Social scientists and cops and wardens all dealt with young people who committed ordinary street crimes and who, if not juvenile delinquents, were for the most part young adults, cohorts really of college students.

Not only does a large block of criminological theory rest on studies of the young, but our criminal justice system, with all its hardware from handcuffs to prison walls, is designed to apprehend and control the mobile, the strong, the runners and the fighters among our criminal populations. We are geared up for the young, the reckless, the psychopathic, the rootless, the tough young *man* (with more attention in recent years to his female counterpart).

Now along comes the problem, still not numerically very large, of elderly criminals, of old or at least older people who commit ordinary crimes from larceny to homicide. How do they fit into the theories of criminology and into the processes of criminal justice? Are they products of differential association? Control theory? Are the guns and leg-irons necessary or even appropriate for these criminals? Do we need a geriatric court as we have a separate court for juveniles? Should we have special police units as we have "diaper dicks" for juveniles? Where do we stand in regard to gang behavior? Is there an elderly counterpart to the school dropout?

The easiest thing to do is to dismiss these problems lightly, to chuckle even when the issues are raised. After all, there is certainly no epidemic of elderly crime. Oh? Perhaps not in the nation as a whole but what about in Miami and other clustering points for the elderly? And, much as we may deplore it, we are collectively getting older. It has been called the "graying" of America and the major issues are seen to be economic support, medical care, housing, and all the other pressures and problems assumed to be the province of gerontologists. And they are. There is no doubt that an aging population will create ripples and waves in our social order now only dimly perceived.

And the bottom line is that the number of elderly criminals will also increase. Even if the crime rate (for any offense) remains the same or for some reason declines, we will still have more elderly criminals simply because we will have more old people. Young-old, middle-old, and old-old will all increase and, indeed, with dietary and medical research going full blast, our old will get older and become a larger proportion of our total population. We are closing grade schools, merging high schools, not building new colleges (though we are building new prisons), but our nursing homes and retirement communities are booming.

Perhaps the most fascinating thing about the problem of elderly crime is that we can see it coming; predict its growth. It is rare we have this opportunity or this challenge. Who predicted an AIDS epidemic? or Crack? But elderly crime, in much more significant numbers than now, is on the way. And, in general, we are still unprepared for it. Sure there are programs and practices designed especially for elderly offenders in some places but, overall, we are still waiting without plan or policy.

This book by Belinda McCarthy and Bob Langworthy, while not the first in the field, is probably the most comprehensive in dealing with both criminological theory *and* with major criminal justice processing points in the study and treatment of elderly offenders. Overall, this is a sweeping book. Both theories and practices are analyzed as they fit elderly criminal populations. As far as I know, this is the only work that has really attempted to cross both fields: criminology and criminal justice. Naturally, anyone in these fields (or between them as many of us are) should read this book. So should gerontologists and criminal justice planners. Now is the time to really think about and prepare for the coming increment in elderly crime. In doing so, this book is a must.

Donald J. Newman
Professor
School of Criminal Justice
SUNY-Albany

Acknowledgments

We would like to thank the Society for Interdisciplinary Research on Elderly Offenders (SIREO) for their assistance in identifying potential contributors to the monograph. We thank the contributors for their scholarship and the spirit of cooperation in which they worked with us through all stages of the editorial process. The University of Alabama at Birmingham supported the typing of the manuscript, and we are grateful for that assistance. Finally, we would like to thank Jeanne Holloway—typist, copyeditor and friend—for her invaluable aid and her unfailing dedication.

Introduction:

Elderly Crime and the Criminal Justice System Response: Conceptualizing the Problem

Belinda McCarthy
Robert Langworthy

THE PROBLEM OF ELDERLY CRIME

Until recently, most writers on crime and aging introduced their research with the question "Should we study older offenders?" Underlying this question were two assumptions: that in order to justify the study of a phenomenon, one had to first make the argument that the phenomenon was significant in size and scope, and second, provide documentation that the phenomena represented a compelling social problem. It is our position that these assumptions have little merit.

The study of deviance is grounded in the knowledge that that which is different is important for study precisely because it is uncommon and infrequent, because it is not the norm. To set arbitrary standards on how frequent or infrequent an event must occur in order to make it worthy of study ignores one of the basic premises of deviance theory: studying the uncommon tells us much about that which is routine. While it is certainly true that some conditions—events that are so rare as to make the identification of a pattern impossible—cannot be systematically studied, this was never the case regarding elderly crime.

National and state level statistics on elderly crime and incarceration patterns, the same data used to study younger offenders, are available to study older offenders as well. Perhaps more importantly, general population data on patterns of deviance among the elderly, such as that compiled by Akers and La Greca in Chapter 4, are now becoming available to assist us in viewing the elderly criminal in a more realistic and reasonable manner. From studies such as these, we can begin examining elderly criminals not only as a minority group within the larger body of offenders, but in the context of aging, and in terms of other deviant and nondeviant behaviors of the elderly.

This research rationale is logically tied to the next assumption. Theoretical problems do not have to be social problems. It matters little whether the criminal justice system is about to be flooded with older offenders, or if the numbers represent only a trickle. Age influences human behavior and it influences the manner in which behavior is perceived. If the criminal justice system is to justly and fairly process offenders, then all factors that may influence criminal behavior and judgments about criminals need to be explored.

What is so significant about the nature of the elderly offender is the fact that the criminal's age may not only influence our routine use of discretion in police, court, and correctional processing, but it may also influence the broader long-range objectives that we wish to achieve. Are retribution, rehabilitation, deterrence, and incapacitation equally important objectives for the punishment of older and younger offenders? Whatever the weight accorded these objectives for old and young, considerations of ultimate purpose can only enhance the policy judgments and programmatic decisions we make for all offenders.

AGE AND CRIME

The Impact of Aging

Once freed from requirements that we must only study that which is plentiful or immediately problematic, we can begin looking at age and crime in a more complex fashion. Clearly, all older persons are not alike. Beyond this simplistic assessment lies a growing awareness that old age and youth are different in a manner not addressed in prior research, research that has often focused on the comparable powerlessness of older criminals and juveniles. Virtually all juveniles are powerless to the extent that they are dependent on families or other adults for power. Being underage results in certain similarities of position. Certain benefits and obligations of adulthood are denied to all minors, regardless of the social and economic position of the individual.

But this is not the case for older persons. Some older persons possess considerable political and economic power, others possess virtually none, and the great majority exist between these two poles. Unlike juveniles, older persons have spent lifetimes engaging in employment and developing careers, establishing social lives, and building families, or dealing with the consequences of their lack of action (or at least lack of success) in these areas. Where prior research on elderly offenders has agonized over the meaning of 50, 55, 60, and 65 as lower limits on "elderliness," the focus should more appropriately be placed on the correlates of aging. What people do or do not achieve over their lifetimes and what they are able to sustain over the years—these more pervasive but less obvious factors offer the most potential for studies of the causes of deviant behavior.

Such studies will not be simple or easy to accomplish, because at the same time that older persons must be considered in terms of where they are on various "power" dimensions, they must also be considered in terms of the impact of age on physical well-being. Studies of older inmates make clear the fact that the healthy inmate is concerned with different aspects of incarceration than the sick individual. When the focus on health expands to physical well-being, looking not just at wellness or sickness but the capacities of the individual, the need to address these issues becomes clear. Energy levels and the functioning of the senses may affect how older offenders respond to law enforcement and court processes. They may influence the perception of time and space, key elements in the adjustment to various forms of confinement. On a different level, they may affect how older persons view themselves and others. Does the mercy killing of a spouse dying a painful death mean the same to the aged killer as it does to the general public? Do some crimes come to mean more or less as age increases and health deteriorates?

The irrationality of considering these complex issues based only on arbitrary age demarcations is apparent. It has often been said that you have nothing if you don't have your health. If age and health are related, how does this influence our attempt to explain crime and deal with offenders? These are questions worth addressing.

The Diversity of Crime

Just as the aged are not all alike, so are their crimes varied and distinctive. Attempts to explain elderly crime must be as diverse in methodology and focus as studies of younger offenders. Much prior research on elderly criminals has focused on arrest rates and incarceration patterns, necessitating an emphasis on street crime and those acts most likely to lead to imprisonment. Field research is needed, not only to make studies of different forms of deviance possible, but also to locate the elderly offender in different contexts, such as the business world. This focus may be especially useful for deviance research, because correlations among business success or failure, aging, and white-collar crime can be explored.

There are many other especially interesting and useful approaches to the study of crime and the elderly. The routine activities approach to criminal behavior, discussed by Kratcoski and Walker in Chapter 5, may prove especially useful because it directs us to an examination of who the elderly are and how they live their lives. From this perspective, distinctions between crime in retirement havens and in the larger community can be explored. Patterns of drug abuse involving prescription drugs will merit attention. And the financial circumstances of older persons, and the economic activities in which they engage (so often alluded to, but infrequently examined in work on property crime and the elderly), can be directly studied.

The Criminal Justice System

Too often critical thinking about criminal justice is prompted by crisis and/or the intervention of federal courts; prison overcrowding is only the most recent example. The use of deadly force, the response to victims of spouse abuse, the guarantee of due process protections to the poor—these matters became the focus of intellectual debate and action only after the problems drew national attention. Although there have been some attempts to use this same crisis-provoking model to draw attention to elderly crime, it should be clear that this approach is neither necessary nor desirable.

The use of discretion in the criminal justice system always merits attention because it places such a heavy burden of responsibility on the decision makers. The need to be just and fair in a system that demands repeated and sequential "in or out" judgments, in a system that holds death and confinement as possible outcomes, in a system that incarcerates large numbers of offenders—together—often for years at a time, this system must constantly re-evaluate the judgments and the outcomes it metes out. And because our knowledge of the aged is just developing, and our understanding of the older offender is so limited, the questions surrounding crime and the elderly are especially important, not just for the offenders themselves, but for the quality of criminal justice system we are creating.

OVERVIEW

Research on older offenders and the criminal justice system response to their deviant behavior has matured considerably during the last decade. The theoretical questions have become more sophisticated and complex, changing from "Should we study older offenders?" and "How many older persons commit crimes?" to "What methodological approaches are best suited to the study of older offenders?" and "What can we learn from the study of elderly crime?"

The purpose of this book is to examine the theoretical and empirical issues surrounding the problems of elderly crime and the processes by which society manages the elderly criminal. The materials selected for this book were selected because each, in its own way, advances thinking on the nature of crime and the elderly, answering some questions while raising others.

Section I provides an examination of the elderly crime "problem" and prior research on the topic. In Chapter 1 Forsyth and Gramling discuss the increased attention devoted to elderly crime in recent years, and then step back to address more fundamental questions: Who are the elderly? What is a crime? What do we mean by elderly criminals? From this perspective, they question the emergence of elderly crime as a social problem. Has an increase in elderly crime led to the phenomena's redefinition as a social problem, or has increased attention to relatively unchanged phenomena promoted the labeling of elderly crime as a social problem? Although their conclusions tend to support the latter view, they perceive many opportunities for research created by the construction of this social problem.

Gewerth in Chapter 2 provides a review of the research literature on elderly offenders and their processing and treatment in the criminal justice system. He points out that the concern with elderly crime is not new, but dates back to the early 1940s. While much research has concentrated on national arrest patterns, some studies have focused on specific offenses such as homicide and shoplifting. Explanations of elderly crime range from diagnoses of organic brain disease and senility, to weakened inhibitions (affecting the elderly sex offender), to broadly applied sociological theories. There has been little systematic attempt to empirically test these explanations.

His review of studies on law enforcement, diversion, prosecution, and correctional treatment of the elderly offender indicates that older offenders may receive differential treatment from criminal justice system actors and that some distinctions need to be made regarding the management of the older offender. Research is needed to ensure that differential treatment is planned, however, and not the result of prejudice or misguided assumptions.

Our "Perspectives in Criminology" chapters address both theoretical and empirical issues regarding crime among the aged. Their selection illustrates the use of diverse methodologies in the study of general categories of deviance as well as victimless, violent, and property crime. Together, these chapters illustrate the variety of theoretical approaches that can be utilized in attempts to understand and explain elderly crime.

Akers, La Greca, and Sellers examine in Chapter 3 the application of contemporary sociological theories of crime and delinquency to elderly deviance. Building upon the assumption that elderly crime is not an enormous social problem, but a theoretical one, they assess the generalizability of contemporary theories of deviance, developing conceptual and/or operational modifications of the theories to reflect characteristics of old age and the aged population. They conclude that social learning, social bonding, and anomie theories offer explanations of deviance that are as coherent and relevant for older offenders as they are for the adolescent age group to which they are commonly applied.

Akers and La Greca then provide in Chapter 4 an empirical analysis of patterns of alcohol use, criminality, and contact with the criminal justice system among the elderly. This research is unique in that a general population sample of the elderly, rather than elderly offenders, is utilized and self-report, rather than official data, is used as the source of data on contact with the legal system. Findings indicate that the relationship between alcohol abuse and crime, and subsequent criminal justice system involvement, is the same for older as for young persons; problem drinkers are many times more likely to engage in deviant behavior and to encounter trouble with the law than nondrinkers.

Kratcoski and Walker turn our attention in Chapter 5 to violent crime and the victim/offender relationship in homicide cases involving the elderly. Drawing from the "routine activities" conceptualization of crime and empirical work on homicide, a series of assumptions regarding homicide among the elderly are developed and tested. Their findings support the routine activities conceptualization of deviance, but at the same time provide evidence that homicide may be an especially complex phenomena, as well as a more rare event, among older persons.

In Chapter 6 Bachand and Chressanthis employ an economic analysis in their examination of property crime among the elderly. Drawing from the work of Becker (1968, 1974) and Ehrlich (1970, 1973, 1974), they assess the impact of economic and demographic factors on the level of property crime among the elderly. The results of their longitudinal analysis support the model developed from economic theory.

Our "Perspectives in Criminal Justice" chapters include research on law enforcement, court and dispositional processing, and consideration of the problems of incarcerating older offenders. These works examine the issues of leniency and severity of treatment at various decision-making points, in terms of the type of processing afforded elderly defendants as well as the actions of the decision makers. Taken together, they raise questions about the meaning of differential decision making and the difficulty of determining what forms of treatment elderly offenders should receive. It is clear from these writings that the lack of a unified system of justice, that is, one in which subsequent decisions must logically flow from preceding judgments, poses serious problems for both descriptive research and normative evaluation.

Langworthy and McCarthy examine in Chapter 7 the treatment of the elderly offender at the earliest stage at which data is available—police disposition of arrests. There are logical reasons to assume either leniency or severity for older offenders at this stage, and the lack of data on factors influencing initial arrest decisions serves only to "muddy the water" on this issue. Concluding that there are no significant differences in the manner in which arrests of elderly and nonelderly persons are disposed of by police, the authors emphasize the need for multistage research on criminal justice system processing of the elderly.

In Chapter 8 Feinberg extends prior research on age and differential decision making in the courts in his examination of three due process protections—not guilty pleas, representation by attorneys, and the use of jury trials—and their employment by the elderly. He concludes that elderly defendants are less likely to be adversarial than younger defendants and offers possible explanations for their behavior.

Champion looks in Chapter 9 at the issue of plea bargaining by the elderly in a new context: the federal courts. This focus offers much opportunity for the advancement of theoretical approaches to differential processing. Unlike research based on the Uniform Crime Reports, or state courts and/or institutions, it permits a closer examination of white-collar and other nonstreet crimes. Findings indicate that older offenders receive much less severe sentences whether they plea bargain or go to trial, and that both older property offenders and violent offenders benefit from this apparent leniency.

In Chapter 10 Johnson considers the ethical dilemmas and moral issues involved in the confinement of older offenders. His chapter provides a much needed discussion of the humanitarian, therapeutic, and custodial objectives of institutional care of the elderly inmate.

Fry's description in Chapter 11 of the factors that facilitate the adjustment of the older offender to prison documents longstanding beliefs that older and younger prisoners adapt differently to confinement. Using Toch's (1977b) Prison Preference Inventory, he found that while younger prisoners tend to value freedom, support, and privacy, older inmates in this sample required safety, structure, and reasonable levels of activity for successful adjustment.

Sabath and Cowles approach essentially the same problem from a different perspective in Chapter 12. They developed a model of elderly offender adjustment that included three major dimensions: involvement, morale, and adjustment. Background variables were presumed to condition the relationship between these factors, but essentially inmates showing greater involvement in institutional life were expected to demonstrate higher levels of morale and more successful institutional adjustment. Findings only partially supported this view; family contact and inmate health were more significant in the explanation of adjustment than personal and program involvement. The policy implications of these somewhat surprising findings are discussed, clearly indicating the need for more research on this issue.

CONCLUSION

Research on crime and the older offender has come a long way. No longer are elderly victims the only consideration when crime among the elderly is discussed. Aging and crime are increasingly being viewed as complex phenomena meriting serious scholarly research. It is our hope that this book will advance the pursuit of knowledge through the stimulation of discussion, debate, and research.

SECTION I

ELDERLY CRIME AND ELDERLY CRIMINALS

1

Elderly Crime: Fact and Artifact

Craig J. Forsyth
Robert Gramling

INTRODUCTION

One of the most notable trends in the criminological literature in recent years has been the increased attention devoted to the subject of elderly crime (Aday, 1984; Bergman and Amir, 1973; Brickfield, 1982; Cullen, Wozniak, and Frank, 1985; Curran, 1983; Dickinson and Wheeler, 1980; Forsyth and Shover, 1986; Fyfe, 1984; Goetting, 1983; Ham, 1980; Krajick, 1979b; Markham, 1981; McCarthy, 1983; Morton and Anderson, 1982; Newman, Newman, and Gewirtz, 1984; Reed and Glamser, 1979; Rodstein, 1975; Shichor, 1984a; Shichor and Kobrin, 1978; Sunderland, 1982; Teller and Howell, 1981; Weigand and Burger, 1979; Wilbanks and Kim, 1984). Scholarly concern has been accompanied by a rise in print media and television coverage of the subject (Alter, 1983; Daugherty, 1982; Long, 1982; *Time*, 1982; *U.S. News and World Report,* 1982). In 1982 elderly crime was the focus of a *60 Minutes* television segment and was also the focus of a *Today* show.

This increased focus on the elderly is also evidenced by the establishment in 1982 of a National Elderly Offender Conference, which has since been held annually. These conferences have received an unexpected amount of media attention (Newman, Newman, and Gewirtz, 1984:241) and, by their existence alone, will insure a continued focus on the topic. Augmenting this was the formation in 1985 of the Society for Interdisciplinary Research on Elderly Offenders (SIREO). SIREO was formed by a group of researchers, educators, and practitioners to encourage the study of elderly offenders. SIREO also plans to publish a journal entitled *Crime and Aging* devoted to papers on this topic (Forsyth and Shover, 1986).

Attention has focused on several discrete conceptual areas of the phenomenon of elderly crime, one of these being the potentially violent aspects of an increase in elderly crime (Hucker and Ben-Aron, 1984; Rodstein, 1975; Wilbanks and Murphy, 1984). Goetting (1983) links the elderly with crimes of interpersonal violence. She explains how problems commonly associated with old age, when combined with alcohol, have led to a disproportionate amount of violence among the elderly. Tardiff and Sweillam (1979) found that violent behavior by the elderly is a frequent reason for admission to a psychiatric hospital.

A second focus of the literature has explained the need to tailor existing programs (judicial, prison, and post-prison) to fit the needs of the elderly. Abrams (1984:xvi) addressed the need for special courts to handle the elderly charged with crimes.

> We need a court informed on geriatrics and gerontology that can assure the proper counseling service, the proper referral service, the proper family and community support when dealing with the frail elderly caught in the judicial administration system. Today, thousands of elderly arrested on charges ranging from shoplifting to creating a nuisance in Social Security Offices are shunted into courts before judges who have little time, patience, or understanding. There is no inquiry into the impact of arterial blockage on cerebral functioning; the frustrations, fears, and confusion of elderly who may not be able to hear or see well; or undetected mini-strokes which cause distortions in the elderly perceptions of right and wrong.

Abrams (1948:xvi) adds that a special court could provide insight into the unique problems of the elderly offender. It could

> provide referral and counseling service for the arrested aged, and could segregate mentally infirm elderly from hardened old criminals. In a time when judicial administrators are calling for assembly-line, high-disposal rates of cases, these courts could provide society's final mark of respect for the aged. . . . A court that understands the physical and emotional changes in the aging process can help take many elderly people out of the high-cost law enforcement system and mete out a more humane justice for society and the aged. If need be, facilities geared to lower-cost care should be established.

Many practitioners and scholars have suggested special programs to deal with the "first timer" and also the elderly now in prison (Fry, 1984; Ham, 1980; Krajick, 1979b; Markham, 1981; Reed and Glamser, 1979). Some feel that crime control programs must be expanded or created to deal with this new problem (Aday, 1984; Curran, 1983; Dickinson and Wheeler, 1980; Goetting, 1983; McCarthy, 1983; Morton and Anderson, 1982; Newman, Newman, and Gewirtz, 1984; Weigand and Burger, 1979; Wilbanks and Kim, 1984).

> The aging offender often represents a special population in terms of criminal patterns and problems of individual adjustment to institutional life, posing special difficulties for the institution in regard to custody, medical care, rehabilitation, and eventual community reintegration (Aday, 1984:295).

The community reintegration problem is extended by Rodstein (1975:639), "Once released, the majority cannot be rehabilitated by education or job training and become welfare cases." Krajick (1979b:46) calls for such post-prison programs for the elderly to be connected to a system of prerelease education.

> The same counselor who has established a position of trust with the convict in prison, and possibly helped him obtain his freedom follows him into the community and helps him with whatever problems he encounters. The relationship may last for years and extend beyond the initial readjustment from prison to community.

Dickinson and Wheeler (1980) and Morton and Anderson (1982) call for the expansion and improvement of existing programs and services. We are likely to see a continuation of these appeals in the future. Programs such as Project 60 in Pittsburgh, the Broward Senior Intervention Program, the Advocate Seniors Programs, and Price Inc., in Florida will multiply (Forsyth and Shover, 1986).

Finally, there has also been an increase in interest in elderly crime as a topic of empirical study (Brickfield, 1982; Burnett and Ortega, 1984; Cullen, Wozniak, and Frank, 1985; Forsyth and Shover, 1986; Fyfe, 1984; Sunderland, 1982). Whatever conceptual area the reader chooses to examine, even a casual perusal of the literature provides convincing evidence that we are seeing the rise and/or construction of a social problem. As such, current theoretical approaches applicable to social problems are the best point from which to examine this increased interest in elderly crime. There are, however, three critical definitional problems which must be examined before theoretical paradigms can be used to examine the issue: Who are the "elderly"? What is a "crime"? What do we mean by "elderly criminals"?

WHO ARE THE ELDERLY?

One of the most troublesome aspects of the literature on elderly crime is the failure of researchers to agree on what constitutes "elderly" (cf. Newman, Newman, and Gewirtz, 1984:xxxiii, 3-5). Some authors define elderly as 65 years of age and older, some make the cutoff at 60 years, still others at 55 years, and a few use 50 years of age and older to define "elderly." This of course leads to confusion, an inability to compare the findings of various researchers, and a great deal of difficulty in making generalizations about elderly crime.

It would seem premature to start designing programs for a population that has yet to be defined. Certainly 50-, 55-, 60-, and 65-year-old people should be recipients of different policy strategies, as should career and first offenders, and Index and Part II offenders.

Obviously the younger the elderly the greater the problem of elderly crime, since the greater the percentage of the population included in crime statistics (see Table 1.1). Moreover the problem does not grow in a straight line fashion as the definitional age limits are lowered, but in a curvilinear ratio since the "younger elderly" commit more crimes than the "older elderly" (see Figure 1.1).

Without belaboring the point, it is sufficient to say that the very first thing a critical reader of elderly crime research should do is to pin down the exact definition of what constitutes "elderly." For the purpose of discussion, we will define "elderly" as 65 years of age or older.

WHAT IS A CRIME?

The most commonly used definition of "crime" is the FBI's Crime Index offenses (murder, forcible rape, robbery, aggravated assault, burglary, larceny/theft, motor vehicle theft, and arson). Again, definitional problems have arisen. Some researchers have combined the less serious Part II offenses with the Index offenses in their discussion of elderly crime (Fyfe, 1984; Shichor and Kobrin, 1978). Since 37 percent of Part II offenses for the elderly (65+) are for either violation of liquor laws, drunkenness, or

Table 1.1.
Index Crimes, Age 50 and Older

Age	Index Crimes 1984	Cumulative Total
65+	16,571	16,571
60-64	13,394	29,965
55-59	19,297	49,262
50-54	26,180	75,442

Source: Federal Bureau of Investigation, 1984.

Figure 1.1
1984 Index Crimes, Cumulative Age 50 and Older

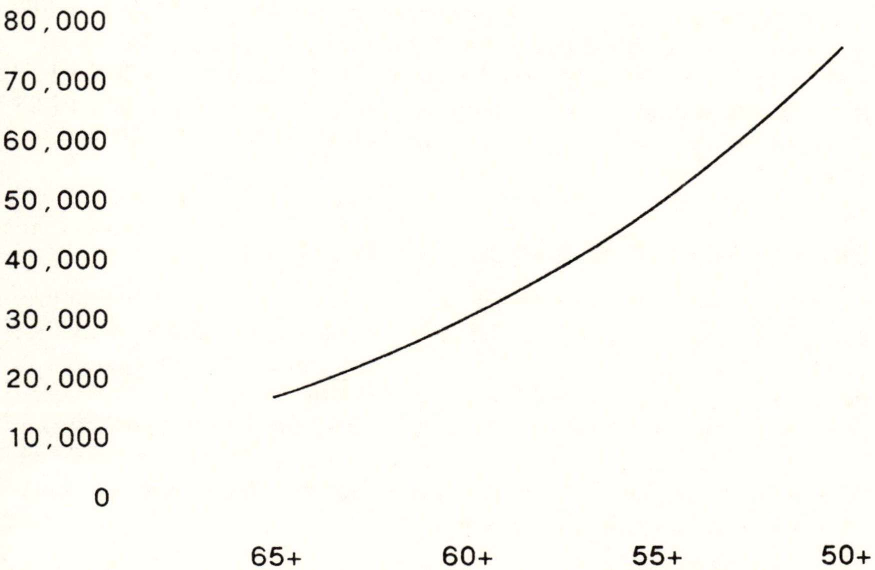

disorderly conduct (Federal Bureau of Investigation, 1985), which are arguably minor or victimless crimes or noncriminal misconduct, this procedure tends to inflate the problem of elderly crime. An additional 27 percent of elderly Part II offenses are for driving while intoxicated, an offense which although serious, should not be included with other crimes. Once again the lack of a clear definitional focus inhibits comparability and generalizability (Newman et al., 1984:5-7).

WHAT DO WE MEAN BY ELDERLY CRIMINALS?

A final problem surrounds the concept of "elderly criminals." Is our concern with the older career criminal or with the individual who commits his first offense after reaching age 65? (Aday, 1984; Rubenstein, 1984). Dealing in the rather sterile world of crime statistics this question is not so problematic. The question becomes critical, however, in the design of programs, or modification of existing ones to meet the needs of the elderly.

Finally, these three definitional problems interact. How does one compare findings concerning elderly (defined as 60 and over) career criminals (crimes defined as Index offenses), with findings about elderly (defined as 65 and over) who may be first offenders? One does not? Since it is highly unlikely that research creativity will ever be channelized into narrow predefined directions, let the reader beware!

Because of these definitional inconsistencies there is considerable variation in the literature as to the magnitude of crimes committed by the elderly (Brickfield, 1982). These inconsistencies taken singularly are harmless, unless they "lead to inappropriate funding, imprudent policy decisions, or misdirected operations" (Sunderland, 1982:40). Researchers and policymakers should be very careful about accepting too easily some of the emerging accounts and explanations of elderly crime, as well as some of the newly touted programs for dealing with them (Forsyth and Shover, 1986).

THE EMERGENCE OF A SOCIAL PROBLEM

The goal for a theory of social problems is to account for the nature, emergence, and maintenance of claims-making and responding activities. Such a theory should address the process by which a putative condition becomes a social problem (Spector and Kitsuse, 1977:76). The social problem of elderly crime has produced two scenarios of claims-making activity to account for its emergence: the traditionalist and the definitionalist accounts. Both arguments can be summarized by $X \rightarrow Y$ (Woolgar and Pawluch, 1985). Whereas;

X = the number of crimes committed by persons 65 years of age and older (we used 65 and older because this is the category that is used most often, i.e., Cullen, Wozniak and Frank, 1985; Forsyth and Shover, 1986; Sunderland, 1982). Y = the attention being paid to elderly crime.

The traditionalist argument: The increase in Y is the result of an increase in X.

The definitionalist or constructionist argument is: X has not increased and Y is a result of a constant activity recently being defined as a problem.

THE CONSTRUCTIONIST ARGUMENT

Basically the constructionist argument is that there has been no significant change in the activity in question, but that activities which were not previously defined as problematic, or rates of activity which were not previously defined as problematic, have been defined as a problem (cf. Blumer, 1971; Lopata, 1984; Spector and Kitsuse, 1977; Woolgar and Pawluch, 1985). The reasons for this redefinition are myriad and range from vested interest through sensationalism to new information (cf. Belknap, 1977; Currie, 1972; Dickson, 1969; Embree, 1977; Rains, 1984; Szasz, 1970). Whatever the reason, from the constructionist approach, the primary issue is the definitional process itself, not the activity. In order to argue the constructionist approach one must show that the activity has remained relatively constant while interest and concern have increased. For example, Best and Horiuchi (1985) present just such a case. Although the actual incidence of Halloween sadism (putting dangerous objects or substances in children's Halloween candy) has been so consistently low over the last 25 years that the probability of a child getting altered candy is virtually zero, the hue and cry fanned by media attention has virtually eliminated "trick or treating."

Forsyth and Shover (1986) argue this approach with respect to elderly crime. They contend that the current focus on elderly crime is a product of three basic factors. The first of these factors is the vested interest of the criminal justice bureaucracy. As the baby boom cohort moved through the high-crime-committing ages (15-24), this caused an increase in the crime rate and correspondingly a growth in the criminal justice bureaucracy. Once this large cohort passed the high-crime-committing years the crime rate began to fall. Bureaucracies justify their existence by the number of clients they process. Therefore, the criminal justice bureaucracy, because it was faced with a declining number of clients, began to cast about for new ones, and elderly crime was a previously untapped resource.

A second factor is the fashion by which scholarship is evaluated in most academic disciplines (cf. Gouldner, 1968). The summa of scholarly activity has always been the publication. Thus, academics are always looking for "hot new areas" of research, where the competition is less fierce and the probability of publication greater (cf. Cole, 1975; Hagan, 1973). The criminal justice interest in elderly crime provided such an area and scholars were quick to respond.

These two factors were exacerbated by the media. Always hungry for news, the media was all too happy to provide coverage of this new "crime wave" (Fishman, 1978; Gordon and Heath, 1981; Humphries, 1981; Pandiani, 1978; Sheley and Ashkins, 1981). Huge percentage increases were reported. These increases were accurate, but misleading since the numerical base was originally so low. For example, a numeric increase from two crimes to four leads to an accurate but misleading 100 percent increase.

The third factor, which has affected both media and scholarly attention, is the uniqueness of the juxtaposition of old age and crime, which appear almost antithetical (cf. Goetting, 1983; Morton, 1976). This is not unlike the idea that brought female criminality to our attention (cf. Adler, 1975; Cullen, Wozniak, and Frank, 1985:159-160; Morton, 1976; Weis, 1976). Thus Forsyth and Shover (1986) argue that elderly crime has remained relatively stable, while the increased focus has stemmed from three sources: criminal justice agencies, the mass media, and scholars.

THE TRADITIONALIST ARGUMENT

The distinctive feature of the social problem argument of the traditionalist is objective conditions and causes (Woolgar and Pawluch, 1985). The traditionalist argument here is that this increased attention being paid to elderly crime is a reflection of significant increases in crimes committed by that group. Documentation usually involves the significant percentage increases in elderly crime (cf. Aday, 1984), as opposed to the constructionist argument which uses small numerical increases.

Typical among such arguments is the oft-cited study of Shichor and Kobrin (1978:213). ". . . arrests for index crimes [committed by the elderly] increased by 224%, while arrests for index crimes among the crime prone youth remained steady at about 40%." Sunderland (1982:42) examined arrest data for the State of Virginia, and pointed to the problem in such reports:

> Depending upon how statistics are reported startling increases can be extracted from arrest reports. For example in my review of 32 categories in recent years in Virginia it was found that in 1975 two robbery arrests were reported of persons over 65 years of age. This increased to three in 1980.

The traditionalist argument would cite a 50 percent increase, the constructionist would use an undramatic numerical increase of one (Forsyth and Shover, 1986).

COMPARING THE THEORETICAL APPROACHES

Few social phenomena present themselves in pure black or white terms, and the social scientist is generally quite accustomed to working somewhere within the gray spectrum. It is quite unrealistic to expect data on elderly crime to totally support one of the two conceptualizations presented here. Probably the most fruitful way to view the two theoretical positions is as extremes of a continuum. If the rise in attention to elderly crime closely parallels the rise in elderly crime our analysis would lend support to the traditionalist model. If the rise in attention to elderly crime greatly exceeds the increase in elderly crime our analysis would tend to support the constructionist model.

Table 1.2 presents basic statistics relevant to the increase in elderly crime (number and percentage in U.S. population 65 years of age and older, number of crimes [Index crimes] committed by the 65-and-over population, percentage this constitutes of total Index crimes, and numbers of crimes per 100,000 of the 65-and-over population) and scholarly interest (number of scholarly articles[1]) for the last two decades. The last line of Table 1.2 presents the percentage increase (where applicable) for the 20-year-period 1965-1984 (Federal Bureau of Investigation, 1965-1984).

Some very definite trends emerge. First, elderly crime is definitely on the increase, or at least has been over the last 20 years. In fact, looking only at the percentage increase of elderly crime, the "alarmist" could become quite

Table 1.2.
Elderly Crime Statistics and Number of Scholarly Articles

	Population*		Elderly Crimes 65+**			
	Total 65+ x 1,000	% of Total	Total x 1,000	% of Total Crimes	# per 100,000	Scholarly Articles***
1965	18,156	9.3	3.92	.5	21.6	0
1966	18,475	9.3	4.64	.5	25.6	1
1967	18,795	9.5	5.29	.5	25.0	0
1968	19,129	9.6	5.37	.5	27.7	4
1969	19,470	9.6	5.74	.5	29.4	4
1970	20,087	9.8	6.85	.5	34.5	4
1971	20,567	9.9	7.50	.5	37.0	3
1972	20,948	10.0	8.19	.6	38.5	3
1973	21,329	10.2	8.23	.6	38.5	5
1974	21,815	10.3	7.81	.5	35.7	4
1975	22,400	10.5	11.70	.6	52.6	4
1976	22,934	10.7	11.52	.6	50.0	8
1977	23,494	10.9	13.03	.7	55.5	11
1978	24,054	11.0	15.12	.7	62.5	9
1979	24,658	11.3	15.89	.7	62.5	14
1980	25,550	11.3	16.56	.8	66.6	16
1981	26,263	11.5	19.13	.8	71.4	10
1982	26,826	11.6	18.27	.8	66.5	14
1983	27,384	11.7	18.65	.9	66.5	12
1984	28,040	11.9	16.57	.9	58.7	28
Total % increase	54.4	NA	322	NA	171	NA

Source:
*U.S. Bureau of the Census, 1966-1985.
**Federal Bureau of Investigation, 1965-1984.
***Forsyth and Shover, 1986.

excited, since elderly crime increased 322 percent between 1965 and 1984. This increase is partly due to the growth of the elderly segment of the population (54.4 percent) and partly to the growth of number of crimes per 100,000 in the elderly population (171 percent). However, before we proclaim an elderly crime wave a cautionary note is in order. While the percentage increase in elderly crime is rather dramatic within the elderly population, this effect is quelled when this increase is seen as part of total Index crimes. Between 1965 and 1984 the percentage of total crimes committed by the elderly rose from .5 percent to .9 percent or four-tenths of 1 percent over a period of 20 years. Perhaps the bottom line is that the elderly are almost 12 percent of the population but commit less than 1 percent of the total Index crimes.[2]

During the same time period interest in elderly crime (evidenced by scholarly publications [Forsyth and Shover, 1986]) rose dramatically. Although a percentage increase cannot be calculated (because the initial measurement was zero) the rise in scholarly publications greatly surpasses the increases in elderly crime.

DISCUSSION

Before drawing conclusions from the data several questions which have major implications for researchers and policymakers must be considered. First, to what extent is the rise in elderly crime an artifact of reporting procedure? Some researchers (Aday, 1984:298; Bergman and Amir, 1973; Hagan, 1974; Shichor, 1984a:30) have suggested that arresting officers have established more lenient policies with regard to the elderly, particularly for offenses where the safety and rights of others are not involved. Others (Cullen, Wozniak, and Frank, 1985; Fyfe, 1984:100) have suggested that these policies may be changing and police are now more likely to arrest the elderly. Additionally, since the elderly are disproportionately arrested for shoplifting (nearly 80 percent of elderly arrests are for larceny/theft, a category that includes shoplifting), the increased use of private security personnel in retail outlets may be impacting arrest rates for shoplifting. Whether this will increase or decrease reported crimes by the elderly is not known. Currently private security personnel make approximately 500,000 arrests yearly (Levine, Musheno, and Palumbo, 1986:205). The question to answer now is—can this increase in elderly crime be due to a change in attitude toward the elderly?[3]

Second, if the increase in elderly crime is not an artifact of the reporting procedure, then are we seeing more career criminals who are becoming older (extended careers), or are we seeing more over-65 first offenders? The answer to this question is critical to the design and implementation of programs initiated to work with the elderly criminal. Third, to what extent is the increase in elderly crime due to an increase in shoplifting, and does this indirectly reflect the economic plight of the elderly?

In summary, it appears that there is no elderly crime wave. In fact, our data tend to support the constructionist argument that at least part of the heightened focus on elderly crime is due to factors other than an increase in elderly crime. But, as stated previously, elderly crime is on the rise. Given the projected escalation in the elderly population (White House Conference on Aging, 1982), we can safely assume that elderly crime will continue to increase, and will do so at a correlative rate. Thus, some of the interest in elderly crime is probably not misplaced, and for once social scientists may be ahead of the game.

NOTES

1. In order to document the scholarly interest in elderly crime we obtained the frequency of publication by examining the Criminal Justice Periodic Index, the Sociological Abstracts, and the Psychological Abstracts between 1960 and 1984 and the bibliography of the two 1984 books on elderly crime (Newman, Newman, and Gewirtz, 1984; Wilbanks and Kim, 1984).

2. Even combining Index and Part II offenses the total in 1984 was below 1 percent.

3. Cullen, Wozniak, and Frank (1985:160) have commented on this change in attitude. In the past the elderly were primarily looked upon as victims. More recently, however, this view of the elderly as "vulnerable and ineffectual" has been challenged. The elderly are seen as

> capable of performing productive roles. This more active image has had the invaluable function of punctuating the myth that senior citizens are exclusively a dependent, surplus population. It seems equally reasonable to suggest that it has also had the function of allowing scholars to entertain the possibility that the elderly are capable of committing crimes, and serious ones at that!

2

Elderly Offenders: A Review of Previous Research

Kenneth E. Gewerth

INTRODUCTION

Within the past few years, a number of researchers concerned with the general problem of "crime and the elderly" turned their attention from the aged as *victims* of crime to the problem of elderly *offenders*. As initially interpreted, their findings were somewhat surprising: It appeared that crime among the elderly (typically defined as those aged 55 and over) was on the increase (Malinchak, 1980; Shichor, *quoted in* Long, 1982; Shichor, 1984a; Shichor and Kobrin, 1978). These results quickly drew the attention of the national media (*60 Minutes* [CBS], 1982; *This Week* [ABC], 1983; *Time*, 1982; *U.S. News and World Report*, 1982) and provoked a strong reaction among members of the academic community and the general public. Journalists began to write articles with provocative titles, suggesting that the United States would soon experience an "elderly crime wave" (Harper, 1982), while officials of at least one lobby group, the American Association of Retired Persons, dismissed the entire issue of elderly crime as a media hype (Brickfield, 1982) engineered by "academicians . . . looking for grants" (Crow, *quoted in* Long, 1982). Other social scientists complicated the issue further by arguing that the "'new elderly offender' [was] best seen as an invention" of criminologists, and that the study of elderly crime was not nearly as important as finding out why criminologists persist in "inventing" new types of offenders (Cullen, Wozniak, and Frank, 1985:159-160).

However, those who consider the problem of elderly crime to be trivial or faddish, or who criticize the social scientists studying it overlook two important facts. First, the problem of crime among the aged may be *newly recognized,* but it is certainly not *new*: Research interest in criminal behavior among the elderly dates back to the early part of this century—the phenomenon was first discussed at a criminology conference in Budapest in 1899 (Pollak, 1941:213). Second, the research that has been done is quite diverse. Some studies attempt to estimate the amount and types of crime committed by older people, or are concerned with issues of causation. Other research efforts focus on how these offenders are processed through the criminal justice system, trying to identify those facts that police, prosecutors, and correctional officials take into account when deciding what to do with an 80-year-old shoplifter or a 65-year-old charged and convicted of homicide. Still other studies describe the difficulties older people encounter when they are jailed or imprisoned, or detail the characteristics of rehabilitation programs targeted at elderly lawbreakers. In this chapter, we shall review some of the major studies in each of these categories.

THE AMOUNT AND TYPES OF CRIME COMMITTED BY THE ELDERLY

Analyses of National Data

Several authors have analyzed nationwide arrest statistics attempting to determine how much and what kinds of crime are committed by older persons. Although the definition of an "elderly offender" varies somewhat, the findings and conclusions are remarkably similar. For example, reviewing arrest and incarceration data, Pollak (1941) and Moberg (1953) both found that arrest and incarceration rates declined with advancing age (Pollak, 1941:213; Moberg, 1953:768). As to the types of crime committed by older offenders, Pollak reported that the arrest rates for those aged 50 and over were highest for the crime of larceny-theft, assault, embezzlement, fraud, and sex offenses (other than prostitution), and lowest for robbery, prostitution, and auto theft (Pollak, 1941:220 [Table 4]). In Moberg's study, typical offenses of the elderly included drunkenness, sex offenses, embezzlement, and fraud (Moberg, 1953:768). Finally, both authors reported that a high proportion of elderly criminals were first offenders (Pollak, 1941:221-222; Moberg, 1953:768).

In another analysis of arrest statistics, Keller and Vedder (1968) examined data from the 1964 *Uniform Crime Reports* (UCR). Ranking the "Top 20" crimes for each of five age categories (25-49, 50-54, 55-59, 60-64, and 65 and over), they found that younger people are arrested in far greater numbers for all crimes except drunkenness. However, the rank order of many offenses in each of the age categories, for example, drunkenness and disorderly conduct ranked first and second, and the relative positions of aggravated assault, larceny, gambling, suspicion, prostitution, and fraud were about the same (Keller and Vedder, 1968:43). Nonetheless, some offenses, such as burglary, robbery, rape, and narcotics violations were more prevalent among the young, while vagrancy, "other assaults" (that is, "assaults without intent to kill or commit great bodily injury") and "other sex offenses" (that is, "statutory rape, offenses against chastity, common decency, morals, and the like") and—somewhat surprisingly—vandalism, were more common among the older groups (Keller and Vedder, 1968:43-44).

In another assessment of the elderly crime problem, Wilbanks computed age-specific arrest rates for elderly and younger offenders using 1980 UCR data. Next he calculated the ratio between the rates for each group. No matter what the offense, younger persons were much more likely to be arrested. For example, the crime with the greatest difference in arrest rates was robbery, where the young were 86.5 times more likely to be arrested as the elderly; for the other Index crimes, the smallest difference in rates was found for larceny-theft, where the young were 8.7 times more likely to be arrested. Overall, the greatest similarity in arrest rates of the two groups was found for gambling, where the young were only 2.8 times more likely to be arrested (Wilbanks, 1984a:4-5).

Several authors have examined trends in elderly arrests using UCR data. For example, Shichor and Kobrin (1978) reported that the number of persons aged 55 and over arrested for Index crimes increased 224 percent from 1964-74. This rate of growth was substantially higher than the rate of increase in Index arrests for all age groups (43 percent). Moreover, the data indicated that a large proportion of elderly arrests were for violent crimes, particularly aggravated assault, while the arrests for serious property crimes by the elderly were largely confined to larceny-theft (Shichor and Kobrin, 1978:213-214). Misdemeanor arrests, however, revealed a different trend. From 1964-74, the proportion of arrests for vagrancy and drunkenness among those 55 and over declined substantially, while arrests for gambling dropped slightly as well. In contrast, the proportion of arrests of the aged for driving while under the influence rose sharply.

In a subsequent analysis of UCR data, Shichor (1984a) found that the percentage change in the number of arrests of those 55 and over was, for some types of crime, greater than the level of increase or decrease in the total population. He found a 5.7 percent increase in the number of elderly arrests during this period. Moreover, the percentage increase in the number of arrests was larger in the elderly group for the crimes of homicide, rape, larceny, motor vehicle theft, and for the less serious sex offenses. In addition, the number of arrests for the crimes of drunkenness and vagrancy decreased more sharply for the elderly group than for the general population.

Wilbanks's (1984a) study of UCR arrest data from 1970-80 presents a slightly different picture of elderly crime. Using a more restrictive definition of an elderly offender (aged 60 and over) and a smaller comparison group (persons 18-59), he calculated the percentage change in the number of arrests for both groups. His analysis indicates: first, a 12 percent *decrease* in the total number of arrests of the elderly; second, an increase in the number of arrests that was larger in the elderly group for the Index crimes of rape, robbery, burglary, larceny, and motor vehicle theft; third, arrests of the elderly for minor sex offenses increases, while the number of elderly arrests for drunkenness, vagrancy, and gambling decreased more sharply compared to those in the 18-59 age group.

Close comparison of Shichor's (1984a) and Wilbanks's (1984a) findings reveals a few other differences (see Table 2.1). For example:

1. Shichor indicates that homicide arrests increased more in the elderly group, while Wilbanks found a greater rate of growth in the comparison group.
2. For robbery and burglary, Shichor found large rates of increase in the comparison group, while Wilbanks found a greater rate of increase in the elderly group.
3. For gambling, Shichor found the largest decrease in the comparison group, while in Wilbanks's analysis, the largest decrease was in the elderly group.
4. Finally, the rates of increase or decrease reported by Shichor are, on the whole, larger than those reported by Wilbanks.

However, it should be noted that there is a great deal more consistency than not.

Shichor (1948b) also compared the trends in elderly arrests for urban, suburban, and rural areas, between 1964 and 1979. In general, he found that most elderly arrests occur in the cities, although the proportion of elderly arrests occurring in the suburbs was on the increase, probably the result of the growth in the suburban population. When Shichor examined the arrest trends for various categories of crime (that is, Index and non-Index crimes, violent and property crimes, etc.) for the different residential areas, two patterns became apparent. For total arrests, non-Index offenses and violent Index offenses, the proportion of elderly arrests declined, relative to the general population. However, for Index crimes, and Index property offenses, the proportion of elderly arrests, again relative to the total population, increased during the period studied. These patterns, according to Shichor, remained stable for all three types of residential areas.

Table 2.1.
Comparison of Results of Shichor (1984a) and Wilbanks (1984a) Study of Elderly Arrest Data in the Uniform Crime Reports

	STUDY				
	Shichor		Wilbanks		Agree on Groups of Greatest Increase
Offense Category	Elderly Group	Comparison Group	Elderly Group	Comparison Group	
All offenses	5.7	102.9 *	-12.0	60 *	Yes
All Index	256.7 *	177.2	129.0 *	104	Yes
Homicide	201.7 *	184.8	68	93 *	No
Rape	355.3 *	208.6	179 *	105	Yes
Robbery	229.8 *	234.1 *	101 *	67	No
Aggravated Assault	165.8	221.8 *	71	111 *	Yes
Burglary	120.1	150.3 *	94 *	93	No
Larceny-Theft	318.0 *	206.3	157 *	130	Yes

Table 2.1. (continued)

	STUDY				
	Shichor		Wilbanks		
Offense Category	Elderly Group	Comparison Group	Elderly Group	Comparison Group	Agree on Groups of Greatest Increase
Motor Vehicle Theft	256.1 *	47.6	72 *	27	Yes
Arson	-	-	117	171 *	-
Violent Index	176.6	222.3 *	68	93 *	Yes
Property Index	296.6 *	166.1	151.0 *	109	Yes
All Non-Index	-4.0	88.1 *	-21	52 *	Yes
Drunkenness	-45.4 *	-25.3	-58 *	-29	Yes
Vagrancy	-88.5 *	-73.9	-83 *	-71	Yes
Disorderly Conduct	-14.5	49.6 *	-9	31 *	Yes
Driving While Intoxicated	328.5	445.8 *	118	209 *	Yes
Liquor Law	18.8	151.6 *	33	83 *	Yes
Gambling	-39.0	-50.9 *	-53 *	-45	No
Sex Offenses	18.1 *	7.8	37 *	35	Yes

*indicates group with greatest increase or decrease.

Adapted from Shichor, David "The Extent and Nature of Lawbreaking by the Elderly: A Review of Arrest Statistics" in Newman, Newman and Gewirtz (eds.) *Elderly Criminals*. MA: Oelgeschlager, Gunn and Hain, Publishers, Inc. 1984. Tables 2.6-2.9 pp. 22-25. Reprinted with permission. Also adapted from Wilbanks, W. "The Elderly Offender: Placing the Problem in Perspective." In W. Wilbanks and P. K. H. Kim (eds.) *Elderly Criminals*. MD: The University Press of America. 1984. Table I p. 12. Reprinted with permission.

Elderly Crimes in Specific Jurisdictions

Several studies have focused on the levels and patterns of elderly crime in specific state or local jurisdictions. For example, Adams and Vedder (1961) reviewed the files of prisoners in a large Southern state prison who were aged 50 and over at the time of commitment. When compared to the total prison population, offenders in the older group had a slightly higher incidence of assault convictions, and a much greater proportion of convictions for embezzlement, forgery, passing worthless checks, perjury, receiving money or stolen goods under false pretenses and receiving stolen property. Convictions for gambling, manslaughter, and various types of sex crimes were also higher in the older group. In contrast, the proportion of convictions for burglary, breaking and entering, and robbery were higher in the general prison population as were convictions for larceny and auto theft (Adams and Vedder, 1961:180 [Table 2]).

Epstein, Mills, and Simon (1970) collected data on all persons aged 60 and over who were arrested in San Francisco during a four-month period in 1967-68 (N = 722). When compared to all those over the age of 18 who were arrested in the city in 1967 (N = 45,677), the elderly group was disproportionately white, and predominately male: The sex ratio in the older group was 15:1 as opposed to 6:1 in the comparison group (Epstein, Mills, and Simon, 1970:36-37). The elderly were most commonly arrested for drunkenness, although apprehensions for gambling, disturbing the peace, and aggravated assault were also frequent (Epstein, Mills, and Simon, 1970:38). The authors also noted, however, that arrests for crimes such as "forgery, ficticious checks, desertion, malicious mischief, arson, extortion, and prostitution" which constituted a large portion of all adult arrests, were absent in the older group (Epstein, Mills, and Simon, 1970:38).

Burnett and Ortega (1984) examined arrest trends among the elderly (that is, those aged 50 and over) in Lincoln, Nebraska, and Kansas City, Missouri, from 1962-67 and 1970-80. Their analysis revealed a decline in the total number of arrests, as well as a 9 percent decline in the arrest rate (per 100,000) during the period studied. Separate analyses of Part I and Part II crimes showed that arrest rates for Index crimes rose, due primarily to a 230 percent increase in arrest rates for property offenses (chiefly larceny). For all Part II offenses, the arrest rate declined substantially, due to significant drops in arrests for alcohol offenses, lesser sex crimes, and other minor offenses such as vagrancy. There were, however, increases in arrest rates for less serious property crimes, such as fraud, embezzlement, forgery, and counterfeiting (Burnett and Ortega, 1984:20). The data also indicated that arrestees aged 50-59 outnumbered those aged 60 and over for most offenses for both males and females. Throughout the study period, the ratio of younger to older offenders remained stable at about 2.5-3.5:1. The only exception appeared to be among females arrested for "personal disorganization" offenses (that is, intoxication, driving while under the influence, vagrancy, disturbing the peace, etc.) where the ratio increased from 3.42 in 1964 to 5.33 in 1980 (Burnett and Ortega, 1984:23).

Sex and race differences among elderly offenders were also the subject of a 1984 investigation by Wilbanks (1984b). Using records from Dade County, Florida, he identified a total of 4,268 cases (791 felonies and 3,477 misdemeanors) where a person aged 60 and over had been charged. Overall, the misdemeanor-felony ratio was 4.4:1 (3,477/791). However, when he computed misdemeanor and felony rates (per 100,000) for various racial and gender groups, the likelihood of being charged with a felony or misdemeanor varied markedly. For example, elderly males had a misdemeanor rate approximately five times larger than the misdemeanor rate for females (1,997.5/352.7) while the felony rate for older males was over ten times that for females (500.1/47.8). Differences between black and white elderly offenders were not as large: misdemeanor rates for black offenders were three times larger than the rate for whites, while blacks were 5.6 times more likely than whites to be charged with a felony (1,013.5/181.8). Looking at various combinations of sex and race, Wilbanks found that both felony and misdemeanor rates were highest for black males followed by white males, black females, and white females.

Finally, comparison of the arrest rate ratios of two groups of older offenders (those aged 60-64 and those aged 75 and over) permitted Wilbanks to demonstrate that race was not as good a predictor of felony offense rates as either gender or age. He was also able to show that the felony arrest rates for black male elderly offenders do not decline as sharply with age as do the arrest rates of other race-gender groups (Wilbanks, 1984:43-44).

As to the types of offenses committed by the elderly, Wilbanks (1984b:45) found that misdemeanor larceny and petty theft were the most common minor crimes, although there was also a significant proportion of "automobile-related offenses" (14.2 percent of all elderly misdemeanors). Looking next at gender and race categories of offenders, white females were most often arrested for three alcohol-related offenses (disorderly conduct, intoxication, and alcohol beverage violations) and two automobile offenses (traffic violations and driving without a license) (Wilbanks, 1984b:45).

Analyses of Specific Offenses

Several studies have focused on specific types of offenses committed by older persons, including homicide, violent offenses (homicide, attempted homicide, or assault), shoplifting, and alcohol-related offenses. The major studies in each of these areas will be reviewed below.

Homicide. Using nationwide data contained in the FBI's *Supplemental Homicide Reports* for 1980, Wilbanks and Murphy (1984) compared elderly (60 and over) and nonelderly (18-59) homicide offenders. The elderly offender rate varied widely across jurisdictions and was strongly and positively correlated to the homicide rate for younger offenders, the proportion of blacks living below the poverty line, the proportion of urban dwellers, and the proportion of blacks in the jurisdiction (Wilbanks and Murphy, 1984:84). Also, the monthly pattern of homicides was similar for both younger and older offenders. The homicide rate among the elderly varied by gender and race, ranging from 19.25 for black males to 0.11 for white females.

Violent Offenses. Hucker and Ben-Aron (1984) compared 16 elderly offenders who had been charged with violent crimes, and 16 nonviolent sex offenders, with a group of offenders, aged 30 or less, who had been charged with violent crimes. They found similar proportions of young and older violent offenders were related to the victim, and were under the influence of alcohol at the time of the crime. However, the typical psychiatric diagnosis was different for the two groups:

> [Y]oung aggressors [were] more likely to receive a diagnosis of antisocial personality disorder [, whereas the] elderly violent group received a diagnosis of either organic or functional mental disorder in nearly three quarters of the cases (Hucker and Ben-Aron, 1984:74).

Shoplifting. At least two studies have examined the characteristics of elderly shoplifters (Curran, 1984; Feinberg, 1984a). Feinberg's (1984a) analysis begins with the examination of larceny arrests of older persons using UCR data, and statistics from the state of Florida. He notes that there has been a substantial increase in the elderly larceny arrest rate and then constructs a profile of older shoplifters. The results are surprising because they seem to contradict several widely held notions about the characteristics of these offenders and the nature of their offenses. For example, previous research portrays shoplifting as a "female-dominated" crime (Feinberg, 1984a:50, n. 5,6). Feinberg's sample, however, contained approximately equal proportions of men and women. His research also challenged other widely held notions: that elderly shoplifters stole necessities (most of the things they took were luxury items); or that the thefts were the product of some aging-related memory impairment (in nearly half the cases studied, more than one item was stolen); or an attempt to overcome feelings of isolation or loneliness (over two-thirds of those studied did not live alone; just under two-thirds were married; and 80 percent had family living nearby). Feinberg also noted that most of the offenders felt guilty about the offense, but did not view themselves as law violators.

The results of Curran's (1984) examination of elderly shoplifters in Palm Beach County, Florida, are generally consistent with those of the Feinberg study. For example, a substantial proportion (60 percent) of the 493 subjects in her sample were male; again, a finding that contradicts the view of shoplifting as a crime typically committed by females. Curran also found that the items taken were generally low value household or personal goods (glue, tape, tools, cigarettes, etc.).

Alcohol-Related Offenses. Epstein, Mills, and Simon (1970), Shichor (1984a), Shichor and Kobrin (1978), and others (Meyers, 1984:64 n. 3,4), have all found a fairly strong link between alcohol use and criminal behavior by the elderly. Based on an analysis of UCR data, Meyers has noted that older persons are commonly arrested for public drunkenness and driving while intoxicated, while arrests for other liquor law violations (such as the sale of alcohol to minors, or other commercial violations) are less frequent (Meyers, 1984:54). Second, he found that while the proportion of elderly persons arrested for alcohol-related offenses is small, this proportional contribution is larger than for other types of crime (Meyers, 1984:54).

Following his examination of UCR data for 1977-78, Meyers (1984) notes that the attempt to uncover a trend in these offenses is complicated for several reasons. First, the growing acceptance of the notion of alcoholism as a disease has led to the decriminalization of offenses such as public intoxication in many jurisdictions, making it more difficult to determine whether declines in arrests reflect changes in the way older alcoholics are processed by the criminal justice system, or changes in the amount of criminal behavior per se. Second, a variety of methodological or demographic factors, such as changes in crime definitions, the number of state and local police agencies participating in the UCR program, or the uneven distribution of the elderly population in the United States, may distort arrest data.

In summary, the most consistent findings from studies of national and local arrest data indicate that: (1) the elderly comprise only a small proportion of the total number of persons arrested; (2) fraud, embezzlement, and larceny-theft seem to be the most frequent crimes for which the elderly are arrested, although some authors have found that assaults and sex offenses are relatively common as well; and (3) there is a fairly clear nexus between the use of alcohol and criminal behavior among the elderly.

THE CAUSES OF ELDERLY CRIMINALITY

According to many authors, criminal behavior in old people is often a symptom of some type of organic brain disease associated with the aging process, such as cerebral arteriosclerosis or senile dementia. The pathological changes produced by these disorders are believed to weaken an individual's inhibitions or cause delusions that lead to episodes of violence or deviant sexual activity. In Whiskin's review of 28 cases involving elderly offenders, half were diagnosed as having organic brain disease (Whiskin, 1968:245 [Table 1]). Similarly, 49 percent of the older criminals studied by

Zeegers (1966), and 9 percent of the cases reviewed by Hucker (1984) were diagnosed as victims of senile dementia.

The frequent use of the diagnosis of "organic brain disease" prompts Whiskin (1968) to ask if the diagnosis is "overworked." He goes on to suggest that these patients are being regarded as "beyond repair" when, in fact, they are not. He suggests that additional study of these cases may reveal many elderly offenders who might benefit from therapeutic intervention.

While organic brain disease and senile dementia are perhaps the most common psychiatric diagnoses in cases involving elderly offenders, they may also, according to Whiskin, exhibit symptoms of depression, functional psychosis, personality disorder, alcoholism, or paranoid schizophrenia (Whiskin, 1968:244).

Many have also tried to explain the high incidence of sex crimes among elderly males. They suggest that these offenses may result from weakened inhibitions (Moberg, 1953:774), perhaps coupled with a "persistent libido," (Pollak, 1941:231) or an attempt to prove "manliness" and rebel against old age (Salzmann, 1963:54). Or, these crimes may arise from the need to compensate for feelings of rejection, impotence, or unattractiveness (Whiskin, 1968:250).

An extensive, if somewhat disorganized, "laundry list" of reasons that the elderly are more (or less) likely to commit crimes is offered by Moberg (1953:773-775). The potential criminogenic factors he identifies range from senility to the possibility that older offenders may be more likely to commit white-collar crimes, thereby lessening their chances of arrest. On the other hand, according to Moberg, older people may be less likely to commit crimes for a variety of reasons, ranging from physical inability to the fact that the increased power and economic independence that comes with age reduces the need to resort to crime. Finally, he notes that crimes by older offenders may be less accurately recorded and that judges and juries may be less likely to convict elderly offenders. There is, of course, ample reason to doubt many of these assertions about the nature of elderly criminality; however, they are significant because they represent an early attempt to explain crimes by the aged using both psychological and sociological concepts.

In *Crime and Gerontology* (1980), Malinchak reviews four of the major sociological theories of crime (cultural deviance, strain, conflict, and labeling) and two of the major theoretical perspectives in gerontology (disengagement theory and activity theory) in an effort to explain "why the elderly turn to crime" (Malinchak, 1980:140). Unfortunately, the treatment of this topic is somewhat mechanical and incomplete. For example, the summary of the cultural deviance perspective includes a discussion of Miller's notion that lower class youth have a distinctive set of "focal concerns'' which lead them into conflict with the law. Malinchak then implies that the elderly also have a set of focal concerns which lead them into conflict with the law, but nowhere is there an indication of what they might be.

Noting that many elderly persons must survive on fixed incomes despite a rising cost of living, Malinchak (1980) speculates that strain theory may be useful for explaining some types of crime by the elderly, particularly larceny and shoplifting. Interpreting conflict theory, Malinchak suggests that the elderly are part of the ''surplus population'' that the ruling class controls by providing various forms of public assistance. According to the theory, the growth of the elderly population will lead to the eventual collapse of this system, forcing more older persons to turn to crime in order to live. Next, taking up the labeling and disengagement theories, Malinchak explains that once people are labeled ''elderly'' by the rest of society, they are treated differently by others, who see them as sick, confused, and nonproductive. Thus labeled, old people are forced to give up or ''disengage'' from a number of important social roles. In reaction to this isolation, according to Malinchak, some old people turn to crime (Malinchak, 1980:155).

Although he does not mention it, Malinchak (1980) could just have easily noted the similarity between the gerontological theory of disengagement and another criminological theory, control theory (see generally, Hirschi, 1969). Control theorists believe that people obey the law because they are ''bound'' or tied to the conventional social order. That is, people develop, over time, ''stakes in conformity'' (Hirschi, 1969:16) such as a job, or a good reputation, all of which would be damaged if they are to engage in criminal behavior. According to control theory, criminal behavior becomes more likely whenever a person's ties or bonds to society become weakened or broken.

Finally, Malinchak makes a brief reference to activity theory, which suggests that the proper adjustment to the ''elderly'' role is contingent upon older people's ability to remain active in their ''golden years'' (Malinchak, 1980:155). He suggests that since old people are not permitted to remain active in conventional social activities and roles, some turn to illegitimate, criminal activities instead.

As indicated by the literature reviewed in this section, the attempts to develop satisfactory explanations of elderly crime have, almost from the beginning, been multidisciplinary in nature: psychological, sociological, and gerontological theories have all served as starting points for this effort. Unfortunately, however, much of the existing work in this area is either outdated or incomplete. Moreover, the little theoretical development that has occurred has taken place more or less in a vacuum: Few analysts have tried to reconcile potentially valuable causal theories with the data on elderly crime.

ELDERLY OFFENDERS IN THE CRIMINAL JUSTICE SYSTEM

Quite apart from the question about the nature and extent of criminal behavior among the elderly is the question of what to *do* with older persons who break the law. All the major actors in the system may, at one time or another, have to decide the fate of an older person. Some of the problems and issues that arise as the aged are processed through the system will be briefly detailed below.

The Police: The Decision to Arrest

Fyfe (1984) contends that police contacts with the elderly are likely to increase in the future, due, in part, to their disproportionate involvement in three offenses (shoplifting, drunken driving, and family violence) which are now regarded as serious social problems. This hardening of public attitudes has placed greater pressure on police to make more arrests. While this may be an acceptable policy when younger people are involved, formal processing may be problematic when the offender is old. "The pressure to arrest," writes Fyfe,

> and the inflexibility of the prescribed arrest process may subject elderly offenders to the trauma of detention prior to court appearances that accomplish nothing. . . .
>
> Further . . . for the police agencies, public reaction to arrests of the elderly . . . is likely to involve both sympathy for arrestees and a perception that the police have reacted unreasonably [citation omitted] the arresting officer in such a case is likely to suffer a negative reaction . . . from his superiors and colleagues as well (Fyfe, 1984:107-108).

Because of these negative consequences, Fyfe recommends careful formulation of policies regarding police treatment of the elderly to ensure they are processed "in a way that is best for the victim, the public, offenders and the police." That may mean, contrary to general trends, that police discretion in elderly offender cases may need to be broadened (Fyfe, 1984:109).

Prosecution and Adjudication

Cutshall and Adams (1983) extracted data on 745 shoplifting cases processed in Washington, D.C., in 1974-1975 to determine if persons aged 50 and over were treated more leniently by prosecutors. Age indeed made a difference: for those 50 and over, charges were dropped in 71.4 percent of the cases, compared to a dismissal rate of 55.1 percent of those aged 26-49 and 61.4 percent for those aged 17-25. The introduction of a number of control variables, such as prior record, the number of offenses charged, the strength of the prosecution's case (as measured by the number of witnesses to the offense) and the seriousness of the offense (as measured by the value of the merchandise stolen) failed to eliminate statistically significant differences in the dismissal rates of elderly offenders compared to those who were 26-49 years old. However, when race was introduced as a control variable, the difference in dismissal rates for the two groups disappeared among whites. Among blacks, the elderly were still treated more leniently than those who were 26-49. Similarly, controlling for gender eliminated the differences in dismissal rates between elderly and middle-aged females. When the elderly were compared with 17-25 year olds, statistically significant differences in dismissal rates persisted among male offenders, those with prior records, and those charged with a single offense, as well as in less serious cases or those where the evidence was strong.

According to Cutshall and Adams (1983), a belief among prosecutors is that the probable outcome in the case (usually probation or a suspended sentence) is not worth the time and effort necessary to proceed. They contend that some "tacit criminological theor[y]" or a stereotypical view of elderly offenders as "[helpless] . . . 'grandma and grandpa' . . . " types might be the causes of the higher rate of dismissals in elderly cases (Cutshall and Adams, 1983:7).

In another article, Cohen (1984) outlines some of the problems faced by an attorney representing an elderly client. Since the aging process may produce a number of pathological conditions affecting the defendant's criminal responsibility or competence to stand trial, investigation of these issues should be of paramount concern to defense counsel. Also addressed are the questions of whether advanced age could be used as a defense to a criminal charge, or if the elderly should receive some form of "special treatment" under the law. Cohen argues that the "variability in capacity and functioning of those who are of the same chronological age" (Cohen, 1984:116) requires a case by case determination of the criminal responsibility of elderly offenders. Moreover, "[l]egal doctrine built on a generalized picture of the [elderly] as sick, dependent, needy and not competent would not comport with the facts and would needlessly contribute to this negative stereotyping" (Cohen, 1984:127). A similar argument would seem to preclude the development of a special court for elderly offenders or the creation of "status offenses" applicable only to the aged.

Diversion

The traditional sentencing alternatives may be inappropriate or of limited value for older offenders. Fines may be onerous if the person is living on a fixed income. Probation programs and services may not be designed to meet the needs of aged persons, and probation officers may lack the training or skills necessary to work with them. Incarceration may be unduly severe given the nonserious nature of most crimes committed by older persons. In addition, the traditional vocationally oriented rehabilitation programs offered to aid offenders are unlikely to be beneficial for older people (Feinberg, 1984b), while confinement itself may be dangerous, since older offenders may be tempting targets for victimization by younger, tougher inmates.

To overcome these problems, a number of jurisdictions have established diversion programs for specific types of elderly offenders; the operations of at least two have been described (Feinberg, Glugover, and Zwetchkenbaum, 1984; Fry, 1984). The Broward Senior Intervention and Education Program was established in April 1979 to aid first offenders (aged 60 or over) who were convicted of shoplifting, while a California program diverted those (apparently 50 and over) "charged with misdemeanor property crimes, victimless sex offenses and less serious public disturbances, such as family dispute[s]" (Fry, 1984:147).

Participants in the Broward County program were required to attend a series of 12 weekly educational and activity sessions at a local community center. These sessions included lectures on current events, discussion groups focusing on health and health-related issues, art and handicraft classes, etc. They also received individual counseling, where social workers helped them identify the causes of their criminal behavior, reduced the trauma and embarrassment resulting from their arrest and conviction, and, where necessary, ". . . provide[d] emotional support and practical information [about] future procedures and expectations" (Feinberg, Glugover, and Zwetchkenbaum, 1984:184). A third, optional component of the program offered individuals the opportunity to do volunteer work in the community. The operational components of the California program are not as clearly described, but presumably are similar.

Proponents of each diversion program claimed success. For example, Feinberg, Glugover, and Zwetchkenbaum (1984) reported that 98.5 percent of the 1,400 individuals processed through the program from April 1979 to April 1982 completed it without incident (Feinberg, Glugover, and Zwetchkenbaum, 1984:188). Fry (1984:151) also reports a success rate of 98.5 percent.

Both programs have been criticized on similar grounds, however. It is possible that the restrictive criteria used to select participants (that is, first offenders, misdemeanants, etc.) and the nonserious nature of the charges involved artificially increased the success rate in both programs. Also, some probation staff resistance to the California program was reported, because they tended to view the elderly clients as more of a "social welfare" than a "criminal justice" problem (Fry, 1984:151). Clearly, more rigorous research is necessary before the effectiveness of diversion programs can be finally assessed.

The Elderly in Jail and Prison

The population of older inmates includes both first offenders convicted later in life, and those who have grown old in the system after being repeatedly incarcerated following a series of convictions, or receiving a long sentence at a very young age. Both types of offenders, however, create difficult problems for the jail and prison officials who must hold them securely, yet provide for their daily care and protection.

Offenders who are awaiting further processing in the criminal justice system or who have been convicted and sentenced to confinement for up to one year are typically held in local or county jail facilities. Jails tend to be small and perpetually overcrowded; conditions of confinement are often quite poor. Also, since jails are designed as short-term facilities, little effort is made to classify and separate different types of offenders. The dangerous and nondangerous, those convicted and those still presumed innocent, repeat offenders and "new fish" are all housed under one roof.

Incarceration would be a traumatic and distressing experience for anyone. But the presence of an elderly offender, who may be afraid, intoxicated, or physically or mentally ill can complicate the efforts of jail staff to gather information critical for their protection (such as the existence of a heart condition or other disability) or necessary for further processing through the system. The lack of classification and overcrowded conditions of confinement make the task of protecting older inmates difficult. Finally, an antiquated physical plant may make day-to-day life inside the jail almost intolerable for the older person (Golden, 1984:143).

How the elderly fare under long-term confinement in prison is a matter of controversy. Weigand and Burger portrayed the elderly inmate as "competent, responsive, quick and shrewd" (1979:59). Panton (1976-77) and McCreary and Mensh (1977) found them to be less psychotic than other inmates. They also appear to cause less trouble (Jensen, 1977), are less likely to participate in riots (Straus and Sherwin, 1975), and are more likely to benefit from rehabilitation programs. On the other hand, Panton (1976-77) found that elderly offenders as a group had lower IQs, a higher divorce rate, poorer work records, a higher incidence of alcohol abuse, a higher recidivism rate, and a higher proportion of persons who were "mentally defective" compared to younger inmates. Eysenck, Rust, and Eysenck (1977) and McCreary and Mensh (1977) found them introverted and neurotic.

Sociologists who have studied the effects of long-term confinement note that older inmates often become increasingly dependent on the prison environment, so much so that readjustment to freedom is difficult (Aday and Webster, 1979). Others, looking at the social status of the elderly in the prison environment, have suggested that the respect they are accorded by younger inmates may act as a stabilizing force within the institution, and reduce the possibility of riots and violence (Straus and Sherwin, 1975).

At all points of the criminal justice process, then, the presence of elderly offenders can raise a variety of difficult administrative problems. It has become clear, however, that the issues concerning when and how older persons should be processed through the system can no longer be addressed on an ad hoc basis. Clearly, researchers and practitioners must initiate a coordinated effort designed to meet the needs of this special group of offenders.

CONCLUSION

As we have shown, the body of previous research on elderly offenders is substantial, and can be traced back nearly a century. The existing literature can be grouped into three broad categories: (1) studies focusing on the amount and types of crime committed by older people; (2) studies that explore the causes of elderly criminality; and (3) those concerned with the problems that arise when elderly people are processed through the criminal justice system. It is important to note, however, that the studies *within* each of these categories can differ significantly, for example, in the age used to define an elderly person, or in the type of comparison group used in the study. These differences make it difficult to draw a clear, consistent picture of the various aspects of the elderly crime problem.

Nonetheless, some tentative conclusions seem warranted. First, most studies of national arrest data indicate that elderly persons are most often apprehended for the crimes of assault, embezzlement, fraud larceny-theft, alcohol-related offenses, and the "less serious" sex offenses. Trends in the data are more difficult to discern, but it seems likely that the level of crime will increase with the passage of time. In some areas of the country, this increase will be no more than one would expect in light of the increasing age of the general population. In other areas, however, particularly where elderly people make up a large proportion of the general population, the growth in the level of elderly crime may be more significant.

Second, studies of arrest data consistently indicate that the elderly are most frequently arrested for offenses involving alcohol, and for property offenses such as larceny or theft; high proportions of property offenders have also been found in samples of elderly prisoners. There seems little reason to suspect, however, that marked changes will occur in the types of crime committed by older people.

Third, to cope with the projected increases in the number of elderly offenders, officials of the criminal justice system may need to develop new programs or modify procedures to meet the needs of this special group. In some jurisdictions the most effective solution may be to develop one or more brief education programs designed to sensitize police and court and correctional personnel to the needs of elderly offenders. In other areas, where the elderly crime problem is more acute, a more extensive change effort may be needed, such as developing diversion programs specifically for elderly offenders or creating specialized units within the police department, prosecutor's and public defender's offices, and the probation department to process these cases.

Finally, there is a great need for additional research. Most pressing perhaps, is the need to learn more about how elderly offender cases are processed through the criminal justice system. What factors do the police, prosecutors, and judges take into account when they decide to arrest, charge, convict, and sentence an elderly person? How should correctional officials deal with older persons who are sent to prison? What policies should probation departments formulate regarding aged offenders?

In addition, we need to know much more about the causes of elderly crime. As currently structured, criminological theories provide us with only the bluntest of instruments with which to analyze and understand the problem of elderly crime. Substantial modification of existing theories—or perhaps the development of new ones—will be required.

SECTION II

PERSPECTIVES IN CRIMINOLOGY

3

Theoretical Perspectives on Deviant Behavior Among the Elderly

Ronald L. Akers
Anthony J. La Greca
Christine Sellers

INTRODUCTION: ARE CURRENT DEVIANCE THEORIES APPROPRIATE FOR THE ELDERLY?

A common theme expressed in the still sparse literature on elderly crime and offenders is that the research has tended to be largely descriptive, with little in the way of theoretical perspectives which account for deviant and criminal behavior among the elderly. Such theoretical perspectives are needed to understand elderly offense behavior better and to place disparate findings on socio-demographic and other characteristics of older offenders in a more coherent famework. Also, such theoretical development will help to relate knowledge of elderly crime and deviance to the larger body of criminological knowledge and to guide public policy discourse and recommendations. The purpose of this chapter is to examine the extent to which current theories of crime and delinquency, if systematically applied to elderly behavior, are adequate for moving toward these goals. The applicability of these theories to the elderly is not immediately obvious because, whatever the stated scope of the theories, they have, in fact,

This chapter was prepared under support from the National Institute of Alcoholism and Alcohol Abuse, Grant Number P50AA05793.

focused on the behavior of younger adults and youth, either in the original statements or in empirical tests.

The contention here is that special theories of elderly crime and deviance are not needed; new perspectives need not be invented to understand why some elderly persons violate the law or social norms—one can draw upon extant perspectives. The intent of this chapter, more specifically, is to present social learning, social bonding (control) theory, and anomie (strain), three of the most important theoretical perspectives on deviant and criminal behavior. These theories are not necessarily age-specific; they can be applied to the later end of the life cycle as they have been applied to account for the behavior at the adolescent or young adult stages. For each, conceptual and/or operational modifications in these perspectives are discussed to make them applicable to or capable of being tested in an older population.

These theories have been tested on research on alcohol use and abuse among the elderly, but they should be applicable to any form of deviant behavior among the elderly. This is not to imply that all alcohol consumption is deviant for this age group; indeed, as for other adult groups, most drinking is light or moderate and does not violate the drinking norms of the majority of the population.

The focus on the elderly here is not based on the assumption that crime or other deviance is an enormous problem among the elderly. Indeed, except for suicide and certain forms of mental illness, deviance rates are low for the elderly. Rather, it is based on the assumption that applying the theories to behavior in this age group enables the examination of the generalizability and empirical scope of the theories and offers explanations of why some elderly commit offenses against the law and social order. The theories account for both deviant behavior and (either explicitly or by implication) conforming behavior. Indeed, it is commonly claimed that social bonding theory takes conformity as the problem to be explained, and social learning theory claims to account for both conforming and deviant behavior.

The key concepts in social learning theory, including such seemingly adolescent-specific notions as peer associations, can successfully account for maintenance and changes of elderly behavior. Social bonding was specifically developed for delinquency and in the context of data on adolescents, but it too has empirical applications to elderly behavior. Anomie theory was formulated as a perspective on adult deviance but almost from the beginning was modified and tested principally with delinquent behavior and subcultures. Some key concepts such as the discrepancy between aspirations and expectations can, with appropriate respecification, be related to elderly behavior. Further, it is suggested that "life crises" or significant "life events" associated with aging (loss of spouse, deteriorating health, retirement, etc.), which have been offered as explanations of elderly alcoholism as one form of deviance, may be viewed as sources of anomic strain toward deviance.

Because the principal theoretical perspectives on crime and deviance have largely focused on the youthful stage of the life cycle, much of the discussion revolves around modifying concepts or measures to apply these perspectives to the older stage of the life cycle. But for many of the concepts, not much modification is needed; although there are clear differences in the societal location and social context of adolescence and old age there are also some similarities. Feinberg (1984a:46-48) summarizes some of the more salient similarities and differences between the two age statuses. He notes, for example, that both age groups when contrasted with young and middle-aged adults share a certain exemption from work responsibilities, relatively unstructured time schedules, limited financial independence, relative freedom from family responsibilities, de-emphasis on production and emphasis on consumption, and emphasis on play and leisure as a way of life. He notes as well important differences between the elderly and the juvenile.

1. Juveniles can anticipate future engagement in economic, familial, and political roles; the elderly can anticipate mainly disengagement from such roles.
2. Juveniles expect and are expected to enter mainstream society; the elderly expect and are expected to leave mainstream society—and not return.
3. In time, the status, financial, and power positions of juveniles become stronger, whereas in time they become weaker for the elderly.
4. Juveniles look up to those currently in power for acceptance and their reference groups rest within the ongoing social order. The elderly are outside mainstream society, like the youth, but above it. Career concerns, the need to postpone gratification in anticipation of long-range goals, the myriad benefits of acquisitional behavior, the lure of certain status passages, and similarly societally touted ideals which function as the proverbial "carrot" leading society's members along prescribed routes have lost their motivational appeal, stripped as they are of their relevance, intrinsic value, and even their pretense by experience and the cool wind of objective reality.
5. Juveniles tend to have close and intimate role models to follow; the elderly tend to lack such idealized role models (Feinberg, 1984a:47-48).

SOCIAL LEARNING THEORY AND DEVIANT BEHAVIOR AMONG THE ELDERLY

The term "social learning" has been applied to any number of social behavioristic approaches, but the social learning theory most relevant to deviant and criminal behavior is that first formulated by Burgess and Akers (1966; Akers, Burgess, and Johnson, 1968) and subsequently developed by

Akers through the three editions of his book, *Deviant Behavior: A Social Learning Approach* (1973, 1977, 1985). This theory integrates Sutherland's (1947) well-known differential association theory of criminal behavior with general behavioral principles emphasizing differential reinforcement.

According to the theory, social behavior is shaped by the stimuli that follow or are consequences of the behavior (instrumental conditioning) and by imitation of others' behavior (observational learning). Behavior is strengthened by reward (positive reinforcement) and avoidance of punishment (negative reinforcement) or weakened (punished) by aversive stimuli (positive punishment) and lack of reward (negative punishment). By a process of differential reinforcement, deviant behavior is acquired and persists, or conforming behavioral skills do not develop, depending on the anticipated, past, and present rewards and punishments attached to it and alternative behavior. This is frequently not an either/or choice, but rather several different kinds of behavior are carried in one's behavioral repertoire based on a matching function in which the frequency of each behavior is dependent on the relative frequency and value of reinforcement and punishment. The person learns definitions (attitudes, orientations, and evaluative knowledge) of the behavior as good or bad, right or wrong, or otherwise favorable or unfavorable to the behavior. These definitions are themselves verbal (vocal and subvocal) and cognitive behavior which can be directly reinforced and are also cue or discriminative stimuli for other behavior. Therefore, just as the reinforcement balance of aversive and rewarding stimuli affect the probability of behavior occurring, the balance of favorable and unfavorable definitions affects behavioral outcomes. The more individuals hold positive definitions which view the behavior as desirable or neutralizing definitions which justify or excuse the behavior rather than negative definitions of it, the more likely they are to engage in it.

As Akers notes, the reinforcers can be nonsocial, for example, direct physiological effects of drugs or unconditioned reinforcers such as food, or affected by nonsocial, individual variations in response. Nevertheless, the theory proposes that the principal behavioral effects come from:

> [T]hose groups with which one is in differential association and which control sources and patterns of reinforcement, provide normative definitions, and expose one to behavioral models. The most important of these are primary groups such as peer and friendship groups and the family, but they also include work, school, church, and other membership and reference groups (Akers, 1985:58).
>
> [T]he groups and individuals that comprise or control the major sources of the individual's reinforcement will have the greatest influence on his or her behavior. Usually these are primary groups, which Sutherland emphasized, but they can also be secondary or reference groups. They may be imaginary groups, persons, and situations portrayed through the books and the mass media. They may also be the more formal bureaucratic organizations like an individual's school or job, including agencies of social control and law enforcement (Akers, 1985:46).

Social learning incorporates a number of variables operative in the behavioral process of acquisition and maintenance of behavior or refraining from it drawn from behavioral psychology and sociology, and "all the mechanisms of learning are recognized" (Akers, 1985:58).[1] However, as can be seen from this summary statement there are four principal concepts in the theory and these have been incorporated into the research by Akers and associates as main sets of independent variables—*differential association, differential reinforcement, definitions,* and *imitation.*

The variables denoted by these concepts are contained in an ongoing behavioral process of interdependence and interaction as suggested in this statement by Akers.

> The process is a complex one with reciprocal and feedback effects, and the sequence of events is variable [depending on the particular behavior and group or individual in question]. [However] associations with others engaging in or supporting particular deviant acts typically precedes the individual's committing the acts. Those associations are most often formed on bases other than coinvolvement in the deviant behavior. However, after that deviant activity has begun and the consequences [reinforcing or punishing] accompanying it are experienced, the associational patterns may themselves be altered so that the fact that one is drawn to or chooses further interaction with others is based, at least in part, on whether they too are involved in the deviant activity and to what degree (1985:60).

Akers (1985) has used this social learning theory to explain a full range of criminal and deviant behavior for both youthful and adult populations, drug use and abuse, alcohol use and alcoholism, violent behavior, sexual deviance, white-collar, organized, and professional crime, suicide, and mental illness. Research on the basic learning principles, differential association, and other similar models and variables provides substantial empirical evidence consistent with the claims in social learning (for reviews of this extensive body of research see Akers, et al., 1979; Akers, 1985; Krohn, et al., 1985; Radosevich et al., 1980). Further, Akers's model has features in common with learning models that have received research support (Andrews, 1980; Chassin et al., 1981; Jessor and Jessor, 1977; McAlister, Krosnick, and Milburn, 1984). Other research has found models based on Akers's theory to have greater empirical support than competing theories (Conger, 1976; Elliott, Huizinga, and Ageton, 1985; Raskin-White, Johnson, and Horwitz, 1982). In collaboration with colleagues, Akers has conducted a series of research projects intended to test directly the basic model and variations based on it, finding strong empirical support for the theory (Akers et al., 1979; Akers and Cochran, 1985; Akers et al., 1986; Krohn et al., 1984; Krohn et al., 1985; Lanza-Kaduce, Akers, Krohn, and Radosevich, 1984; Lauer et al., 1982).

Almost all of this impressive body of empirical support has come from studies of delinquency, drug use, smoking, and drinking by teenagers.

Nevertheless the social learning model should be applicable to any age group, including the elderly. It is a theory of a dynamic process of acquiring and maintaining conforming and deviant behavior patterns without specific reference to or limitation by age, sex, or other socio-demographic variables. Nothing in the theory restricts its application to youth. The fact that the research has been largely confined to youthful subjects is more a matter of methodology, investigator preferences, and the traditionally greater concern for deviance among the young. It can be appropriately formulated for older subjects. Indeed, we have successfully tested a social learning model of drinking and deviant drinking among the elderly (Akers et al., 1986). The same theoretical concepts and propositions have been used as was used in earlier tests of the theory with adolescent substance use (Akers et al., 1979; Akers and Cochran, 1985; Krohn et al., 1985).

However, when the model is applied to elderly subjects some of the empirical referents or measures of the theoretical constructs have to be modified somewhat to make them more applicable to elderly samples. For instance, in the earlier studies of teenagers, imitation of parental and peer models was measured. Such imitation would be expected to be essentially unrelated to alcohol behavior in an old population; current parental modeling would be nonexistent or irrelevant. One could ask about recollection of parental drinking behavior when the respondents were growing up, and respondents in this study were asked about drinking patterns at different stages of the life cycle. To the extent that these recollections can be taken as accurate (Wilsnack, Klassen, and Wilsnack, 1984) it was expected from social learning theory that those who have been and are heavy drinkers to have been raised disproportionately in heavy drinking families and lifelong abstainers to have been raised mainly in abstinent families (Cotton, 1979). Obviously this is not the same thing as measuring the current modeling of drinking behavior of the parents of teenagers. Also, while it is common to find teenagers who have had no experience with alcohol, and take their first drink during adolescence, initiation of drinking by an old person after a long lifetime of total abstinence is apt to be a very low frequency event. Similarly, adolescence, rather than old age, is the time of life when those who become involved in more serious delinquency and crime first exhibit some deviant patterns. Those who are involved in crime, alcoholism, and other forms of deviance after entering the elderly years are apt to have established such behavior patterns earlier in life. While new behavior patterns are taken on and different life-styles may be assumed in late life (especially after retirement), these are not very likely to include initiation of new criminal or deviant behavior. While observational learning and the facilitative effects of modeling continue at all stages of life, imitation's effects are most likely to be seen in the initiation or acquisition of behavior. Therefore, a social learning model of elderly crime and deviance will include no or very brief reference to modeling.

Such a model would, however, give prominence to the other major social learning concepts of differential reinforcement, differential association, and definitions. Differential association with deviant and conforming, law-abiding and law-violating, peers and friends should be as important for this age as it is for adolescents. The norms to which one is exposed and the definitions favorable and unfavorable to deviance adopted by the individual, and the balance of reinforcement for conformity and deviance are important for the elderly just as they are for the adolescent population, but the important reference groups are different. For both the teenagers and the elderly most interaction is with others in the same general age group. But the range of ages is greater for the elderly, and the disproportionate interaction with other elderly people is more likely for those living in retirement communities. Further, whereas the peer groups for the young are heavily school-related, the relevant groups for the elderly are leisure, social work, and political groups. For both, the family is important, but for the youngster it is parents and siblings; for the older adult, it is spouse, adult children, and perhaps siblings.

Rewards and costs attached to behavior are important for both age groups. As with younger age groups, there are social rewards for drinking among the elderly, but the context will vary a bit. Alcohol can promote socialibility in the fairly restrictive residential settings such as nursing homes in which the elderly are sometimes located (Chein, Strotsky, and Cole, 1973). Changes in life-style whether or not experienced as crises can interact with these social rewards to affect drinking by the elderly. Alcohol is a social facilitator that is expected to relax the individual and "break the ice." It can serve as the focus for something to do or some place to go. It serves these functions for any adult age group, but can become especially relevant for the old person who must make new friends and adapt to a new social environment upon retirement and relocation, or as friends and spouses become immobile, are institutionalized, or die. In retirement communities peer groups de-emphasize one's status to prior retirement; residents see themselves as equals and attach little significance to one's past achievements or status in the general community (Perkinson, 1980). This may be welcomed by those who make friends easily and who enjoy the opportunity to join new groups. Others find this a more difficult adjustment to make. In either case, alcohol can play a role in establishing the relationships, and thereby be reinforced.

Thus, in this research on elderly drinking it was hypothesized from social learning theory that the elderly would drink alcohol and encounter problem drinking the greater the extent to which he or she associated with other drinkers (and heavy drinkers), perceived the social and physical rewards from drinking to be greater than the punishing or negative outcomes of drinking, and defined drinking in positive or neutralizing terms. The social learning model explained 59 percent of the variance in elderly drinking and successfully distinguished the problem drinker from the nonproblem drinker. This was about the same level of explained variance obtained in the earlier Akers study of adolescent drinking (Akers et al., 1979), although for adolescents peer association was the strongest social learning variable while for the elderly differential reinforcement was the strongest independent variable.

There is every reason to believe that a social learning model would also be empirically supported by data on elderly criminal and seriously deviant behavior. The theory would predict that elderly offenders differentially associate with other offenders, are differentially reinforced for committing the offenses, and have a balance of definitions favorable to commission of the offenses. In other words, social learning would explain the deviant (as well as conforming) behavior of the elderly just as it would explain the behavior of adolescents, young adults, and middle-aged adults.

The key social learning concepts are measured very similarly for all age groups, the modalities of association (frequency, duration, priority, and intensity), the social and nonsocial rewards and punishers, and the positive, negative, and neutralizing definitions. However, there are some differences in the specific content of the definitions and the groups with which one is in association and which provide social reinforcement for the behavior. Also, while the overall social learning model is the same for all age groups, the relative explanatory power of the theoretical variables in the best fitting empirical model may differ somewhat for elderly and youthful behavior.

SOCIAL BONDING THEORY AND ELDERLY DEVIANCE

Although control theories have long made reference to other populations, they have mainly been formulated for and tested with juvenile delinquency in mind. Nye's (1958) theory, with its emphasis on internal and indirect control and family relationships, and its test on self-reported delinquency is a clear indication of this. Reckless's (1967) containment theory is also focused on delinquency; its major emphasis on self-concept as an inner containment and its test with the "good boy" insulated self-concept versus the "bad boy" vulnerable self-concept refers specifically to teenage boys from 12 to 16.[2] Social bonding theory, which has become the most influential control theory of deviance, was originally formulated by Hirschi (1969) specifically as an explanation of juvenile delinquency. Thus the scope of the theory was restricted to delinquent acts of adolescents. Hirschi's own data came from a self-report delinquency study among secondary school students. With only one exception (Minor, 1977), all subsequent research testing of bonding theory has used youth crime and status offenses, including teenage substance use, as the dependent variables.

However, social bonding's underlying logic is applicable to deviant/conforming behavior at any age; there is little reason to believe it cannot be more broadly applied beyond the law-abiding or unlawful behavior of juveniles. The bonding principles should be able to produce the same explanation for similar behavior among juveniles or the elderly. What are these principles?

The basic principle is that "delinquent acts result when an individual's bond to society is weak or broken" (Hirschi, 1969:16-30). The bond is comprised of various elements or subsets of bonds; the stronger these bonds are the more the person will conform to social norms; the weaker they are, the more likely one is to violate the rules. Hirschi's contention is that it is really only the first part of this statement which is of interest to control theory—conformity is the behavior that needs to be explained, while it can be taken for granted that deviant acts will occur unless the bonds are strong. The elements of social bond which constrain individuals from the inclination to deviate are identified by Hirschi as attachment, commitment, involvement, and belief.

Attachment to social groups creates a sensitivity to others' opinions which binds the individual to social norms. To other control theorists this may be referred to as internal control or internalization of norms through socialization or self-concept (Reiss, 1951; Nye, 1958; Reckless, 1967). To Hirschi, reference to the constraint from outside the individual through attachment to others is a more objective way of dealing with personal control than is reference to some internal self factor or inner containment. The greater the degree of integration into a group, that is, the stronger the attachment to others, the greater the extent to which the general social norms exert a constraining power over the individual. To Hirschi, the fact of attachment, of integration itself, rather than the nature of the group (delinquent or nondelinquent) to which one is attached produces the conformity. *Commitment* refers to investment in conventional lines of action and attainment of a reputation or status in society that would be jeopardized by the commission of delinquent acts. When these stakes in conformity are low, there is less to lose if caught in deviant behavior, and therefore, less control on deviant behavior. *Involvement* refers to engrossment in, or preoccupation with, conventional activity. Hirschi argues that one may be too busy with conventional activities to have time for deviant activities. In this dimension of the social bond, Hirschi focuses mainly on the time spent doing conventional things rather than the investment that this time represents, but, obviously, there is considerable overlap between this concept and commitment (Krohn and Massey, 1980). *Belief* refers to the degree of acceptance of the norms and values of society. Social bonding theory assumes that deviants and conformists alike share a common value system. In other words, deviants believe that certain acts are wrong, yet they violate the norms forbidding them anyway. According to bonding theory, there is variation in the extent to which people believe they should obey the rules of society; the less strongly one believes in obedience to the rules the greater the likelihood one is to violate them. Deviance is not a function of beliefs demanding violation of the rules, but rather "is made possible by the absence of (effective) beliefs that forbid [it] . . . " (Hirschi, 1969:198).

The research on social bonding theory has demonstrated moderate support for its central propositions. Hirschi's own data (1969) support the theory, although he found that attachment to delinquent peers did not constrain delinquency very well, and subsequent research has found little support for the central contention that stronger peer attachment, regardless of the life-styles and behavior of the peers, lowers chances of delinquency. Attachment to delinquent peers, not surprisingly, increases the probability of delinquency. However, the same sizeable body of literature that finds the type of peers to which one is attached does make a difference (counter to social bonding theory) usually also finds that attachment, commitment, beliefs, and involvement are negatively related to delinquency (Agnew, 1985a; Akers and Cochran, 1985; Conger, 1976; Datesman and Scarpitti, 1975; Elliott, Huizinga, and Ageton, 1985; Hepburn, 1976; Hindelang, 1973; Jensen, 1972; Krohn and Massey, 1980; Krohn et al., 1985; Linden, 1978; Liska and Reed, 1985; Poole and Regoli, 1979).

Given the above, there is reason to believe that the social bonding theory can explain conforming or deviant behavior of older people. Stronger bonds ought to produce greater conformity in any segment of society. Weaker ties to family, friends, and society should free individuals of any age to deviate. This does not mean that older and younger age groups undergo identical social processes or that the social context of the two are the same. While adolescents may be tied to certain specific institutions in the conventional order, very different types of institutions may be more salient for older adults. The abstract concepts and propositions of the theoretical model may remain the same, but the empirical indicators of social bonding must be modified somewhat to accommodate the social situations in which most of the elderly live. Although the content of beliefs is largely unaffected by one's age group, there may be great differences between adolescents and older adults in the specific kinds of attachments, commitments, and involvements in which they take part.

Thus, while attachment to family is expected to be important for both adolescents and the elderly, Hirschi places heavy emphasis on the adolescent's attachment to parents and peers. For the senior person, attachment would be to spouse, adult children, and siblings as well as to elderly peers. Hirschi's measure of commitment are rather adolescent-specific. Although Hirschi asserts that commitment refers to one's stake in conformity in general, such that one's actual accumulations can be jeopardized by deviance, he rationalizes that the concept can be applied to a juvenile's ambitions for the future which may also be threatened by deviance. When studying adolescents, future ambitions and status, then, is what one must measure. For the most part, adolescents have not yet attained a status or reputation for themselves in society at large. Although they may have achieved status within their school or peer groups, their class, economic, and occupational status is "borrowed" from the parents. Future status has greater significance for teenagers, and their aspirations and expectations are more realistic measures of their stake in conformity than what little they have achieved while still in secondary school. For the elderly, commitment is more past and present oriented. While it cannot be said that older people have no aspirations or sense of future accomplishment, for the most part, their long-range goals have already been either achieved or abandoned. An older person's stake in conformity rests on what has already been achieved in investment and reputation in conventional society.

The empirical indexes of the concept of involvement also are affected by differences in age groups. For adolescents, involvement in school activities is of primary importance. Older people rarely engage in degree-earning educational pursuits, but they do become involved in various other activities that require an investment of time and energy, such as hobbies, volunteer service, church activities, and work. These should produce the same constraints on deviance among the elderly that school work and extra curricular activities produce for adolescents. In the abstract, involvement is an integrating bond which increases stakes in conformity and controls involvement in criminal and deviant activities for both age groups, but the concrete activities that indicate this involvement differ.

With these variations in the empirical referents for the theoretical concepts in the model in mind, then, the social bonding theory would explain adolescent and elderly deviance in the same way. For the elderly, as for teenagers, the weaker the bonds of attachment, commitment, involvement, and beliefs the greater the probability of the commission of criminal offenses and other deviant behavior. The more integrated or bonded the elderly person the more likely he or she is to refrain from such behavior and continue in conformity.

We have tested a social bonding model of elderly drinking, problem drinking, and law violation (as measured by reported contact with the criminal justice system). The level of explained variance for elderly drinking was similar to that for bonding models of adolescent substance use (27 percent); the model was also supported but more weakly for problem drinking and contact with the criminal justice system.

ANOMIE, STRAIN, AND DEVIANT BEHAVIOR AMONG THE ELDERLY

Beginning with Durkheim's classic study of suicide (1951), anomie as a social structural condition has been a pivotal perspective on deviance. But its special application to a range of conforming and deviant adaptations stems primarily from Merton's (1938) "means/ends" paradigm which moved toward the contemporary elaboration of anomie to what is often referred to as "strain" theory. From this perspective the gap between culturally induced success goals and the acceptable means to achieve these goals as well as the relative inaccessibility of acceptable means to certain segments of society places strain on individuals to deviate from the norms by pursuing illegitimate means to achieve success.

Merton's references were to deviance in general without special emphasis on youthful populations. However, subsequent theorizing and empirical research in this tradition has been with special reference to juvenile delinquency and delinquent subcultures. In Cohen's (1955) version of strain theory, the anomic situation producing participation in the delinquent subculture results from the fact that lower class boys (the principal carriers of the subculture) are judged by unattainable middle-class criteria. In Cloward and Ohlin's (1959, 1960) version, differential opportunity theory, the discrepancy between educational and occupational goals and the legitimate opportunities to achieve them to which the adolescent has realistic access exerts strain to commit deviant acts by utilizing illegitimate means. The type of deviant behavior chosen or the type of delinquent subculture in which the adolescent becomes involved depends upon the availability of illegitimate opportunities. Those who experience "double failure" in both opportunity structures will take on Merton's "retreatist" adaptation by becoming involved in drug and alcohol abuse. Whatever the source of the strain, the expectation is that the individual will become alienated, develop a sense of powerlessness, or otherwise experience strain and then seek deviant means to accomplish success goals or retreat to drugs to escape the failure. Empirical research on one or more of the varieties of anomie theory has been focused on delinquency; in general the research findings provide weak or inconsistent support for the theory (Akers and Cochran, 1985; Elliott, 1966; Elliott, Huizinga, and Ageton, 1985; Liska, 1971; Short, 1964; Short and Riveria, 1965; Simmons, Miller, and Aigner, 1980; Winslow, 1967). Nevertheless, the theory has continued to receive widespread attention as a major perspective on deviance and efforts continue to revise it to enhance its explanatory power (Agnew, 1985b).

As noted, the anomie perspective shares with the other two perspectives discussed in this chapter an empirical focus on delinquency. But as with the other two, there is little theoretical reason to confine its application to adolescents. Unlike the other two perspectives, however, there is some research literature on the elderly which, while not always consciously addressed to strain theory, has direct relevance to it. Much of the thinking related to strain for the elderly comes from inferential formulations found in Rosow's (1974) classic work *Socialization to Old Age*. Rosow discussed a rather gloomy picture of aging that revolved around three key dimensions of aging. First, retirement, loss of spouse, and other events associated with aging all represent a change of role(s) and status for the elderly. Second,

American society does little to socialize people to the new status of retirement and aging. Roles are lost but there is little substantive new role activity to take their place. The participation that is there for the elderly often revolves around leisure/recreational activity that has little intrinsic, meaningful content. Third, Rosow saw that growing old was a devalued status in a youth-oriented society. All of these factors of aging have been hypothesized as predictors of anomie in older adults.

Direct research on anomie and the aged is characterized by some sense of dealing with the ideas formulated by Rosow and preceding work that parallel Rosow's thinking (see Meier and Bell, 1959). The operational link to anomie is taken from two of the main empirical formulations of anomie—Seeman's (1959) or Srole's (1956). Seeman proposed that anomie was characterized by five recurring modes or components: powerlessness, meaninglessness, normlessness, isolation, and self-estrangement. Srole developed a scale for the direct measurement of "anomia," which he saw as ". . . the individual's generalized pervasive sense of self-to-others belongingness at one extreme compared with self-to-others distance and self-to-others alienation at the other pole of the continuum" (see Leonard, 1977:304). For both Seeman and Srole, anomie has some underlying dimension of unhappiness and powerlessness or inability to know how to cope with a situation of changing rewards and means to achieve those rewards. These two formulations have special appeal for gerontologists who focused on anomie as one of the consequences of aging.

Data on the level of anomie in the elderly or the correlates of anomie for this age group have produced conflicting conclusions. Leonard (1977) found anomie to be related to aging. On the other hand, Pope and Ferguson (1982-83) found no such relationship between age and anomie. However, their cut-off point for "aging" was 40 years since they were also looking at middle-aged as well as older adults. Pope and Ferguson believed that the supposedly greater level of anomie among the elderly is really an artifact of the cohort effect of education and that anomic responses are not inherent in growing older.

As this makes clear, most of the literature on anomie and old age relates to describing or trying to account for the social psychological condition of anomie among the elderly as the *dependent* variable rather than using it as an *independent* variable in the explanation of elderly deviance or crime. One area in which there has been some attempt to relate deviant response to anomic strain among the elderly is alcohol abuse. Indeed, this seems to be the area where the anomie perspective is most apt to be applied to adult populations; the most common explanation of alcoholism or problem drinking is that it is a response to stress, normlessness, alienation, and external locus of control (Apao and Damon, 1982; Phillips, 1976; Seeman and Anderson, 1983; Williams, Calhoun, and Ackoff, 1982). As applied to the elderly this perspective emphasizes the stress that is believed to accompany the occurrence of "life crises" or "life events" associated with growing old—retirement, death of loved ones, health deterioration, lowered standard of living, social isolation, and so on. The hypothesis is that a significant portion of elderly alcohol abuse is a "late onset" of drinking problems in the elderly years as a response to the stress or strain of these events (Borgatta, Montgomery, and Borgatta, 1982; Dupree, Broskowski, and Schonfeld, 1984; Glatt, Rosin, and Jauhar, 1978). The research evidence in support of this hypothesis is primarily from clinical studies (Dupree, Broskowski, and Schonfeld, 1984; Hubbard, Santos, and Santos, 1979). Survey studies have not supported it (Borgatta, Montgomery, and Borgatta, 1982; Meyers et al., 1982), and we have not found support for it in our own research (La Greca, Akers, and Dwyer, 1986). We have found that problem drinking is related to other deviance among the elderly (see Chapter 4 of this volume), but we have not found alcohol problems to be related to life crises faced by the elderly.

Another form of deviant behavior to which anomie theory and life events would seem to be especially relevant is elderly suicide. All sociological theories of suicide rates are variations on the Durkheimian theme of higher suicide rates resulting from lack of social integration (egoistic) or regulation (anomic), and some social psychological theories of suicide refer to personal disorganization, hopelessness, alienation, disrupting loss, or other concepts that overlap with anomie (Akers, 1985). Suicide rates among the elderly have always been high in modern society (Hendin, 1982; Stack, 1982), and theoretically, anomie among the elderly should also be high. There have been few attempts to test this hypothesis or to explain elderly suicide specifically. Usually, it is assumed to be accounted for by the general theory used to account for suicide at any age. But in those instances where it is given special treatment, there is strong emphasis on life crises or events of old age such as illness, death of a spouse, or institutionalization for treatment, which make the elderly vulnerable to suicide (Miller, 1979).

The theoretical link between life events, anomie, and problem drinking is still very much undeveloped in the literature, and the link to other forms of deviant or criminal behavior is seldom made. We have not developed and tested an anomie/strain model for elderly deviance in the way we have with social learning and social bonding models. However, we speculate that the central concepts of normlessness, alienation, and powerlessness, and the stress of significant life events which have been used with adult and elderly populations to some extent already could be combined with strain models that have been developed and tested primarily with adolescents to produce a coherent anomie perspective on elderly deviance.

As we have pointed out for social learning and social bonding models, some strain concepts that have been applied to juveniles or the way they are measured would have to be modified. For instance, a key measure of the concept of anomie with adolescents is the perceived discrepancy between occupational and educational aspirations and expectations. The notion is that a perception of blocked or obstructed opportunities to achieve the goals to which the adolescents have been socialized to aspire is experienced as anomic strain which is deviance producing, to achieve success by illegitimate means or to retreat to drug abuse. For the elderly the concept of anomie as a discrepancy between future aspirations and expectations is not very relevant. This is not to say that the elderly do not have goals and future plans. However, these are not very likely to include occupational or educational goals which can be blocked.

The more relevant concept for the elderly is anomie as a type of retrospective or current discrepancy between life goals and actual achievements. Have the educational and occupational aspirations with which one began as a youth or young adult been realized or thwarted? The measure then is not expectation of limited opportunities, but of limited accomplishments, perhaps as a result of blocked or limited opportunities in life. In some ways this is closer to the original anomie concept than the future-oriented measures used with juveniles. Other anomie concepts would appear to be directly applicable. For instance, external "locus of control" (the belief that one has little control over events and that control lies externally in the hands of others or in fate) has been used by some researchers as an indicator of perceived powerlessness (see Akers and Cochran, 1985) in studies of adolescent deviance. This concept (and the specific measures) can be applied intact to the elderly.

The hypothesis from the anomie perspective regarding elderly deviance would be the same as that regarding adolescents. The theoretical expectation is that those elderly experiencing higher levels of anomie are more likely to engage in criminal or other deviant activities. Our expectation, based on empirical research on juvenile delinquency, is that elderly deviance will be related to anomie, but that the relationship will be weak.

CONCLUSIONS

To repeat the theme with which we began, we believe that the major theoretical perspectives on deviance are applicable to elderly crime and deviance. Special theories relating only to this age group are not necessary. Social learning, social bonding, and anomie theories offer explanations of deviance among this age group that are as coherent and relevant as they are for the adolescent age group to which they have been almost exclusively applied. The concepts and propositions of the theories are abstract enough not to be age-specific, and there are enough commonalities between adolescence and old age that these perspectives hold promise in accounting for substance abuse, crime, and milder forms of deviance among the elderly.

However, as we have shown, in each instance some conceptual and/or measurement modifications need to be made when the models developed for adolescents are applied to the elderly. We have made these modifications and adaptations for two of the perspectives, social learning and social bonding, and have tested them on alcohol behavior among the elderly. The findings are very similar to those from tests of the theories with adolescent substance use—strong support for social learning and moderate support for social bonding. Research on delinquency has found limited support for anomie theory, and we would expect similar results from research on elderly deviance. We have not yet adapted a specific anomie model, but we have tested the effects of stress-producing elderly life events on alcohol problems, and find little support for the theory.

Only a beginning has been made. The interest in deviant behavior among the elderly may fade, and the impetus to find good explanations for it may wane. But to the extent that interest in and research on criminal and deviant behavior among the older population continues there will be an increasingly pressing need for going beyond the descriptive and exploratory work which now characterizes the field to develop theory that is logically consistent, empirically sound, and policy relevant. To accomplish these objectives, we can take advantage of the theoretical models that have already been developed, even though they have concentrated on persons at the other end of the life cycle. We do not have to produce new theory.

NOTES

1. For a full statement of the theory see Akers, 1985; for a general statement of behavioral sociology see Baldwin and Baldwin, 1981.

2. See Feinberg, 1984a, for a brief reference to containment theory and elderly shoplifters.

4

Alcohol, Contact with the Legal System, and Illegal Behavior Among the Elderly

Ronald L. Akers
Anthony J. La Greca

INTRODUCTION

The research literature has shown for a long time a relationship between alcohol and criminal or deviant behavior (Akers, 1984; Collins, 1981a, 1981b), but very little of this research deals with the issue in the older ages, and "little attention has been paid to the role that alcohol plays in offenses by the elderly" (Wilbanks, 1984b:7). Indeed, there has not been much research of any kind on elderly offenders.

Newman, Newman, and Gewirtz wrote in 1984 that:

> of all the problems and dilemmas created by the greying of America, one that has received little professional attention is the involvement of greater number of elderly persons with the criminal justice system. [There is a good deal of research on elderly victims, but the elderly as offender] has been relatively neglected (p. xix).

In another volume published at the same time, Wilbanks and Kim (1984) reach a similar conclusion:

The research reported here was funded by a grant from the National Institute on Alcoholism and Alcohol Abuse, Grant Number P50AA05793.

> Considerable media attention has focused on crime by the elderly in the past two years. . . . However, little scholarly material exists on the topic, and the media . . . make claims (e.g., that there is a geriatric crime wave and that the elderly offender is more likely to be violent) in a vacuum of knowledge on this topic (p. v).

Although there has been some additional work done, these descriptions of research on elderly offenders are still largely accurate. What research there is shows that there are relatively few elderly offenders, comprising a small proportion of all arrests and having an arrest rate much lower than younger age groups. There is no new "elderly crime wave," nor is there any strong basis to expect that the rate of elderly criminal behavior will increase dramatically in the near future (Cullen, Wozniak, and Frank, 1985; Wilbanks, 1984-85). However, that same research shows that a high proportion of the elderly (usually defined as 60 years of age and older, but sometimes as 55 and over) who come into contact with the legal system through arrest or criminal complaint do so for alcohol offenses such as DWI and public drunkenness (Newman, Newman, and Gewirtz, 1984; Meyers, 1984; Shichor, 1984a; Wilbanks and Kim, 1984).

Wilbanks (1984a) reported that drunkenness and DWI alone account for 52 percent of all arrests of the elderly, compared to 29 percent of the arrests of other persons 15-59. Shichor and Kobrin (1978) found drunkenness, driving while intoxicated, and disorderly conduct to be major categories of arrests of the elderly, and Shichor (1984a) found that the three offenses of DWI, drunkenness, and liquor law violation accounted for 57 percent of elderly arrests (55 and over), while accounting for only 28 percent of arrests of those under 55. For both groups, there have been dramatic increases in arrests for DWI or DWI offenses. Because of the decriminalization of public drunkenness offenses, arrests for these offenses have declined for all ages, but it has been less for the elderly than for younger age groups, and the proportion of arrests of the elderly for alcohol-related offenses continues to be greater than for younger age groups. This does not mean that the elderly are more likely to drink and drive than younger age groups; in fact, they are much less likely to do so (Meyers, 1984). It does, however, point to the fact that elderly alcohol offenders are involved in repeated arrests for conduct resulting from intoxication (Wilbanks, 1984-85).

Thus the research indicates that alcohol-specific offenses are the most common reasons for the elderly to be arrested and detained in jail. But none of it examines the relationship between alcohol consumption and the commission of arrestable offenses or actually being arrested. Also, the literature has neglected the related issue of noncriminal contact of the elderly with the legal system. Except for the Meyers (1984) study which asked respondents in a telephone interview about driving and drinking, all of the extant research utilizes official data on offenses. At this time, to our knowledge, there is no published research on self-reported offense behavior among the elderly. Self-reported offense behavior has become the standard technique in research on delinquency and has been used on some adult populations, but self-report instruments have not been developed for elderly populations.

We believe ours to be the first research to provide an examination not only of the incidence of alcohol offenses, but also of the link between alcohol and offense behavior in a general population sample of the elderly. Further, self-reported rather than official data were used. These are of two kinds. First, self-reported contact with the justice system as obtained for the full sample. This includes citations, arrests, convictions, and incarceration. Since this does not measure offense behavior directly it is referred to as contact with the criminal justice system rather than criminal behavior. But this type of contact with the justice system is not the only one of interest. How much experience do the elderly have with the legal system in general, including the civil justice system? There is virtually no research on elderly contact with the civil legal system. Therefore, respondents were also asked about their experience as litigants in civil suits, as jurors, and as witnesses. Second, data were collected from one community on self-reported illegal behavior.

METHODS AND PROCEDURES

Sample

The findings reported here come from a study of various sociological aspects of elderly life in four types of communities. These four communities were selected to represent community settings that are typical of the living situations of the noninstitutionalized elderly population (La Greca and Dzegede, 1980). These are a retirement community in New Jersey, a retirement community in Florida, and two age-integrated communities in Florida.

The main data collection instrument was a structured, closed-end interview conducted in the homes of the respondents. Our operational definition of elderly is 60 years of age or older. Probability samples were drawn from each of the age-heterogeneous communities by random-digit telephone enumeration.

Nonrandom samples were drawn from the two retirement communities. The completion rate in the two age-integrated communities was 74 percent, and in the two retirement communities the completion rate was 40 percent; this lower rate resulted primarily from restrictions placed on our access by the management and associations in the communities.

The valid first-year interviews on which the present analysis is based are as follows:

	N =
New Jersey retirement community	216
Florida retirement community	516
Alachua County, Florida	352
Pinellas County, Florida	326
Total	1,410

Alcohol Behavior

Frequency of drinking of alcohol in the past year was measured on a nine-point scale from abstinence to daily drinking. This frequency variable is dichotomized with those reporting no drinking at all or only once or twice in the past year and categorized as nondrinkers or abstainers, and all others categorized as drinkers.

The frequency of drinking was also cross-classified with the quantity of alcohol consumed on a typical day in which drinking occurred. An index was produced from the cross-classification with five values of abstinence, light, moderate, heavy, and excessive drinking. Problem drinking is a dichotomous variable of no problems or one or more problems in the past year from a checklist of problems of dependency or functioning connected with alcohol.

Contact with the Legal System

Contact with the criminal justice system is an index based on whether or not the respondent reported having received a moving violation traffic ticket, having been arrested, been convicted, been placed on probation, or been incarcerated in jail or prison during the past year. The index is also dichotomized with no contact and contact for one or more of these reasons.

Contact with the civil justice system is an index based on reported experience with the legal system in the past year as a litigant in a suit, as a juror, as a court witness or similar contact. Again, for purposes of testing the statistical association, this variable is dichotomized.

Offense Behavior

Offense behavior is measured by self-reports of committing five offenses—assault, shoplifting, public intoxication, intoxicated while driving, and illegal gambling "since turning 60." This was seen as the equivalent of the wording often used in self-report delinquency studies of "have you ever" committed the offense. These items were included in the interviews conducted at only one of the four communities in the study.

ANALYSIS OF DATA AND PRESENTATION OF FINDINGS

Distribution of Drinking Behavior Among the Elderly

The data analysis presented here is largely descriptive and exploratory. Neither the theoretical issues nor the data at this point warrant advanced quantitative techniques, and only univariate and bivariate analyses are presented. The frequency distribution on the legal contact and offense behavior items are skewed with very few reporting illegal behavior or contact with the criminal justice system, and they were dichotomized in the statistical analysis. Although Personian correlations are reported, they should be read keeping in mind that they are not entirely appropriate for variables measured this way. Therefore, gamma is also reported as a more appropriate measure of association for ordinal and categorical data.

Contact with the justice system and criminal behavior are treated here as the dependent variables and alcohol behavior as the independent variable. However, no causative argument is put forth, and no case is made for causal ordering. The measures of alcohol behavior and contact with the legal system both refer to the past year, and there is no way of knowing if they occurred together or in what order they occurred. The measure of offense behavior refers to anytime during the elderly years; however, it is known that for most of those in this sample, the pattern of drinking behavior in the past year is essentially what it was during the previous decade. Thus, their drinking behavior at the time of engaging in the law violations was most likely the same as that reported for the past year.

Table 4.1 presents the percentage distribution of the alcohol variables. The first part of this table shows the distribution by collapsed categories on the drinking frequency variable. Slightly over 60 percent of the sample reported at least some drinking in the past year. Four out of ten drink at least weekly. The vast majority of the drinkers are light to moderate consumers, but 6 percent of the total sample and 10 percent of the drinkers drink heavily or excessively. A little over 3 percent of the sample (5.5 percent of the drinkers) report at least one problem in the past year related to drinking alcohol. These findings are consistent with those from other surveys of elderly drinking behavior (Barnes, 1979; Borgatta, Montgomery, and Borgatta, 1982; Holzer et al., 1984; Meyers et al., 1981-82). While the majority of elderly persons are drinkers (as are the majority of younger age groups) few are deviant drinkers who drink excessively or encounter problems with their drinking.

Distribution of Elderly Contact with the Legal System and Offense Behavior

The research literature reports that for other age groups criminal behavior and involvement in the criminal justice system are more apt to

Table 4.1.
Percentage Distribution of Drinking Behavior Among the Elderly (N = 1410)

	Percent	Percent
Frequency of Drinking During Past Year		
Abstaining		38.2 %
Monthly drinking (up to 2-3 times a month)		19.6
Weekly drinking (up to 3-4 times a week)		21.1
Daily drinking		21.1
Frequency/Quantity of Drinking During Past Year		
	Total Sample	Drinkers Only
Abstaining	38.2 %	---
Light drinking	30.5	49.3
Moderate drinking	25.0	40.4
Heavy drinking	5.7	9.2
Excessive drinking	.7	1.1
Alcohol-Related Problems During Past Year		
Total sample		3.1 %
Drinkers only		5.5
Drinking After Age 60		
No drinking		36.7 %
Decreased drinking		3.9
No change in drinking		54.6
Increased drinking		2.9
First began drinking		1.1
First began heavy drinking		.8

Source: Compiled by authors.

occur among heavier drinkers (Collins, 1981a). Since the elderly have low rates of heavy and problem drinking, one would expect to find low frequencies of reported offense behavior and contact with the criminal justice system. This assumption was validated by the data.

Table 4.2 presents the percentages of the sample who have had contact with the legal system in the past year. Very few have been cited, arrested, or incarcerated (5.2 percent). Considerably more have had experience with the legal system (17.5 percent) as civil litigants, but it is apparent that not very many of the elderly have had recent encounters of any kind with the law.

Table 4.3 presents the univariate distribution for self-reported illegal behavior. As expected the elderly very infrequently commit any of these

Table 4.2.
Percentages of Self-Reported Contact with the Criminal or Civil Justice Systems in the Past Year Among the Elderly (Four Communities)

	Percent	N
Contact with Criminal Justice (arrested, convicted, or incarcerated)	5.2	1,366
Contact with Civil Justice (litigant, probate, custody)	17.5	1,343
Contact with either Criminal or Civil Justice System	21.3	1,322

Source: Compiled by authors.

Table 4.3.
Percentages of Self-Reported Offense Behavior Since Turning 60 (One Community)

	Percent	N
Assault	2.0	304
Shoplifting	1.3	304
Drunk in Public	2.0	304
Drunk Driving	2.6	304
Illegal Gambling	4.6	304
Any Offense	5.9	303

Source: Compiled by authors.

acts. Only about 6 percent of the elderly in the one community in which these questions were asked report committing at least one of the five offenses. The offenses include those for which the elderly are most likely to be arrested if discovered, but the responses paint a different picture from the official crime statistics of the relative frequency of these offenses. Whereas official data indicate that when the elderly are arrested it is most apt to be for drunkenness or driving while under the influence of alcohol, gambling is the most frequently reported offense in this sample (4.6 percent). Driving while intoxicated is the next most frequently reported offense, but the same number report assaulting someone as report public drunkenness.

Alcohol and Contact with the Legal System

Table 4.4 presents the bivariate relationships between the measures of drinking behavior, as well as socio-demographic variables, and contact with the criminal and civil justice systems. This table shows that elderly men in these four communities are more likely than the elderly women to have had some kind of contact with the legal system in the past year as a suspect or defendant, but there is no difference by sex in other types of reported contact with the legal system. Although the differences are not great, there is a tendency for higher status elderly to have more contact with both the civil and criminal justice systems. The differences by race must be viewed with great caution because only 5 percent of our sample is nonwhite, but apparently nonwhite respondents are a little more likely to have been cited or arrested.

The table shows that there is at best a slight relationship between drinking patterns and elderly experience with the legal system for civil issues. This is not surprising, and there is no theoretical reason to expect a general

Table 4.4.
Association of Drinking Behavior and Socio-Demographic Variables Contact with the Criminal and Civil Justice Systems Among the Elderly (All Communities)

Drinking Behavior	Contact with Criminal Justice Systems G =	r =	Contact with Civil Justice Systems G =	r =
Drinking Behavior				
Drinking/Abstaining	.31	.06	.06	.03
Frequency of Drinking	.13	.04	.10	.04
Frequency/Quantity Index	.16	.05	.07	.02
Problem Drinking	.45	.08	.12	.00
Sex	.38	.08	.02	.00
Race	.10	.00	-.13	.01
SES	.22	.05	.15	.07
N =	1,366		1,343	

Source: Compiled by authors.

association of drinking with ordinary contact with the system as a civil litigant. However, one would expect a clearer relationship between alcohol behavior and the experience of having been arrested, and as Table 4.5 shows that is what is found. The clearest relationship is between problem drinking and contact with the legal system due to an arrest, conviction, or criminal sanction. It is a moderate relationship (G = .45 and r = .08), but it is the strongest in the table. This indicates that nondrinkers are the least likely to be apprehended for law violations and a disproportionate number of those who have been arrested or have had other types of contact with the criminal justice system come from among those who report having drinking problems.

This is shown more clearly in Table 4.5 in which contact with the justice system is cross-tabulated with drinking and problem drinking. The vast majority of respondents, regardless of drinking behavior, had had no experience whatsoever as an apprehended offender. However, the risk that a drinker will be among that small number who have had such experience is

Table 4.5.
Percentage Distribution of Alcohol Drinking and Problem Drinking by Self-Reported Contact with the Criminal Justice System Among the Elderly (All Communities)

	Contact with Criminal Justice in Past Year		
	None	One or More	N =
Alcohol			
Abstaining	96.6	3.4	527
Drinking	93.7	6.3	839
Total	95.0	5.0	1,366
Chi-Square = 5.5 df = 1 P<.05 Gamma = .31 r = .04			
Problem Drinking (Drinkers Only)			
None	93.7	6.3	728
One or More Problems	85.0	15.0	40
Total	93.2	6.8	768
Chi-Square = 4.5 df = 1 P<.05 Gamma = .45 r = .08			

Source: Compiled by authors.

nearly twice that for the abstainer; the proportion (15.0 percent) of problem drinkers who have had such contact is more than double that of other drinkers (6.3 percent), and nearly three times that of the abstainer (3.4 percent). Very few elderly get caught up in the legal system regardless of drinking habits, but relative to abstainers and moderate drinkers, the elderly person who abuses alcohol stands at a greatly increased risk of doing something that will result in a citation, arrest, or other official action. These findings were expected and concur with prior research on younger age groups.

These findings are supplemented by our analysis of the relationship between self-reported deviant behavior and alcohol among the elderly in one of the communities included in our study. Table 4.6 presents the bivariate associations between the drinking variables and reported commission of at least one of the offenses. As with the measures of contact with the criminal justice system, law violative behavior is positively related to alcohol consumption and most strongly related to problem drinking (G = .63 and r = .13). The proportion of abstainers (4.6 percent) admitting to one or more of the offenses is less than that of drinkers (5.2 percent) and is only one-fourth that (20.0 percent) of problem drinkers (See Table 4.7).

Table 4.6.
Association of Drinking Behavior with Self-Reported Offense Behavior Among the Elderly (One Community)

Drinking Behavior	Offense Behavior G =	r =
Drinking/Abstaining	.27	.07
Frequency of Drinking	.32	.10
Frequency/Quantity of Drinking	.32	.12
Problem Drinking	.63	.13

Source: Compiled by authors.

CONCLUSION

There is a relationship in this sample of elderly respondents between drinking and crime, as measured both by contact with the criminal justice system and commission of illegal behavior. (The gamma values are moderate to strong, and the correlation coefficients are moderate to weak.) The relationship is strongest for problem drinking. Although the percentages are small in each case, the problem drinker is many times more

Table 4.7.
Percentage Distribution of Alcohol Drinking and Problem Drinking by Self-Reported Offense Behavior Among the Elderly (One Community)

	Any Offense Since Turning 60		
	None %	One or More %	N =
Alcohol			
Abstaining	95.4	4.6	174
Drinking	92.2	7.8	129
Total	94.0	5.9	303
Chi-Square = 1.4 df = 1 P>.05 Gamma = .27 r = .06			
Problem Drinking (Drinkers Only)			
None	94.7	5.2	114
One or More Problems	80.0	20.0	5
Total	94.1	5.8	119
Chi-Square = 1.8 df = 1 P>.05 Gamma = .63 r = .13			

Source: Compiled by authors.

likely to commit deviant behavior and to get into trouble with the law than the abstainer.

With so little data, any new findings on alcohol and crime among the elderly are welcomed, however tentative they may be. These conclusions are tentative and must be interpreted in light of the fact that they are based on analyses of cross-sectional data, that there are few problem drinkers included in the study, and that the number reporting experience with the legal system is also small. Small cell sizes are especially to be noted for self-reported criminal behavior which was measured in only one of the four communities in the study. Also, generalization to other types of communities must be made with caution. With these limitations in mind, we have found some support for the hypothesis that alcohol consumption is related to contact with the criminal justice system and illegal behavior among the elderly just as it is for younger adults and adolescents. Although the proportions of both problematic drinking and problematic behavior decline with age, the link between the two does not.

5

Homicide Among the Elderly: Analysis of the Victim/Assailant Relationship

Peter C. Kratcoski
Donald B. Walker

INTRODUCTION

Violence and the fear of being a victim of violence have become pervasive in American society. Beginning in the early 1960s, the homicide rate in the United States began a steady upward trend, and homicide was at its highest peak of the century in 1980. Although the rate has leveled off and even shown some slight decline in the early 1980s, it still remains the highest among Western industrial societies. While scholars, especially in the social sciences, have always demonstrated an interest in violent behavior, this interest has shown an increase, especially among criminologists, parallel to the increasing rates of violence since the 1960s. This attention has been focused not only on the offender, but also on the victims of violence. Despite this increased attention to violent crime, one significant social category has been largely ignored until quite recently—the elderly. Studies of the role of the elderly in crime tended to focus on them as victims. More recently the roles of elderly persons as offenders have begun to attract the interest of criminologists (Newman, Newman, and Gewirtz, 1984:xx).

Both the past history of neglect and the current renewed interest in the relationship between the elderly and crime are reasonably easy to understand. In the past, the social structure of American society has been dominated by the young and our culture has been youth-oriented. Similarly, the problem of crime has been a problem associated with youth. However, the past decade has seen a shift in the social structure toward a more mature population. In 1974, 10.3 percent of the U.S. population was 65 years of age or older, while ten years later that population had grown to 11.9 percent. By 1984, the over-65 age category numbered 28 million persons (American Association of Retired Persons, 1985:1). This aging of the population has produced not only a significant interest in the field of gerontology but has also awakened the concern of criminologists regarding the involvement of the elderly in criminal activities. As Shichor (1984a:17) notes, "Since the early 1970s an increasing amount of attention has been paid to crime and the elderly. The majority of this research has dealt with victimization." However, as he points out, "Recently, there has been greater emphasis on the problem of elderly offenders, the patterns of offenses in which they are involved, and their handling by the criminal justice system" (1985:399).

Although the elderly continue to contribute only a small proportion of offenses to the overall problem of crime (only 3 percent of all arrests in 1980 were persons 55 and over), the increased interest in the elderly offender can be attributed to a number of factors. First, the sheer number of elderly offenders will increase in future years even if the rate of elderly crime remains low as a consequence of the increasing elderly population. As noted previously, the elderly constituted 11.9 percent of the population in 1984; this percentage is predicted to increase to 12.2 percent in 1990, and to reach 13.0 percent by the year 2000. Second, although the current arrest level of elderly offenders remains low, the end result still is a significant volume of arrests. For example, in 1984, there was 174,169 arrests of persons 60 years of age and older. This represents 1.9 percent of the total arrests for that year (Federal Bureau of Investigation, 1985:173). Abrams indicates:

> Elderly crime will undoubtedly increase in the years ahead as the elderly population grows. There is no way now of predicting whether the rate of crime within the elderly population itself will increase or decrease. However, crimes committed by the elderly are of sufficient importance to warrant increased research in the field . . . (Abrams, 1984:xviii).

It does appear that there has been an increase in the involvement of the elderly in more serious offenses, thus suggesting a fourth factor contributing to the increased interest in elderly crime. Feinberg supports this conclusion by indicating:

> Although it may be true that fewer elderly persons are arrested for Index Crimes as compared to other age groups, their rate of increase is higher, and just as steady. This is a critical distinction since Index Crimes tend to reflect a more serious criminal problem (Feinberg, 1984b:87).

A final factor influencing the interest in elderly offenders is the population that is affected by such crime. As noted previously, the interest in the involvement of elderly persons in the problem of crime originally focused on the elderly victim. Inasmuch as crime is largely committed against persons of similar social characteristics as the offender (for example, social class, race, age) increasing numbers of elderly offenders are likely to produce greater numbers of elderly victims. As Feinberg noted, "The limited evidence on the subject of victim-offender relationships suggests that they are often similar in race, age, social background and even previous arrest history. It logically follows that the victims of elderly criminals may themselves be elderly persons" (Feinberg, 1984b:90).

In summary, while the problem of the elderly offender has been a neglected area of research in criminology, it is receiving increased attention in recent years. One might attribute this to the aging of the U.S. population and hence a projected increase in the sheer volume of elderly offenders, increasing involvement of elderly persons in serious crime, and a projected increase in the volume of elderly victims. Newman, Newman, and Gewirtz (1984:xxii) state, "It is rare that social scientists have an opportunity to see a problem emerging and can, from the beginning, study, evaluate, and suggest policies. We are at that stage with elderly crime."

This research seeks to contribute to the overall growing body of knowledge about elderly crime as an emerging social problem by exploring a particular form of elderly crime—homicide. Most recent research on factors contributing to increases in crime among the elderly has not focused on violent crime. A study of homicide by the elderly is particularly difficult to complete because of the scarcity of cases. Thus it is necessary to show the population from several cities or regions or to extend the research data base over a period of several years in order to accumulate the number of cases needed to make meaningful comparisons and draw conclusions.

SUMMARY OF LITERATURE

The specific focus of this research is the elderly homicide offender. Since, as noted previously, the study of crime among the elderly has been a neglected topic, it is not surprising that the elderly homicide offender has also received little attention. Hucker and Ben-Aron offer the following rationale for this neglect:

> The elderly are usually seen as vulnerable to the violence of others rather than aggressive themselves. Certainly violent crimes by members of this age group are rare. Probably for this reason violent behavior by the elderly has been little studied (Hucker and Ben-Aron, 1984:69).

As a consequence of this lack of both empirical and theoretical foundation, researchers currently working in the area of elderly homicide must proceed with caution. One approach to this problem is to first consider what we know about homicide in general, and then assess what impact the age variable might have on these findings.

Contemporary studies of homicide, with few exceptions, have found that offenders and victims are most likely to be young black adult males, that offenders and victims tend to be of low socioeconomic status and reside in inner-city slums, that approximately half of homicides occur in the home of the offender or the victim, that offenders and victims are usually acquainted and live in the same neighborhood, and that stranger-to-stranger homicides occur most often during the commission of another felony, such as robbery or burglary (Barlow, 1984:139).

Now, it is important to raise the point that homicide is not a unidimensional phenomenon:

> Based on the nature of this relationship, (victim/offender) criminal homicides can be broadly categorized into two general types. The first, "primary" homicide, involves family or acquaintances and is usually an act of passion. . . . The second category, "nonprimary" homicides, are often instrumental in nature in that they generally occur in the commission of another crime (Parker and Smith, 1979:615).

The distinction between primary and nonprimary homicide becomes significant in comparing the patterns of elderly homicide to those of other age categories.

Hagan adds two other significant observations regarding homicide:

> The spark that sets off this kindling could be any number of interpersonal conflict situations. . . . While ordinarily such disputes do not lead to violence, the addition of two other fuels to the fire can spell danger: alcohol and guns. Alcoholic consumption is present in the majority of homicides, assaults, and rapes (Hagan, 1986:180).

Luckenbill provides a general framework for analysis by noting:

> By definition, criminal homicide is a collective transaction. An offender, victim, and possibly an audience engage in an interchange which leaves the victim dead. Furthermore, the transactions are typically situated for participants to interact in a common physical territory (Luckenbill, 1977:176).

The participants are disproportionately poor, young, black males. In primary homicide the interchange involves a quarrel between acquaintances in which drinking and guns play a vital role. The physical territory generally is in or near either the victim's or the offender's home.

Aging and Crime

According to Hirschi, one of the most solid facts of criminology is the effect of age on crime. He indicates:

no fact about crime (i.e., age) is more widely accepted by criminologists. Virtually all of them, of whatever theoretical persuasion, appear to operate with a common image of the age distribution. This distribution thus represents one of the brute facts of criminology (Hirschi and Gottfredson, 1983:552).

The common image of the impact of age on crime is that of an inverse relationship—crime declines as a direct consequence of the age variable. Further, "available data suggest that the age-crime relation is invariant across sex and race" (Hirschi and Gottfredson, 1983:556). Rowe and Tittle, in their study of self-reported criminal behavior, provide additional support for these observations:

Results indicate a clear negative relationship between age and criminal propensity which is in part attributed to generational differences and partly to life cycle changes. Efforts to account for the association show this relationship to be exceptionally stable and resistant to explanation (Rowe and Tittle, 1977:223).

From these observations it becomes apparent that the age variable is a significant factor affecting criminal behavior. However, as Rowe and Tittle point out, "Despite the widespread assumption of an age crime relationship and some theoretical basis for expecting such a relationship, no systematic study of age and crime is available in the sociological or criminological literature" (1977:223). Although this situation has been somewhat rectified in the past ten years, serious weaknesses still exist in our understanding of the role of the elderly offender in criminal behavior. One step toward a further understanding of this problem is to examine the impact of age on a particular pattern of crime. This research seeks to add to the body of knowledge about elderly crime by presenting a descriptive analysis of elderly homicide offenders and the circumstances under which they commit murder.

Hammack and the Elderly Offender: A Conceptual Model

The "routine activities" approach to crime presents a theoretical framework for organizing a number of expectations regarding elderly homicides. Messner and Tardiff describe the routine activities approach formulated by Cohen and Felson in the following manner:

Cohen and Felson argue that the volume of criminal offenses will be related to the nature of normal, everyday patterns of interaction. Underlying this approach is the basic premise that there is a symbiotic relationship between legal and illegal activities. . . . It follows that the frequency and nature of crime will reflect the structure of social activities more generally (Messner and Tardiff, 1985:241-42).

Following this argument, one would expect that since the elderly have withdrawn from the broader social system more so than younger age categories, their activities will be disproportionately centered around the home. To the extent that increased contact within the home is likely to exacerbate existing family tensions, it suggests that elderly homicides will be disproportionately domestic homicides. As Messner and Tardiff observe:

> Of particular importance in the structuring of routine activities is the extent to which activities are concentrated around the household and around family relationships. Persons with different sociodemographic characteristics are likely to spend differing amounts of time at home. The likelihood of being killed at or near home should be related, therefore, to these very same sociodemographic characteristics (Messner and Tardiff, 1985:243).

One concludes, therefore, that elderly homicides will be disproportionately located in the home and that offender and victim will be involved in familial relationships. The same set of arguments leads to the conclusion that elderly homicides will also be disproportionately intraracial. Both the nature of marriage (intraracial) and withdrawal from wider social contacts (interaction with strangers) support this expectation. The facts that interracial homicides are primarily felony in nature and that elderly persons have a low involvement in robberies and burglaries further support the notion that elderly homicides are primarily intraracial in nature.

Turning next to the problem of gender differences, the question which arises is what differences one might expect in homicide incidents between elderly males and elderly females. Given the fact that women are far less likely to be involved in homicide events, one would expect that elderly women would be less likely than elderly males to appear as homicide offenders. However, consistent with a "routine activities" framework, one would expect the ratio of elderly male to elderly female offenders to be less than the ratio of younger male to younger female homicide offenders. This expectation is also consistent with the prediction that elderly persons are more involved in domestic homicides and less involved with felony type and stranger homicides than are younger persons. Support for this supposition is found in the literature. Shichor found that "Male arrest rates in the younger group were 7.0 times higher than that of females; in the elderly group this rate was 7.8. Younger male arrest rates were 4.8 times higher than elderly male rates; among females the comparable figure was 5.4" (1985:406).

The final sociodemographic factor to be considered is that of the age of the victim. Similar to race, one would expect that the victims of elderly homicide offenders would be drawn from the elderly. If elderly homicides are less felony type and less likely to involve strangers, then it follows that the nature of interactions which elderly persons have would be within their same age category.

The remaining two factors to be considered are the presence of alcohol in the event and the type of weapon used. The "routine activities" approach does not lead directly to specific conclusions relative to these factors. However, one might infer from the general literature on homicide that alcohol would play a role in elderly homicides as it does in homicide events in general but would be less significant in elderly homicides. Given the expected domestic nature of elderly homicides, one would expect that drinking behavior, particularly on the part of the victim, would be less significant than in homicides between friends and acquaintances. Although the use of firearms might be viewed as an "equalizer" in confrontational situations, again one might expect that such would be the case more in felony type and friend/acquaintance quarrels than in domestic situations. One might expect that in an explosive domestic quarrel, the offender would resort to whatever weapon might be closest to hand.

Drawing from the preceding review of the literature, the following can be offered for empirical investigations.

1. The elderly offender-victim homicide relationship will involve a significantly greater proportion of spouse/family homicides than will nonelderly offender-victim homicides.
2. A significantly greater proportion of elderly homicides than nonelderly homicides will occur in the home.
3. A significantly greater proportion of elderly versus nonelderly homicides will be intraracial in nature.
4. There will be a significantly higher proportion of male elderly than female elderly homicide offenders.
5. The ratio of male/female elderly homicide offenders will be significantly lower than the ratio of male/female nonelderly offenders.
6. Elderly homicide offender-victim relationships will be significantly higher within their same age category than will nonelderly offender-victim relationships.
7. The victims of elderly homicide offenders will be significantly less involved in alcohol consumption at the time of the incident than will the victims of nonelderly homicide offenders.
8. There will be a significantly lower proportion of firearms used in elderly homicides than in nonelderly homicides.

RESEARCH DESIGN

The research on which this article is based is part of a larger, ongoing research effort which involves the analysis of more than 2,600 cases of nonjustifiable homicide recorded in the coroner's office of Cuyahoga County, Ohio, for the years 1970-1983. For the purposes of this study, 919 cases in which the assailant was unknown were removed from the data base providing 1,670 cases for analysis. These cases were then categorized into three age groupings: 5-14, 15-59, and 60 and older. The age 60-and-over category is defined as "elderly homicide offenders" and contains 82 cases. Of these cases, 65 involved male offenders and the remaining 17 involved female offenders. The only important distinction between the distribution of the 60-and-over category and the overall population of homicide offenders in the study is a higher proportion of white males. Of the elderly assailants, 34 percent are white males, compared to 19 percent white male assailants in the 15-59 age bracket. The distribution of females in the 60-and-over category is essentially the same as for the other age groupings.

Cuyahoga County is a highly industrialized area and is a commercial center. The county includes the city of Cleveland and its suburbs. In 1970, the population of Cleveland was 750,000, and the county's population was 1,721,300. The city's population declined to 563,800 in 1980, a 23 percent decrease, while the county's population increased 10 percent, to 1,898,800. In 1980, the population of the county was 82 percent white and 18 percent nonwhite. However, Cleveland, which has 30 percent of the county's population, had a 56 percent white population and a 44 percent nonwhite population in 1980.

RESULTS

Approximately one-third of the nonjustifiable homicides committed in Cuyahoga County during the time period of this study were unsolved. As a result, information pertaining to the assailant was not available for these cases, and they were excluded from the analysis. Even for those cases in which the assailant was known, the file information was not always complete. Thus, the number of cases for each variable included in the analysis will vary slightly from table to table. The number of cases for each comparison is given in each table.

The first area of examination is the offender-victim relationship. Table 5.1 shows the proportion of spouse-relative homicides by age group. As expected, elderly homicides in the sample involve greater proportions of spouse/relative homicides than do those of the nonelderly. While 33 percent of the victims of the age 60-and-older homicide offenders are either spouses or relatives, the proportion for the 5-14 age category is 20 percent, and for the 15-59 age bracket it is 22 percent. Further examination of Table 5.1 reveals that persons in the three age categories are almost equally likely to kill acquaintances, but those 60 and older are nearly twice as likely to kill their spouses as persons in the other age groups.

Again as expected, the data presented in Table 5.2 reveals that elderly homicides are disproportionately committed in the home. While approximately half of homicides by nonelderly assailants occurred in the home, more than two-thirds of homicides by elderly assailants occurred there.

Table 5.1.
Age of Assailant by Relationship of Assailant and Victim (N = 1578)

Relationship of Assailant and Victim	Age of Assailant						Total
	5 - 14		15 - 59		60 and older		
	N	%	N	%	N	%	
Spouse	1	5	190	13	18	24	209
Relative	3	15	126	9	7	9	136
Acquaintance	12	60	908	61	44	57	964
Stranger	4	20	257	17	8	10	269
TOTAL	20	100	1481	100	77	100	1578

Significant at .001 level, chi-square test.
Source: Compiled by authors.

Table 5.2.
Age of Assailant by Location of Act (N = 1660)

Location	Age of Assailant						Total
	5 - 14		15 - 59		60 and older		
	N	%	N	%	N	%	
Home	11	50	834	53	55	68	900
Public	11	50	732	47	26	32	769
TOTAL	22	100	1566	100	81	100	1669

Significant at .001 level, chi-square test.
Source: Compiled by authors.

Table 5.3 compares the age of the assailant with the sex and race of the assailant. Although the data is inconclusive, it appears that homicides committed by elderly assailants are probably more intraracial in nature than those committed by assailants in the 15-59 age bracket. This can be inferred from a number of features of the data, including the high proportion of offender/spouse homicides, the high proportion of homicides in the home, and the low percentage (10 percent) of stranger-to-stranger homicides by

Table 5.3.
Age of Assailant by Sex and Race of Assailant (N = 1647)

Sex and Race of Assailant	Age of Assailant: 5 - 14 N	%	15 - 59 N	%	60 and older N	%	Total
White Male	5	25	300	19	25	34	330
White Female	2	10	49	3	1	1	52
Non-White Male	13	65	969	63	34	47	1016
Non-White Female	0	0	236	15	13	18	249
TOTAL	20	100	1554	100	73	100	1647

Significant at .001 level, chi-square test.

Source: Compiled by authors.

those age 60 and older. All of these factors point to intraracial homicide incidents.

In Table 5.3, it is shown that elderly homicides are predominatly committed by males, and this held true for the other age groups as well. Eighty-one percent of homicidal assailants age 60 and older were males; the comparable figures for the 5-14 and 15-59 age categories were 90 percent and 82 percent. However, in regard to the ratio of male/female assailants, the ratio in the 5-14 age group was 9 males to 1 female, while the ratio in the 15-59 category was 4.6:1 and in the age 60 and older category it was 4.3 to 1. Therefore, while the comparisons in Table 5.3 showed significant differences in the ratio of male/female assailants by age, the key difference appeared in the 5-14 age group. The difference in the male/female assailant ratio between the 15-59 age group and the age 60 and older group is not significant.

When the offenders and victims are compared by age categories, it is apparent that, regardless of the age of the offender, the victim is most likely to be drawn from the 15-59 age bracket. Eighty-eight percent of the offenders in the 15-59 age category killed victims from the same age category. However, contrary to expectations, the elderly offenders did not always choose victims within their own age group. Fifty-two percent of the victims of assailants age 60 and older were age 15-59, while only 44 percent of the victims were age 60 or older.

Table 5.4 shows the blood alcohol content of the victim. Forty-one percent of the victims of assailants age 15-59 had evidence of alcohol in

Table 5.4.
Age of Assailant by Blood Alcohol Content of Victim (N = 1566)

Blood Alcohol Content of Victim	Age of Assailant						
	5 - 14		15 - 59		60 and older		
	N	%	N	%	N	%	Total
Unknown/NA	3	14	235	16	16	21	254
Negative	15	68	633	43	34	46	682
Some Alcohol Use	3	14	203	14	10	13	216
Legally Drunk .10-.20	1	4	221	15	6	8	228
Above .21	0	0	177	12	9	12	186
TOTAL	22	100	1469	100	75	100	1566

Significant at .001 level, chi-square test.
Source: Compiled by authors.

their blood at the time of their death. In contrast, only 33 percent of the victims of assailants age 60 and older had been drinking. Also, 27 percent of the victims of assailants age 15-59 were legally intoxicated (.10 alcohol content in the blood), while 20 percent of the elderly assailants' victims were in an intoxicated condition. Hence, while it is apparent that alcohol plays a significant role in homicide in general, it is of less significance in elderly homicides, as was expected.

Table 5.5 indicates that there is no significant difference in the percentage of elderly assailants who used firearms, when the age 15-59 and age 60 and older categories are compared. Although the distribution in this table is significant at the .001 level, the difference between the 5-14 age bracket and the other two age categories accounts for the significance. While the assailants age 15-59 used firearms in 88 percent of their killings, those age 5-14 used firearms in only 60 percent of their offenses.

Table 5.6 describes the circumstances of the homicide events in relation to the age of the assailants. The data suggest that the circumstances surrounding elderly homicides are more complicated and varied than one might at first surmise. While the vast majority of the homicides in the 15-59 age category occurred during or after a quarrel (92 percent), this circumstance was true for only 67 percent of the homicides involving elderly assailants. Other factors explain some of the motives of the older assailants. For example, 15 percent of the elderly assailants later committed suicide. In

Table 5.5.
Age of Assailant by Mode of Killing of Victim (N = 1460)

Mode of Killing	Age of Assailant 5 - 14 N	%	15 - 59 N	%	60 and older N	%	Total
Firearms	12	60	1196	88	67	89	1210
Cuts and Stabs	8	40	125	9	6	8	139
Pushes, Falls, Asphyxiation, Explosives and Other	0	0	44	3	2	3	111
TOTAL	20	100	1365	100	75	100	1460

Significant at .001 level, chi-square test.
Source: Compiled by authors.

Table 5.6.
Age of Assailant by Circumstances of Death (N = 1213)

Circumstances of Death	Age of Assailant 5 - 14 N	%	15 - 59 N	%	60 and older N	%	Total
During or After a Quarrel	9	41	1015	92	55	67	1079
Felony Murder	2	9	64	6	6	7	72
Unknown/Other	11	50	30	2	21	26	62
TOTAL	22	100	1109	100	82	100	1213

Significant at .001 level, chi-square test.
Source: Compiled by authors.

each of these cases, the victim was the wife of the assailant. Several other cases involved mentally ill offenders killing imaginary evil spirits who resided in the victims.

DISCUSSION

The research findings just presented reveal that the data supports a number of previous characteristics of homicides by elderly assailants. The expectations generated by the "routine activities" approach are sustained. Elderly homicides are disproportionately located in the home, they involve familial relationships (particularly spouses) to a great extent, and are likely to be strongly intraracial in nature. Elderly homicide, like homicide in general, is predominantly a male offense. However, contrary to expectations, the ratio of male to female offenders does not change as one moves from the 15-59 age bracket to the 60 and older age bracket.

Although the factors surrounding elderly homicides would lead one to expect that they would occur between persons of this age category, our data reveal that, like assailants in the 15-59 age category, assailants age 60 or older are also likely to kill persons ages 15-59. However, as shown, the proportions are not nearly as dramatic. The findings are, therefore, in the expected direction, with the elderly assailants five times more likely to kill persons aged 60 or older than assailants 15-59.

While the victims of elderly offenders were drinking to a lesser extent than the victims of assailants in the 15-59 age category at the time of death, data on the drinking involvement of assailants was available for only a portion of the population of this study. An analysis of the records of eighteen of the elderly assailants obtained from their presentence investigations revealed that 39 percent of them had been drinking at the time of the killing. Given the nature of elderly versus nonelderly homicides, it could be that alcohol is a significant factor in homicides in general, but that the homicide events of the nonelderly are characterized more by quarrels following drinking between both victim and assailant, while the consumption of alcohol in elderly homicides is a prevalent characteristic of only the assailant.

With respect to the use of firearms, the data failed to support the assumption that the elderly are more inclined than other assailants to use firearms. This assumption is based on the fact that homicides are generally the result of sudden, confrontational scenarios in which the assailant utilizes whatever weapon is available. We also failed to find that the elderly used firearms significantly less frequently than assailants of other age groups. Our data indicates that nearly 90 percent of all assailants age 15 and above used firearms as the mode of killing. The significant difference in mode was actually in the below 15 age bracket. It could be surmised that firearms are so readily available in Cuyahoga County that they are the choice of weapon for assailants of virtually all ages.

It was also surprising to find a high percentage of murder/suicides among the elderly. The question which remains to be answered is whether murder/suicides is a function of domestic homicide in general. Although the data has not yet been gathered which would answer this question, we expect it is a function of elderly domestic homicide to a far greater extent.

It appears that elderly homicide may be a more complex event than homicide committed by younger persons. Homicides committed within the context of the family tend to be of a spontaneous nature, regardless of the age of the victim and assailant. However, this generalization may be less valid for the elderly than for other age groups.

The information necessary to test a number of important questions related to homicides by the elderly is presently being gathered. We have the opportunity to supplement the information from the coroner's files with more in-depth information from presentence investigations. We are particularly interested in the assailant's occupation, past criminal history (especially the presence or absence of violent/assaultive behavior and weapons violations), prior mental condition and the presence/absence of alcohol or drug use both in the past and at the time of the offense. From this information, we hope to be able to answer a number of questions. For example, it is a known fact that one's criminal behavior declines with age. However, this decline may account only for lower felony/homicides among the elderly rather than violence within the family. If a significant proportion of elderly offenders has a prior history of violent and weapons offenses, it would suggest that patterns of violence learned earlier in life remain present and manifest themselves in violence within the family at a later age.

6

Property Crime and the Elderly Offender: A Theoretical and Empirical Analysis, 1964–1984

Donald J. Bachand
George A. Chressanthis

INTRODUCTION

The elderly more often than not are portrayed as victims of crime. Yet recent research appears to be placing greater emphasis on elderly criminal activity, especially as the demographics of the population indicate a "graying" of our population. Recent research investigating the elderly as the offender includes works by Bachand (1983, 1984), Burnett and Ortega (1984), Hucker and Ben-Aron (1984), Newman, Newman, and Gewirtz (1984), Shichor (1984a), and Wilbanks and Kim (1984). However, these works represent only a small fraction of the total research needed to scientifically investigate a wide range of topics concerning elderly criminal behavior.

The foreword to Newman, Newman, and Gewirtz (1984) identifies five areas in this field needing further research, including one area of specific interest and relation to this investigation: ". . . correlation between

We wish to extend our appreciation to the Saginaw Valley State College Computer Center and in particular William Anspach, Daniel Wilson, and Jeanetta Washington for their time and efforts. We are also grateful for the helpful suggestions from Robert Langworthy, Belinda McCarthy, Donald Newman, and Thomas Steinmeier on earlier drafts of this work. The usual disclaimers apply.

economic recession and crimes among the elderly. Does elderly crime increase when inflation rises, or when unemployment rises?'' (p. xvii). An analysis of this question as well as other concerns will be addressed in this study.

The purpose of this chapter is to theoretically develop and empirically test factors that significantly affect property crime arrest rate patterns in the United States by criminals of the ages 55-59, 60-64, and 65 and older from 1964-1984. This chapter includes an analysis of arrest rate patterns over time not only for total property crime but also for burglary, larceny, and motor vehicle theft for each age category given above.

This chapter proceeds in the following fashion. The section entitled ''Theoretical Model'' describes the development of a theoretical model and the derivation of hypotheses to be tested in the empirical section. The section entitled ''Empirical Model and Results'' explains the methods of estimation and discusses the findings from the single-equation and seemingly unrelated regression equations estimation procedures. The chapter concludes with the section ''Conclusions and Implications'' and contains conclusions and policy implications.

THEORETICAL MODEL

Introduction

The theoretical foundations for this present analysis on elderly criminal behavior pertaining to property crimes are based on the works of Becker (1968, 1974) and Ehrlich (1970, 1973, 1974) which are general theoretical economic analyses of the participation of individuals involved in illegitimate activities. An elaboration of these models as to their direction in explaining criminal behavior is important if the reader is to understand the approach taken in this investigation involving elderly criminal behavior. Differences in model specification between the general theoretical frameworks and the one presented here will be discussed.

DISCUSSION OF THE MODELS PRESENTED BY BECKER AND EHRLICH

The seminal work by Becker (1968, 1974) represents the starting point for our discussion with respect to theoretical foundations involving the behavioral patterns of elderly criminal activity in property offenses. Criminals in the Becker model are utility maximizers who face an array of constraints or potential restraints on their behavior to engage in criminal activity. Society, on the other hand, evaluates and weighs the costs imposed by criminals onto society and attempts to effectively deal with limiting the costs from criminal activity in an optimal fashion. Thus the model represents a conflict between the criminals and society with each having diverging objectives of behavior. Therefore the model presented by Becker involves not only the elaboration of behavioral relations as to activity of criminals but also in indicating the optimal fashion by which society can limit the scope and damage of crime.

The model presented by Becker can be summarized into five categories of relations which constitute the framework to incorporate the behavioral relations behind the costs of crime. Becker (1974:5) lists these five categories of relations: (1) the number of crimes or offenses and the cost of offenses, (2) the number of offenses and the punishments meted out, (3) the number of offenses, arrests, and convictions and the public expenditures on police and courts, (4) the number of convictions and the costs of imprisonments or other kinds of punishments, and (5) the number of offenses and the private expenditures on protection and apprehension. The following is a brief explanation of each relation and insights into the implications of the Becker model with respect to elderly criminal behavior.

First, the amount of damage to society from crime would tend to increase with the level of activity. Likewise, the social value of the gain to offenders also tends to increase with the number of offenses. Therefore, the net cost or damage to society would be the difference between the harm and gain functions. The magnitude of the net damage to society will provide the impetus behind measures instituted to restrict activity. Elderly criminal behavior in burglary, larceny, and motor vehicle theft, though showing indications of increasing levels of activity in the period from 1964 to 1984, has never resulted in a percentage of activity with respect to the total figures of more than 2 percent in each crime category per age group of 55-59, 60-64, and 65 years and older.

Second, the supply of offenses involves an approach which relates the number of offenses by any person to the likelihood of conviction, punishment if convicted, income which could be derived from other legitimate and illegitimate activities, and the willingness to commit an illegal act. The elderly criminal faces different incentive and disincentive mechanisms than other criminals. Their likelihood of being apprehended and convicted are less than for younger criminals for the same crime. Punishment resulting from convictions are more likely to be less severe than for younger criminals due to the leniency given to elderly criminals and other factors which are further elaborated concerning Becker's fourth relation. The elderly also face different opportunities with regard to generating income from other activities than criminals of younger age. Retired individuals on fixed incomes have few opportunities to supplement their income through the labor market and must rely on individual savings and government transfer payments.

Third, increases in the amount of resources spent on policemen, court personnel, and specialized equipment will imply discovering more offenses and convicting more offenders. However, the empirical evidence investigating the impact of police force size and expenditures on crime patterns reveal ambiguous results when reviewing the entire literature on this question as indicated by Avio and Clark (1976), Carr-Hill and Stern (1973), Greenwood and Wadycki (1973, 1976), Jones (1973, 1974), Swimmer (1974a, 1974b), Land and Felson (1976), and McPheters and Stronge (1974). Furthermore, increases in the number of police resources devoted to crime prevention does not necessarily translate into lower property crime arrest rates among the elderly offenders. Police forces spend the vast majority of their time and energies dealing with younger criminals and more traditional antisocial behavior. Evidence from Bachand (1983, 1984), Moberg (1953), Shichor (1984a, 1985), Shichor and Kobrin (1978), and Visher (1983) all indicate that the elderly are more leniently treated by the police than younger criminals. The reasons for this could involve social biases that tend to favor the elderly as offenders because of their usual role as victims of crime and the perception by many in law enforcement that the problem of elderly criminal behavior is not an issue worth pursuing.

Fourth, punishments are designed to impose costs on the offender and thus reduce the expected net gain to an individual engaged in criminal activity. However, most punishments not only impose costs on the offender but also to the rest of society as well. The cost of imprisonment involves, for example, guards, supervisory personnel, buildings, food, and health care, and thus society must balance these costs with the gain from its desire to limit criminal activity. Elderly criminals are not constrained by the same punishment mechanisms as seen in younger age groups. The analysis of leniency on elderly criminals by Bachand (1983, 1984), Moberg (1953), Shichor (1984a, 1985), Shichor and Kobrin (1978), and Visher (1983) all indicate that the elderly are treated more leniently not only by the police but also the judicial system. Lesser sentences to the elderly mean smaller opportunity costs with respect to foregone earnings and foregone consumption. Elderly criminals likewise have far less to lose than younger criminals because of reduced opportunity in the labor market and thus may be more willing to engage in criminal activity, all things being equal. Furthermore, the costs to society of incarcerating elderly offenders are potentially greater than for younger offenders due to the special physical and psychological needs of the aged and the greater probability of death while in prison. Therefore, the lenient treatment of elderly offenders by society may be a result of the recognition of the balancing of these costs and benefits of imprisonment, especially since the vast majority of elderly criminal activity is of the property crime variety which society regards of less significance than violent crimes.

Fifth, there exist an array of private means for individuals to protect themselves against crime such as expenditures on protection and apprehension services. Those services that can reduce the number and incidence of crimes include guards, locks, alarm systems, extended insurance coverage, neighborhood watch groups, and alterations in behavioral patterns which may reduce the likelihood of being placed in situations where crime has a greater probability of occurrence. The impact of these private expenditures on elderly criminal activity will be a shifting of offender activity to those areas that are less amenable to extensively placed measures to reduce the number of incidents of crime. The emphasis by the elderly offender on larceny rather than burglary may be in part an indication of the placement of these private expenditures to reduce criminal activity.

The general theoretical model of individual criminal behavior presented by Ehrlich (1970, 1973, 1974) represents an elaboration of the works by Becker (1968, 1974) by explicitly introducing both gains and losses in illegal activity and gains in legal activity rather than strictly emphasizing the costs of punishment alone as done in Becker. Schmidt and Witte (1984) characterized the contributions of Ehrlich as they pertain to property offenses with the following statement: "Time allocated to illegal activity decreases with increases in probability of apprehension, penalty, and wage rate; increases with increased wealth and illegal gains; fines are relatively more effective for risk averse individuals" (p. 180).

Ehrlich (1974:69-70) provides a detailed explanation as to the four extensions of his work with that of Becker and other previous contributors. First, Ehrlich's model investigates the relationship between both punishment and reward in establishing the costs and gains from legitimate and illegitimate pursuits which goes beyond Becker and his emphasis on punishment. Moreover, Ehrlich attempts to theoretically predict and empirically verify such a systematic association between these forces. Second, his model theoretically investigates individual decision making under uncertainty with respect to the choice between competing alternatives which connects involvement in participation in illegitimate activities with the general theory of occupational choice. The individual must decide the optimal allocation of resources under uncertainty as to the participation of activities that involve both market and nonmarket alternatives. Ehrlich differs from Becker in treating the decision made on these choices as integrated rather than being mutually exclusive activities. Empirical estimates could then be derived which measure not only the direction but also the relative magnitude of the response of specific offenders to changes in observable opportunities. Third, his model distinguishes between the deterrent and preventive effects of punishment by imprisonment, while emphasizing empirical verification of the former effect. Fourth, Ehrlich statistically analyzes the interaction between crime and law enforcement activity and institutes a simultaneous-equation empirical model in estimating supply-of-offenses functions and a production function of law enforcement activity. These empirical estimates provide an indication as to the effectiveness of deterrence activity through law enforcement and its impact on limiting the social damage from crime.

Therefore, the overall impacts of the Becker and Ehrlich theoretical frameworks on the specification of a theoretical model concerning elderly criminal behavior (individuals 55 years and older) with respect to property offenses (larceny, burglary, and motor vehicle theft), account for the existence of strong leniency effects. These effects result in the virtual elimination of any impacts from deterrence activity by law enforcement personnel and punishments via the judicial system. The following relationships remain to be identified and specified in the theoretical model: (1) the specification of the gains attributed to illegitimate activities, (2) the specification of the gains attributed to legitimate activities, (3) the specification of the joint analysis between the incentive and disincentive mechanisms as they pertain to criminal activity, and (4) the delineation of the opportunities available for individuals to commit crime and thus indicating the time constraint imposed that will determine the degree to which an individual can be involved in criminal activity.

This theoretical model will look different from the framework presented by Becker (1974) and Ehrlich (1974) for two very important reasons. First, while Ehrlich developed a general model of criminal behavior and employed empirical tests to estimate reasons behind such behavior for specific crime categories in the aggregate (total crime activity that is nonage-specific), this present analysis is only interested in modeling the determinants of illegitimate activity for elderly property crime offenders and in pursuing an empirical investigation into these relationships for the elderly offender. Therefore, the incentive and disincentive mechanisms that exist operate very differently for elderly criminals than for the population as a whole and especially for the young offenders with naturally varying results as discussed in the elaboration of the model by Becker (1968, 1974). The major differences involve the omission of law enforcement and punishment variables due to strong leniency effects toward elderly property crime offenders. Second, the empirical research of Ehrlich (1973, 1974) tested the model using a cross-sectional framework of the analysis of crime variations across states in the United States for specific crime categories. This research employs a time-series analysis of specific property crime categories according to elderly age brackets in a national perspective for the United States and thus will be concerned with slightly different control variables. The remainder of this section will involve a discussion of the variables needed to be included in the specified theoretical model which captures the essence of the four remaining relationships to be identified as indicated earlier.

Specification of the Theoretical Model

The definition of the property crime activity rate for this research will be the number of burglaries, larcenies, and motor vehicle theft arrests per thousand population for elderly offenders in these age categories: 55-59, 60-64, and 65 and older years of age. This research breaks down the total property crime activity rate measure into the individual property crime arrests per age grouping. This was based on the assumption that the nature of the gains and losses from legitimate versus illegitimate activities vary according to the type of property crime and age of the offender. Differences in the nature of these relationships should be most dramatic between the youngest and oldest elderly groups.

The use of the inflation rate as an explanatory variable can be employed to capture many aspects of the four relationships to be specified in the theoretical model. The relationship between the inflation rate and the property crime rate leads to ambiguous results due to the different interpretations and impacts of the variable on the test statistic which may vary according to the age classification of the offender. An increase in the inflation rate increases the value of goods stolen and thus may make property crimes more appealing relative to other activities that are not rising in value in proportion to the inflation rate. The inflation rate may also represent trends in income and wages or transfer payment movements thereby creating disincentives for property crimes. The existence and distribution of transfer payments play a major role in the income of the elderly and have been explicitly specified in the theoretical models of other empirical crime studies. Berk, Lenihan, and Rossi (1980a, 1980b), DeFronzo (1983), and Jurik (1983) found that increases in transfer payments reduce some aspect of criminal behavior such as crime rates or recidivism, although none of these analyses specifically investigated elderly criminal activity. The elderly receive social security payments (reduced payments from 62-64 years of age and full payments from 65 years and older), medicare transfers for health care for people 65 years and older, and food stamps along with other transfers. These transfer outlays are generally periodically adjusted for changes in the consumer price index as in the case of social security and thus the inflation rate variable would be capturing this trend over time. Moreover, the reaction to inflation rate changes may vary according to the age of the offender. People 55-64 are more likely to be working than individuals 65 and over. Therefore, employed individuals are in a better position to contractually adjust for changes in the inflation rate through legitimate activities not only in the workplace but also in investments in preparation for retirement than individuals 65 and over who are principally drawing down on wealth accumulated over this working life (Ando and Modigliani, 1963). People 65 years and over on the other hand may see their real spending power of their fixed income fall as the inflation rate increases thus providing greater incentives for engaging in property crimes. Furthermore, changes in the inflation rate may cause modifications in the composition of crime. Friedland and Rutenberg (1978), Gutmann (1977), and Henry (1976) found greater incidences of tax evasion and other "underground" economic activities associated with government regulation and inflation although Simon and Witte (1979) and the U.S. Department of the Treasury, Internal Revenue Service (1979) found results to be inconclusive. Thus, the issue of the impact from changes in the inflation rate on property crimes is one of placing the relationship in proper perspective.

The next explanatory variable included to capture a supply of offense relationship and the time constraint imposed on individuals concerning their availability to engage in criminal activities are unemployment rate variables for individuals 55-64 years of age and an employment participation rate variable for people 65 years and older expressed as a percent of the total number of people 65 and older who are working in the labor force. These variables are necessary to capture changes in the return of work versus leisure (legitimate alternatives) and illegitimate activities as well as measuring variations in the amount of time available to engage in property crimes. The inclusion and interpretation of these variables is consistent with Ehrlich (1970, 1973, 1974) as elaborated earlier. Increases in unemployment rates among the 55-64 year old groups should be associated with higher property crime rates as individuals not only find that the value of legitimate activities decreases relative to illegitimate activities but also as the amount of leisure time available to engage in these activities likewise increases. The relationship between employment rate participation among the 65 and older group and property crime rates should be negatively associated as individuals realize greater gains from legitimate labor market activities and as available leisure time decreases.

Before moving on to the next explanatory variable, a digression is in order concerning the decision not to include a race variable as done in Ehrlich (1974) and other empirical studies. This investigation does not employ a race variable because it is felt that the inflation rate and labor market variables should be sufficient to capture the economic conditions in the environment for each age classification under which individual decisions are made on whether to engage in illegitimate property crime activities versus legitimate market alternatives over time.

The last variable to be included in the supply of offenses function is a population variable that captures changes in the population size of each age group with alterations in property crime rate activity over time. The use of population size as an explanatory variable can be seen in many theoretical and empirical studies on criminal behavior. The population size variable is assumed to have a positive impact on the property crime rate over time. The relationship could be negative indicating that although the incidence of crime may increase with population over time, its rate of incidence may not.[1]

Thus, the model for property crime activity rate of elderly offender categories (55-59, 60-64, 65 and older) can be specified using four explanatory variables: inflation rate, unemployment rates for individuals in 55-64 age categories, employment participation rate for individuals in the 65 and older age category, and population size. The functional form of the property crime activity equations for each age group is given below.

$$y_{1t} = f_1(x_{1t}, x_{2t}, x_{5t}, u_{1t}) \quad (6.1)$$

$$y_{2t} = f_2(x_{1t}, x_{3t}, x_{6t}, u_{2t}) \quad (6.2)$$

$$y_{3t} = f_3(x_{1t}, x_{4t}, x_{7t}, u_{3t}) \quad (6.3)$$

where,

y_{1t}, y_{2t}, y_{3t} = property crime arrest rate for people respectively 55-59, and 65 and older over time

f_1, f_2, f_3 = function operators

x_{1t} = inflation rate over time

x_{2t}, x_{3t}, x_{4t} = population size for people respectively 55-59, 60-64, and 65 and older over time

x_{5t}, x_{6t} = unemployment rate for people respectively 55-59 and 60-64 over time

x_{7t} = employment participation rate of people 65 and older expressed as a percent of the total number of people 65 and older over time

u_{1t}, u_{2t}, u_{3t} = disturbance or error terms respectively for each equation over time

EMPIRICAL MODEL AND RESULTS

The purpose of this section is to determine whether the explanatory variables (inflation, population, and labor market participation) delineated in the theoretical model significantly impact property crime activity patterns in the United States from 1964 to 1984 according to three categories of elderly criminals: 55-59, 60-64, and 65 and older years of age. Four property crime categories will be analyzed for each age grouping: total property crime, burglary, larceny, and motor vehicle theft.

This section is divided into three subsections. First, the data will be introduced with source listings and discussions pertaining to the appropriateness of the empirical variables relative to those measures mentioned in the theoretical model. Second, single-equation estimation findings will be introduced measuring the impacts of the explanatory variables on the four categories of property crime listed above for each of the three age groups. Third, joint-estimation or seemingly unrelated regression (SUR) equations estimation as suggested by Zellner (1962) will be undertaken on the four categories of property crimes by combining the regression equations for each age group per crime category over time into one generalized least-square regression equation. Comparisons of the single-equation and the SUR estimation results will then follow.

Data

The dependent variable is calculated as the total number of arrests per thousand population according to each age grouping and crime category over time. The arrest data were collected from the U.S. Department of Justice *Uniform Crime Reports: 1964-1984*. Annual population estimates for the United States for people 55-59, 60-64, and 65 and older were gathered from the Bureau of the Census (1971, 1972) in their *Population Estimates and Projections* publications. Only two series were used to compile the population data in order to reduce biases due to changes in assumptions of population characteristics over time: 1964-1969 and series B projections from 1970-1984. The population data combined with the arrest figures form the arrest rates per crime category and age group over time.

The same population figures were used to capture population changes over time per age group as one of the explanatory variables as listed in the theoretical model. The use of the population variable on both sides in the regression equation as an explanatory variable and as the denominator in the formulation of the dependent variable (property crime arrest rate statistic) can lead to some potentially damaging effects with regard to statistical estimation. First, any bias in the population explanatory variable will cause a bias in the property crime arrest rate statistic in the opposite direction, since the population variable shows up in the denominator of the test statistic. This potential problem thus suggests that a review of the legitimacy and accuracy of the population data base should be undertaken to ensure that these biases are limited in design and insignificant in impact. The application of the Bureau of the Census (1971, 1972) *Population Estimates and Projections* publications would imply any errors in measurement have been minimized due to the widely known integrity of this data source. Moreover, tradition and common use of this source implies an acknowledgment of the accuracy of these figures by other researchers and institutions interested in developing arrest rate statistics according to age, such as the U.S. Department of Justice (1986) in its special release on arrest rates according to age and race. The second potential statistical problem is the development of heteroscedasticity (or heterogeneous variances) in the error term when estimating a regression equation which runs counter to the assumption of the error term exhibiting homogeneous variances in the linear model. Heteroscedasticity may arise in dealing with grouped data of different sizes over time as is potentially the case here in this investigation with the use of subgroups of population and the analysis of their interaction with each other, even though the original observations indicate homoscedasticity. However, two factors exist that would appear to nullify the concern over heteroscedasticity appearing in the regression equation. First, heteroscedasticity does not usually occur in time-series studies, unlike cross-sectional studies, because changes in the dependent variables and changes in one or more of the independent variables are likely to be of the same order of magnitude. It is possible for variances to fall over time as measurement techniques improve. Second, these groups are of fairly small size which will also tend to lessen the probability that heteroscedasticity exists. An excellent source for a more complete discussion of heteroscedasticity is Johnston (1984:169, 293-304).

The inflation rate variable is the consumer price index (1967 = 100) for all items found in the Bureau of the Census (1985), *Statistical Abstract of the United States: 1967-1986*. The labor market participation variable in the 55-59 and 60-64 theoretical equations is represented by the national unemployment rate over time. The employment variable in the 65 and older equation is the percent of people 65 and older who are employed over time. The sources for these measures come from the Bureau of the Census (1966-1985), *Statistical Abstract of the United States: 1967-1986* and the Bureau of the Census (1975), *Historical Statistics of the United States, Colonial Times to 1970*.

Single-Equation Estimation

A review of the econometric literature on crime reveals an enormous amount of research completed on the subject ranging from property to violent crimes. Long and Witte (1981) compiled an extensive review of the existing literature and noted that only five property crime and two robbery studies were completed using a time-series approach (Danziger and Wheeler, 1975; Fleisher, 1963, 1966; Glaser and Rice, 1959; Land and Felson, 1976; Phillips, Votey, and Maxwell, 1972; and Weller, Block, and Nold, 1978). None of these studies, however, investigated elderly criminal activity and thus there appears to be an intellectual vacuum that needs to be filled in the empirical analysis of elderly criminals.

This research begins by assuming that the dependent variables are originally measured in multiplicative functional form which can then be easily transformed to a log-linear form (eqs. 6.4-6.6.). This form is commonly applied to demand and supply function econometric analysis because of its flexibility and additional information provided by the coefficients as not only representing the relationship between explanatory and dependent variables but also in exacting elasticity or sensitivity measures which are especially important for policy analysis. This elasticity measure is defined as the ratio of the percentage change of the dependent variable over the percentage change of the explanatory variable which can be greater than, less than, or equal to unity (elastic, inelastic, or unit elastic, respectively). The relationship between these two variables becomes more sensitive or elastic as the measure increases with the limits being zero (perfectly inelastic or no sensitivity) and infinity (perfectly elastic or extreme sensitivity). The sign (positive or negative) merely indicates the nature of the association between the two variables. Using equation 6.4 as an example, a_1, a_2, and a_3 represent the property crime arrest rate elasticity coefficients for people 55-59 years old with respect to the consumer price index, population of the 55-59 year old age group and the national unemployment rate, respectively. Thus this investigation will not only examine to see whether estimated signs of the coefficients conform to a priori predictions but also to inquire into the meaning of the magnitude and hence elasticity measure of the coefficients.[2] Therefore, the single-equation models to be estimated are as follows:

$$\log y_{1t} = \log a_o + a_1 \log x_{1t} + a_2 \log x_{2t} + a_3 \log x_{5t} + e_{1t} \quad (6.4)$$

$$\log y_{2t} = \log b_o + b_1 \log x_{1t} + b_2 \log x_{3t} + b_3 \log x_{5t} + e_{2t} \quad (6.5)$$

$$\log y_{3t} = \log c_o + c_1 \log x_{1t} + c_2 \log x_{4t} + c_3 \log x_{6t} + e_{3t} \quad (6.6)$$

where,

$\log y_{1t}, \log y_{2t}, \log y_{3t}$ = the logarithm of the arrest rate for burglary, larceny, and motor vehicle theft for the elderly 55-59, 60-64, and 65 and older, respectively.

$\log a_o, \log b_o, \log c_o$ = CONSTANT

$\log x_{1t}$ = LCPI (the logarithm of the consumer price index, 1967 = 100).

$\log x_{2t}, \log x_{3t}, \log x_{4t}$ = LPOPGR1, LPOPGR2, LPOPGR3 (the logarithm of population for the elderly 55-59, 60-64, and 65 and older, respectively).

$\log x_{5t}$ = LUSUR (the logarithm of the national annual unemployment rate).

$\log x_{6t}$ = LPUSEM65 (the logarithm of the percent of the elderly 65 and older who are employed).

e_{1t}, e_{2t}, e_{3t} = error terms for each respective equation.

The expected signs of the constants and parameters are given below according to expectations derived from the theoretical model.

$\log a_o, \log b_o, \log c_o \gtrless o$ $\quad a_2, b_2, c_2 > o$

$a_1, b_1, c_1 \gtrless o$ $\quad a_3, b_3 > o$ $\quad c_3 < o$

The single-equation estimation results are listed on Table 6.1, 6.2, and 6.3. Statistical information regarding the performance of the regression

Table 6.1.
Single-Equation Estimation Results for the Arrest Rate of All Property Crime Categories for the Elderly 55-59 Years of Age: 1964-1984

	Dependent Variables				
	Property	Burglary	Larceny	Motor Vehicle Theft	
	(1)OLSQ	(2)OLSQ	(3)OLSQ	(4)OLSQ	(5)CORC
CONSTANT	-39.641 ***a	-21.943 **	-42.926 ***	-37.101 **	-28.563
	(-6.132) b	(-1.987)	(-7.251)	(-2.364)	(-1.102)
LCPI	.291 **	.175	.289 **	.263	.113
	(2.213)	(.781)	(2.404)	(.824)	(.273)
LPOPGR1	4.083 ***	2.012 *	4.419 ***	3.497 **	2.600
	(5.373)	(1.550)	(6.351)	(1.896)	(.867)
LUSUR	.152 **	-.058	.183 **	-.155	.158
	(1.785)	(-.397)	(2.358)	(-.751)	(.739)
RHO					.498 ***
					(2.567)

Table 6.1 (continued)

	Dependent Variables				
	Property	Burglary	Larceny	Motor Vehicle Theft	
	(1)OLSQ	(2)OLSQ	(3)OLSQ	(4)OLSQ	(5)CORC
N	21	21	21	21	20
S.E.E.	.064	.110	.059	.156	.136
D-W	1.679	1.521	1.726	1.192	1.470
Adj. R^2	.976	.725	.983	.766	.386
F	276.765 ***	18.614 ***	377.470 ***	22.875 ***	4.674 **

[a]***Indicates significance at the .01 level, **.05 level, and *.10 level.

[b]Figures in parentheses are t-statistics. One-tail tests were performed on all tests of hypotheses except for LCPI in which a two-tail test was employed.

Source: Compiled by authors.

Table 6.2.
Single-Equation Estimation Results for the Arrest Rate of All Property Crime Categories for the Elderly 60-64 Years of Age: 1964-1984

	Dependent Variables					
	Property		Burglary	Larceny		Motor Vehicle Theft
	(6)OLSQ	(7)CORC	(8)OLSQ	(9)OLSQ	(10)CORC	(11)OLSQ
CONSTANT	-11.946**	13.568	10.709*	-14.290**	16.424	-17.224*
	(-1.972)	(.659)	(1.457)	(-2.304)	(.698)	(-1.445)
LCPI	.681***	1.009**	.916***	.661***	1.048*a	.365
	(3.603)	(2.176)	(3.995)	(3.416)	2.056)	(.980)
LPOPGR2	.845	-2.167	-2.044**	1.101*	-2.510	1.168
	(1.118)	(-.866)	(-2.230)	(1.424)	(-.882)	(.786)
LUSUR	.218*	.394***	.065	.229**	.398***	.163
	(1.720)	(3.033)	(.423)	(1.763)	(3.172)	(.653)
RHO		.627***			.687***	
		(3.596)			(4.227)	
N	21	20	21	21	20	21

Table 6.2. (continued)

	Dependent Variables					
	Property		Burglary	Larceny		Motor Vehicle Theft
	(6)OLSQ	(7)CORC	(8)OLSQ	(9)OLSQ	(10)CORC	(11)OLSQ
S.E.E.	.096	.083	.117	.099	.082	.190
D-W	1.060	2.312	1.803	.962	2.381	1.634
Adj. R^2	.949	.770	.772	.951	.729	.706
F	125.771***	20.808***	23.615***	130.780***	16.934***	17.023***

[a]Significant at the .05 level for a one-tail test.

Source: Compiled by authors.

Table 6.3.
Single-Equation Estimation Results for the Arrest Rate of All Property Crime Categories for the Elderly 65 and Older Years of Age: 1964-1984

	Dependent Variables					
	Property		Burglary	Larceny		Motor Vehicle Theft
	(12)OLSQ	(13)CORC	(14)OLSQ	(15)OLSQ	(16)CORC	(17)OLSQ
CONSTANT	-65.733***	-54.843*	-41.033**	-67.158***	-53.189*	-97.068***
	(-4.094)	(-1.698)	(-2.031)	(-4.086)	(-1.506)	(-4.329)
LCPI	-.141	.225	.006	-.140	.312	-1.247**a
	(-.438)	(.321)	(.016)	(-.425)	(.404)	(-2.772)
LPOPGR3	6.351***	4.961*	3.554**	6.481***	4.722	9.774***
	(3.926)	(1.444)	(1.746)	(3.914)	(1.250)	(4.327)
LPUSEM65	.764	1.194	.544	.783	1.280*	.233
	(1.063)	(1.285)	(.602)	(1.065)	(1.338)	(.222)
RHO		.489**			.538***	
		(2.508)			(2.854)	
N	21	20	21	21	20	21

Table 6.3. (continued)

	Dependent Variables					
	Property		Burglary	Larceny		Motor Vehicle Theft
	(12)OLSQ	(13)CORC	(14)OLSQ	(15)OLSQ	(16)CORC	(17)OLSQ
S.E.E.	.108	.104	.136	.110	.106	.151
D-W	1.227	1.674	2.038	1.201	1.685	2.207
Adj. R^2	.956	.818	.828	.956	.782	.908
F	144.979 ***	27.560 ***	33.090 ***	144.695 ***	22.284 ***	66.605 ***

[a]Significant at the .01 level for a one-tail test.

Source: Compiled by authors.

equations are provided beneath each respective equation: number of observations regressed over time (N), standard error of the equation (S.E.E.), Durbin-Watson statistic (D-W) which determines the degree to which first-order serial correlation may exist in the equation, adjusted R^2 (Adj. R^2) which measures the degree to which the explanatory variables explain the movement of the dependent variable while adjusting for statistical degrees of freedom of the equation, and the F-statistic (F) which tests the significance of the complete regression.

The estimation procedure proceeded as follows. First, ordinary least-squares (OLSQ) were applied to each equation. Second, the equations were then tested to determine whether first-order serial correlation exists by analyzing the D-W statistic as suggested by Durbin and Watson (1950, 1951). First-order serial correlation means the e_t is correlated to e_{t-1} with rho being the measure of serial correlation. Such an occurrence is common in time-series analysis. However, the Durbin and Watson test is not entirely conclusive for all ranges of the test statistic. Johnston (1984) recommends adjusting for first-order serial correlation in the event of an inconclusive result at the .01 and .05 levels. Such a procedure was applied with the adjustment being the Cochrane-Orcutt (1949) method (CORC). The application of this procedure loses one observation.

The estimation results quite strongly indicate that the regressors used are significant in explaining movements of the property crime arrest rate data. All the equations are significant to at least .05 significance level, while having a high adjusted R^2, and a low standard error of the equation.

The inflation rate (LCPI) is an important positively signed regressor for the 55-59 larceny and total property crime categories (larceny being the dominant property crime) and all the 60-64 age group property crime equations except for motor vehicle theft. Surprisingly, the inflation rate did not show any significance in the 65 and older age group equations except for motor vehicle theft. However, the reason for this is answered in the SUR estimation section.

The statistically significant negative sign on the 65 and older motor vehicle theft coefficient can be explained in the following manner using the implications from the theoretical model. Car thefts represent big-ticket items unlike the price of goods stolen under larceny. Therefore, the incidence of auto theft will be more sensitive to changes in income than other items. The 65 and older persons, on fixed income, who heavily rely on income transfer payments will see a negative transfer adjustment to income with a decline in consumer prices and thus increasing the burden to the elderly of acquiring automobiles in a legitimate fashion if one assumes mean car prices do not follow the general overall consumer price index. The burden of buying automobiles falls as consumer prices rise since this will be translated into increases in transfer adjustments to income and thus less incidence of illegitimate auto theft behavior. The elastic coefficient of −1.247 for LCPI in the 65 and older motor vehicle theft equation adds weight to the validity of the preceding argument since price changes for the oldest elderly are more likely to also represent income changes than younger elderly who are earning income through wages and legitimate labor market activities. The differences in the elasticity coefficients for LCPI in the 55-59 and 60-64 age groups for the other crime categories reveal variations that are consistent with the "life cycle" notion of wealth accumulation by Ando and Modigliani (1963). Individuals are their wealthiest before retirement and then declines as retirement uses up stored wealth. People 60-64 do not have as much access to the extensive transfer payment system as people 65 and older where the system protects people from real decline in income. This may explain the change in results for LCPI between the 60-64 to 65 and older age groups for total property crime, burglary, and larceny crime categories.

The population variables (LPOPGR1, LPOPGR2, or LPOPGR3) are significant in all the 55-59 and 65 and older per crime categories while having an expected positive coefficient. The 60-64 age group OLSQ burglary and larceny equations indicated a significant coefficient for LPOPGR2 although it was negative for burglary. The elasticity coefficients on the 65 and older population group equations are the highest of the three groups, followed by the 55-59 and 60-64 age groups. The interpretation of the sign and magnitude of the coefficients for the population variable in each property crime arrest rate regression per age group can take two directions. First, there simply exists a positive and elastic relationship between population and arrest rates. Second, the sign and magnitude of the coefficients, especially those regarding the 65 and older estimation results, could indicate a greater response of the legal system in dealing with elderly property crime. A 1 percent increase in the 65 and older population translates into an increase in arrest rates of 4.96 percent for total property crime, 3.55 percent for burglary, 6.48 percent for larceny, and 9.77 percent for motor vehicle theft. The very high elastic response in the 65 and older motor vehicle theft regression equation may be attributable to the following impacts: (1) reveals a more intense display by law enforcement to combat the incidence of this type of property crime, (2) indicates a relationship arising from the supply of offense function as to the severity of this particular crime which involves large-price ticket items, or (3) signifies a type of property crime that is inherently more risky than other property crimes and thus more susceptible to arrest. An exact answer is difficult to extract given the aggregate testing of relationships that are inherently made as individual decisions about the choice of behavior.

The unemployment variable displays a significant positive sign in the 55-59 and 60-64 age group equations. This counters previous results obtained by Ehrlich (1973), Land and Felson (1976), and Swimmer (1974a, 1974b) who all stated the opposite result that unemployment has no appreciable effect on the incidence of crime. The employment variable does not exhibit any consistent significance in the 65 and older equations. However, these results changed through SUR estimation results.

The weakest performing regressions are those explaining motor vehicle theft. Although the results are dramatically altered under SUR estimation, it may reveal that this particular type of crime may be very different than burglary and larceny. Auto theft entails greater risks in committing the act, implies the existence of knowledge of required networks of operation to dispose of stolen cars, and is in general a crime where the expected net benefits are more difficult to evaluate than under other property crimes.

Seemingly Unrelated Regression Estimation (SUR)

The method of estimating seemingly unrelated regression equations as developed by Zellner (1962) was performed on each crime category across each age group. An explanation of the SUR estimation procedure is provided in the Appendix. These results are presented in Tables 6.4-6.7. The procedure entails jointly estimating equations (6.4)-(6.6.) for one crime category across each age group. The theoretical justification for employing this procedure rests with the belief that if the researcher suspects that the error terms in these equations are highly correlated, then SUR estimation derives greater statistically efficient estimates than under ordinary least-squares. Statistical efficiency of the estimates through SUR estimation increases with greater error correlation as information from the other regressions are being used in the calculation of coefficient estimates. Correlation estimates were run on each of the OLSQ regression equations per crime category across age groups and were found to be significant enough to warrant SUR estimation. The results of the correlation matrix relevant for each crime are provided at the bottom of each SUR estimation table. We suspected a high correlation since the population group that is restricted to 55 and older would be fairly homogeneous in regards to their motivation to commit crime. Ehrlich (1974) applied SUR estimation at a given time period across all categories of property crime equations which included robbery and another SUR estimation application for violent crime equations (murder, rape, and assault). This application of the SUR method may be theoretically flawed since the individual who commits one kind of crime may be very different than a person who commits another type of crime, as in the case of robbery versus larceny.

The SUR estimation results reveal that the inflation rate is a very significant regressor on the property crime arrest rate and is positive in all cases except two (burglary and motor vehicle theft for the 65 and older age group). The SUR estimation results also reinforce the impact of changes in population on the arrest rate while again indicating that the oldest age group generates the highest population elasticity coefficients in all the crime categories. The unemployment rate and even the employment variable for

Table 6.4.
SUR Estimation Results for the Arrest Rate of Total Property Crime for the Elderly 55-59, 60-64, and 65 and Older Years of Age: 1964-1984

	Dependent Variables		
	Property (55-59) (18)SUR	Property (60-64) (19)SUR	Property (≥65) (20)SUR
CONSTANT	-2.455	-3.223 **	-26.871 ***
	(-.822)	(-1.808)	(-5.145)
LCPI	1.018 ***	.979 ***	.595 ***
	(12.706)	(13.498)	(4.781)
LPOPGR1	-.307		
	(-.877)		
LPOPGR2		-.261	
		(-1.187)	
LPOPGR3			2.310 ***
			(4.312)
LUSUR	.104	.129 ***	
	(.247)	(3.591)	
LPUSEM65			-.109
			(-.521)
N	21	21	21
S.E.E.	.101	.933	.114
D-W	.948	1.023	1.038
Adj. R^2	.934	.971	.990
$F_{3,17}$	95.524 ***	221.000 ***	623.963 ***

Correlation Matrix of the Error Terms from the Single-Equation OLSQ Estimation Results

	error(1)[a]	error(6)	error(12)
error(1)	1.000	.581	.534
error(6)	.581	1.000	.852
error(12)	.534	.852	1.000

[a]The number within the parentheses represents the equation number from which the error term was taken when deriving the correlation matrix.

Source: Compiled by authors.

Table 6.5.
SUR Estimation Results for the Arrest Rate of Burglary for the Elderly 55-59, 60-64, and 65 and Older Years of Age: 1964-1984

	Dependent Variables		
	Burglary (55-59) (21)SUR	Burglary (60-64) (22)SUR	Burglary (≧65) (23)SUR
CONSTANT	-19.664 ***	-.022	-32.133 **
	(-3.961)	(-.060)	(-2.286)
LCPI	.137	.537 ***	-.482 [a]
	(1.161)	(4.080)	(-1.682)
LPOPGR1	1.764 ***		
	(3.029)		
LPOPGR2		-.680 *	
		(-1.514)	
LPOPGR3			3.400 **
			(2.402)
LUSUR	.061	.195 **	
	(.684)	(1.894)	
LPUSEM65			-1.319 **
			(-2.105)
N	21	21	21
S.E.E.	.101	.114	.143
D-W	1.359	1.470	1.788
Adj. R^2	.998	.998	.999
$F_{3,17}$	2827.667 ***	5661.000 ***	2829.945 ***

Correlation Matrix of the Error Terms from the Single-Equation OLSQ Estimation Results

	error(2)	error(8)	error(14)
error(2)	1.000	.805	.521
error(8)	.805	1.000	.552
error(14)	.521	.552	1.000

[a]Significant at the .10 level for a one-tail test.

Source: Compiled by authors.

Table 6.6.
SUR Estimation Results for the Arrest Rate of Larceny for the Elderly 55-59, 60-64, and 65 and Older Years of Age: 1964-1984

	Dependent Variables		
	Larceny (55-59) (24)SUR	Larceny (60-64) (25)SUR	Larceny (≧65) (26)SUR
CONSTANT	-4.606 *	-4.046 **	-26.748 ***
	(-1.596)	(-2.205)	(-4.948)
LCPI	1.049 ***	1.015 ***	.689 ***
	(13.313)	(13.401)	(5.390)
LPOPGR1	-.107		
	(-.318)		
LPOPGR2		-.199	
		(-.877)	
LPOPGR3			2.205 ***
			(3.992)
LUSUR	.023	.119 ***	
	(.544)	(3.046)	
LPUSEM65			.038
			(.173)
N	21	21	21
S.E.E.	.101	.201	.118
D-W	.877	.917	.958
Adj. R^2	.953	.975	.990
$F_{3,17}$	136.025 ***	264.175 ***	624.270 ***

Correlation Matrix of the Error Terms from the Single-Equation OLSQ Estimation Results

	error(3)	error(9)	error(15)
error(3)	1.000	.520	.507
error(9)	.520	1.000	.844
error(15)	.507	.844	1.000

Source: Compiled by authors.

Table 6.7.
SUR Estimation Results for the Arrest Rate of Motor Vehicle Theft for the Elderly 55-59, 60-64, and 65 and Older Years of Age: 1964-1984

	Dependent Variables		
	Motor Vehicle Theft (55-59) (27)SUR	Motor Vehicle Theft (60-64) (28)SUR	Motor Vehicle Theft (≧65) (29)SUR
CONSTANT	-25.789 **	-7.520	-54.825 ***
	(-2.439)	(-.916)	(-3.084)
LCPI	.441 *[a]	.596 **	-.854 **
	(1.971)	(2.257)	(-2.314)
LPOPGR1	2.173 **		
	(1.749)		
LPOPGR2		-.036	
		(-.035)	
LPOPGR3			5.860 ***
			(3.239)
LUSUR	-.132	.213	
	(-.873)	(1.205)	
LPUSEM65			-1.756 **
			(-2.325)
N	21	21	21
S.E.E.	.143	.174	.152
D-W	1.173	1.567	1.831
Adj. R^2	.998	.998	.999
$F_{3,17}$	3772.111 ***	2829.022 ***	5661.000 ***

Correlation Matrix of the Error Terms from the Single-Equation OLSQ Estimation Results

	error(4)	error(11)	error(17)
error(4)	1.000	.674	.437
error(11)	.674	1.000	.499
error(17)	.437	.499	1.000

[a]Significant at the .05 level for a one-tail test.

Source: Compiled by authors.

the 65 and older group registered statistically significant coefficients of the correct sign. Overall, these equations exhibit extremely high adjusted R^2 and F-statistics which suggest that these equations together with the performance of the coefficients support the theory derived in the section "Theoretical Model."

CONCLUSIONS AND IMPLICATIONS

Conclusions

The purpose of this chapter was to apply economic theory in the theoretical development and empirical testing of factors that would significantly impact and explain property crime patterns in the United States from 1964-1984 by elderly criminals of the ages 55-59, 60-64, and 65 and older years. This investigation determined that changes in the inflation rate, population, unemployment rate, and employment participation patterns are key independent variables in explaining trends in property crime arrest rates. This study departs from previous analyses in the literature in specifically isolating the aged as criminals in empirical testing in an annual time-series framework by relating changes in the inflation rate and unemployment rate to property crime arrest rate patterns over time. Thus this investigation has not only undertaken the process of developing a theoretical model and testing hypotheses from the model but also in empirically evaluating those tests for elderly criminals. It appears that the theoretical model has been empirically supported given the estimation results in explaining changes in total property crime, burglary, and larceny arrest rate patterns for all the elderly categories listed above in the United States from 1964-1984. Empirical findings regarding the motor vehicle theft regression equations demonstrated weaker overall statistical qualities than those of the other crime categories. This divergence of empirical findings would seem to indicate that elderly criminal behavior regarding motor vehicle theft operates under different incentive and disincentive mechanisms than observed under burglary and larceny and hence should be theoretically modeled and empirically testes separately in order to conform to the specific decision-making characteristics that are distinctive to motor vehicle theft.

Policy Implications

Extracting policy implications from the empirical findings in this study are indeed difficult. Clearly, the incidence of elderly property crime activity nowhere approaches that for younger age categories and thus it cannot be implied that society faces an elderly crime wave. However, the empirical results do hint that the issue of rising arrest rate patterns by the aged over time is not only due to the existence of an increasingly larger aged population but also in providing an indication as to the cause of this social problem which may in fact be symptomatic of a larger and far more complex underlying structural problem within our society in dealing with the specific needs of the aged. If in fact this is true, then the issue of elderly criminal activity is of secondary importance to the primary factors that must be addressed. The application of an integrated socioeconomic approach to elderly criminal activity could provide the answer to this question which would not only point the direction of future research in this field but also provide policymakers a more firm foundation as to the course of policy prescriptions in dealing with elderly property crime.

APPENDIX

Zellner's Seemingly Unrelated Regression (SUR) Equations Estimation Procedure

The method of estimating seemingly unrelated regression equations as developed by Zellner (1962) is a procedure for jointly estimating a set of equations when the researcher suspects a theoretical relationship between these regressions as measured by the correlation of the error terms between each regression. Consider the following set of equations as seen in this study.

$$y_{t1} = f_1(w_{t1}, w_{t2}, \ldots, w_{tk1}) + u_{t1} \quad \text{(A.1)}$$

$$y_{t2} = f_2(x_{t1}, x_{t2}, \ldots, x_{tk2}) + u_{t2} \quad \text{(A.2)}$$

$$y_{t3} = f_3(z_{t1}, z_{t2}, \ldots, z_{tk3}) + u_{t3} \quad \text{(A.3)}$$

where,

$y_{t1}, y_{t2}, y_{t3},$ = dependent variables per regression, respectively

$w_{t1}, \ldots, w_{tk1}, x_{t1}, \ldots, x_{tk2}, z_{t1}, \ldots, z_{tk3}$ = explanatory variables per regression, respectively

u_{t1}, u_{t2}, u_{t3} = error terms per regression, respectively

f_1, f_2, f_3 = function operators per regression, respectively

k_1, k_2, k_3 = the number of explanatory variables per regression, respectively

t = time period, where the number of observations per regression is $t = 1, 2, \ldots, n$

The application of the Zellner SUR estimation procedure will yield feasible generalized least-squares estimates if the above defined regressions are linear, contain the same number of observations, and follow certain technical statistical assumptions as given in Johnston (1984:337-341).

The application of single-equation estimation techniques such as ordinary least-squares on the regressions separately when in fact a theoretically derived and empirically demonstrated relationship exists between these regressions will imply the calculation of coefficient estimates of less statistical efficiency than those obtained through SUR estimation. The gain in efficiency yielded by the Zellner estimator over ordinary least-squares increases directly with the correlation between disturbances from the different equations and decreases as the correlation between the different sets of explanatory variables increases.

The intuitive appeal of the SUR estimation procedure is the use of all information which is theoretically relevant to the estimation of a regression equation carried in the other empirically correlated regressions. Thus the SUR estimation procedure does not waste valuable and relevant information unlike the single-equation estimation procedure.

The application of the SUR estimation procedure in this investigation by combining property crime arrest rate regressions per crime category across the three age groups is considered to be more theoretically valid than the application in Ehrlich (1974) which combined aggregate national cross-sectional property crime regression equations containing robbery, burglary, larceny, and auto theft and another SUR estimation for violent crime regression equations containing murder, rape, and assault. The incentive and disincentive mechanisms that operate under robbery, for example, differ sharply from other property crimes such as burglary or larceny. Thus, it is not clear whether SUR estimation of different property crimes and a violent crime like robbery represents a theoretically proper application of the Zellner estimation procedure.

NOTES

1. Inclusion of a population variable on both sides of the equation (as a denominator in the dependent variable and as an independent variable) may result in an empirical distortion of impacts. This issue is discussed at length in the empirical section of the chapter.

2. Elasticity coefficients are also known as regression coefficients. In the present case an elastic variable is one in which a unit change in the log of an independent variable results in more than a unit change in the log of the dependent variable. An inelastic variable, by contrast, is one in which a unit change in the log of an independent variable results in less than a unit change in the log of the dependent variable.

SECTION III

PERSPECTIVES IN CRIMINAL JUSTICE

7

Police Disposition of Arrests: An Exploratory Study of the Treatment of the Older Offender

Robert Langworthy
Belinda McCarthy

INTRODUCTION

Despite growing interest in crime, justice, and the elderly offender, the impact of advanced offender age on police use of discretion has been largely ignored by empirical research. The implications of our failure to examine the impact of police discretion at this early stage of processing are considerable, because police use of discretion may affect our understanding of the type and volume of crime committed by older offenders. Perhaps more important, a lack of understanding of how police dispose of arrest cases limits our ability to assess the extent to which elderly offenders are exposed to differential treatment at arrest and subsequent stages of the criminal justice system.

Interest in the elderly offender has led to considerable research on elderly arrest patterns and trends, much of which focuses on a comparison of these findings with similar data on younger offenders to determine the impact of age on criminal conduct (Keller and Vedder, 1968; Shichor, 1984a; Wilbanks, 1985). However, in this examination no attention has been paid to the process by which offenders become "arrest statistics." Instead, it is assumed that arrest patterns represent the criminality of older offenders in the same manner that they reflect the offenses of younger criminals.

By ignoring the decision-making process that produces an arrest, studies of older offender arrest patterns tacitly accept the proposition that the decision to arrest is not influenced by age, and that offenses involving older and younger offenders are similarly disposed of by the police. Because arrest studies are our primary source of information about the involvement of offenders in crime, this assumption is a hazardous one. If police treat older offenders more leniently or more harshly than younger offenders, then arrest statistics will not reflect the criminal conduct of older offenders in a manner that is comparable to their representation of younger offenders. Any attempt to determine how older offenders are different from younger offenders based on these statistical comparisons will be seriously flawed, distorting our understanding of patterns of crime and the elderly.

Police use of discretion in the handling of older offenders may also be distorting the results of empirical research on the treatment of the older offender in the criminal justice system. Although research on all aspects of elderly crime is limited, much of what has been accomplished has focused on the extent to which elderly offenders are treated more leniently or more harshly by courts and correctional agencies. When such research focuses on prosecution practices, police practices regarding arrest and the disposition of arrest are ignored; it is assumed that cases are referred for prosecution on an equitable basis, that is, that older and younger offenders are equally likely to arrive at that stage of justice system processing. If police use of discretion does lead to greater or lesser screening of older offenders before judicial hearings begin, then findings regarding leniency or severity of treatment that ignore prejudicial handling are flawed. If, for example, it is understood that older offenders in a particular jurisdiction are usually given "a break" by arresting officers and that only the most serious older criminals are referred for prosecution, then prosecutors may be especially likely to fully prosecute the cases of the older offenders they receive. While this might look like harsh treatment by the courts, it would be more accurately viewed as a response to earlier leniency in the system. Without information on the leniency or severity with which police handle older offenders, studies of subsequent court processing are basically operating in a void.

The purpose of this study is to begin to address these gaps in the empirical literature by examining one aspect of the use of police discretion and the elderly. By focusing attention on the most visible aspect of police behavior involving the elderly, the arrest disposition, one can advance understanding of criminal justice system processing and the elderly, and the degree of differential treatment meted out in the criminal justice system.

REVIEW OF THE LITERATURE

Research on Police Use of Discretion

Prior research on police discretion indicates that a variety of factors influence the police decision to arrest. These include offender characteristics and demeanor, and incident characteristics.[1] Although most research indicates that incident characteristics are more important than offender traits and behavior, there is evidence that some offender characteristics play an important role, to the extent that certain groups of criminals may be treated more leniently than others. In this regard, leniency refers to a decision not to arrest in a situation in which an arrest could have been made.

Generally speaking, women have been found to be recipients of leniency more often than males, and there is mixed evidence that white offenders may be treated more leniently than blacks and other minorities. The age variable has even been addressed in some of this research, but the focus has been on juvenile versus adult distinctions, rather than the impact of old age. This research generally indicates that juveniles are treated more leniently than adults.

Unfortunately, virtually no research has been undertaken on the arrest disposition process. While we may assume that the same factors influence arrest and arrest disposition processes, this assumption requires a strong caveat: It is quite possible that arrest and arrest disposition processes complement each other in much the same way that arrest disposition and prosecution processes may balance each other. That is, leniency for a particular group at the arrest decision may be followed by harsher treatment of the few members of that group that are arrested.

Arguing against the likelihood of two stages of inversely related differential police treatment is the fact that unlike police-to-prosecution decision making, both arrest and arrest disposition decisions are made by the same organization. These decisions should demonstrate greater uniformity than decisions flowing from different organizations, since the same policy directives are guiding behavior. A second factor supporting expectations of noncompensating uses of discretion at the arrest and arrest disposition stage is the fact that much of what we know about arrest decision making supports the contention that incident characteristics greatly outweigh the importance of offender characteristics. This being the case, one might expect the dispositional decision to introduce offender characteristics into the decision-making process, rather than to counteract them.

Differential Treatment and the Older Offender in the Criminal Justice System

Expectations regarding how older offenders might benefit or suffer from their status of senior citizen can be drawn both from an understanding of the limited role of offender characteristics in the arrest decision and from an understanding of current criminal justice system processing and the older offender. There is empirical support for expectations of findings showing no differential treatment, and findings indicating leniency or severity of treatment.

The greatest argument against expectations of differential treatment is the fact the other personal characteristics of offenders seem to be of limited importance in police decision making. Indeed, one would expect juvenile status, gender, and race to have a greater impact than old age. Advanced age at present does not warrant screening into a separate justice system, as is the case for juveniles, nor is it a status with the magnitude of role expectations and limitations as gender. Because elder status is a "softer" and more amorphous status than race, which is clearly identifiable, decisions based on this more ambiguous classification would be expected to be less distinctive.

On the other hand, there is a clear difference between factors of limited value and factors of no value. Prior research on police decision making does indicate a role played by personal characteristics, and an understanding of the role played by age in subsequent criminal justice processing provides support for the assumption that advanced age will be important in police decision making as well. Wilbanks (1985) found that older offenders are treated more severely by the courts up to the sentencing stage, at which point they appear to benefit from lenient treatment. Cutshall and Adams (1983) found that prosecutors were more lenient in their treatment of older offenders, being more willing to dismiss charges against them. Lindquist, White, and Chambers (1986) produced mixed results in their study of felons and misdemeanants, with some classifications of older misdemeanants actually receiving more severe sentences than their younger counterparts.

Logical arguments are available to support differential treatment in the direction of leniency or severity. Age was among the first discriminators employed by the criminal justice system to legitimately distinguish classes of offenders. Juveniles are treated differently than adults ostensibly because of age-related assumptions regarding criminal responsibility and *parens patriae* notions that children should be cared for and nurtured by society. While the age discrimination notion has not been applied by the criminal justice system to persons at the other end of the age spectrum much of the logic is already in place to establish a separate system for older offenders with an eye toward leniency and compassion. Cohen (1984), for example, suggests that older offenders could, in some cases, be excused from criminal liability due to infirmities of aging. Likewise, we see the evolution of a geriatric profession whose aim is to give aid and comfort to elderly citizens in need in a manner similar to the evolution of child protective services agencies. If older people are viewed by the larger society as somewhat less responsible and more in need of protection then it seems likely that police will be inclined and expected to go easy.

Another basis for believing that older people would be treated less harshly is that similar punishments are differentially severe depending on age. This thesis suggests that older offenders may be treated with more leniency because of the perception that punishments are disproportionately felt. This argument suggests the obvious—a year of incarceration given someone who is 70 years old takes a considerably larger proportion of that person's remaining years than the same punishment assigned to a 20-year-old offender.

The contrasting case can also be made; that is, there are reasons to expect older offenders to be dealt with more harshly. One might argue that the older offenders should know better and are, therefore, more culpable than younger people (Cohen, 1984:118,119). Black's (1976) treatise on the sociology of law provides another basis for expectations of harsh treatment for older offenders. Black suggests that marginality increases vulnerability to the law. He notes that "A marginal man is . . . more likely to have the police called against him, . . . to be arrested, prosecuted, . . . to have heavy damages demanded of him, or to be severely punished" (p. 51). Older people, like young people, are marginal; they do not participate in the productive activities of the society and until very recently had little or no political clout. If Black's thesis is true then one would expect older people to be treated more harshly than younger people because they are less well integrated into the society.

In summary, there is a sound theoretical basis for the development of different assumptions about the way police may treat older people. There is, however, very little empirical information concerning the way older suspects are treated by the police. Ideally, an analysis of police treatment of older suspects would provide insight into both the way the police officer who makes arrests (or elects not to make an arrest) exercises discretion with regard to older suspects as well as the police department's disposition of that arrest. However, the data to examine the individual officer's decision to take an older person into custody presently do not exist. Simply put, police encounters with older suspects occur so infrequently that observational data collected describing the nature of police/citizen interactions fail to be able to describe the nature of police and older suspect interactions.[2] However, it is possible to describe what happens to arrests after they have been made and that is the approach selected in this analysis.

RESEARCH DESIGN AND METHODS

The data used in this analysis are from the 1981 California Offender Based Transaction System (OBTIS) statistics. The full data set includes 200,661 adult felony arrest dispositions and provides information concerning arrest disposition (police release, nolle pros, dismissed, convicted, etc.), age, sex, racial characteristics of defendants, as well as geographic and agency identifiers. From this data set we extracted all adult felony arrest cases in which the defendant was 50 years old or older (n =

6,538) and a 3.4 percent sample of the rest to generate an under 50 years of age (n = 6,546) comparison group.

Table 7.1 is a summary description of the variables used in the study. As noted above the offender data were divided into two groups depending on whether they were under or over 50 years of age. The dependent variable in the analysis is arrest disposition. Since we are concerned with police disposition of arrests it is coded to distinguish between police release of persons arrested for felony offenses and other dispositions (nolle pros, dismissed by courts, or convicted) of felony arrests. Arrests disposed of by the police were coded 1; arrests disposed of later in the criminal process were coded 2. Race is coded as 1 for whites and 2 for those who are not white. Hispanics were not distinguished in the data file and are, therefore, included in the white tally. Those coded as not white include 74 American Indians and 44 Asians and Pacific Islanders. The data set contains 8,497 whites (64.9 percent) and 4,294 nonwhites (32.8 percent). Males were coded 1 and females 2. As in any arrest data set this one is dominated by males, 86.3 percent, while females constitute just 13.6 percent of the cases. The arrest charge is the original offense charged by the arresting officer. Arrest codes are in a rough inverse order of seriousness with less serious offenses coded with higher numbers and more serious offenses coded with lower

Table 7.1.
Description of Variables

Variable	Description
Arrest disposition	police release = 1; other disposition (nolle pros, dismiss, convict) = 2. Number of police releases = 1,086; other dispositions = 11,854.
Race	white = 1, not white = 2. Hispanics included in whites. Number of whites = 8,497, not whites = 4,294.
Sex	male = 1, female = 2. Number of men = 11,289, women = 1,778.
Arrest charge	the charge brought by the arresting officer. The charges are coded in an inverse order of their seriousness with more serious offenses having lower codes than less serious offenses.
Age at arrest	computed by subtracting the year of arrest from the year of birth. The average age for those under 50 years (n = 6,546) is 26 and for those 50 years or older (n = 6,538) the average age is 56.

Source: Compiled by authors.

numbers. The final variable used in the analysis is age at arrest. This variable was used to differentiate the two age groups and is then used as an independent variable within age groups. The age at arrest variable was computed by subtracting the year of birth from the year of arrest. The average age of persons arrested who are under 50 years of age is 26 while for those over 50 the average age is 56.

Limitations of Data

As noted at the beginning of this chapter, we are concerned with whether police treat older suspects differently than younger suspects. The initial question was followed with several theoretical positions that could be used to generate hypotheses regarding police treatment of older suspects. This being the case it is reasonable to ask why an exploratory analysis was conducted rather than a test of theory. The answer has to do with the limits of the available data. The data being used in this analysis describe what happens to arrests once prior decisions have been made resulting in an arrest.[3] Without knowledge of how the initial arrest decision is structured theories of discriminatory handling of older suspects cannot be tested. This shortcoming is not peculiar to this study but attends all studies that examine summary arrest statistics. It is known, for example, that fewer older persons are arrested than younger persons (Shichor, 1984a:29) but without interactional or observational studies it is not known whether to attribute the differential to a lower rate of offending by older people, population composition, reluctance of officers to arrest older people, or to some combination of all the above factors. Likewise, it is known that arrested older persons are more likely to be arrested for violent crimes than younger arrested persons (Shichor, 1984a:21). But again the differential could not be interpreted—it cannot be said whether the difference is a behavioral difference associated with age or differential treatment by the police. Clearly, if police only arrest older persons when they are suspected of having committed serious offenses then the distribution of older suspects across crime categories will be biased in favor of more serious violent offenses. The analysis, like the studies that developed the conclusions noted above, cannot interpret the findings theoretically because the structure of the initial arrest decision is not known. If officers are instructed to treat everybody equally and if they follow those instructions then there is no problem—the intake data will accurately reflect the behavior of the population and the arresting officers. However, if officers are instructed, either formally or informally, to go easy on older people then the only older people through the department's doors will be those whose guilt is beyond question which may very well result in lower release rates of older suspects. Therefore, the inability to specify the structure of the initial arrest decision makes it impossible to test theory but does not inhibit the exploration and documentation of the behavior of police with respect to disposition of arrested older suspects. Analysis of these data will make it possible to document the apparent similarity or difference in treatment and structure the speculation as to explanations of the data which should be useful in future analytic endeavors—which is, after all, the purpose of exploratory research.

Data Analysis

The analysis unfolds in two stages. First is an examination of police disposition rates of older and younger suspects by sex, race, and by charged offense. This analysis examines the percent of older and younger suspects that are released by police to provide a vehicle for describing dispositional differences. The second phase is a multivariate analysis that compares models that predict the disposition of older and younger suspects by police. This latter stage of the analysis is designed to determine if the same set of variables are useful in predicting police dispositions of both older and younger suspects or if it appears that older suspects are treated differently than younger suspects. The total analysis, thus, offers the opportunity to compare and describe the disposition of older and younger suspects by police.

FINDINGS

Table 7.2 presents the percent of older and younger suspects released by police by sex, race, and arrest charge. The first impression is that older suspects are less likely to be released by police than younger suspects. That is, disposition of older suspects' arrests occurs after deeper penetration into the criminal justice system. Overall, younger suspects are one and a half times more likely to be released than older suspects. This relationship holds for males and whites but becomes even more pronounced for females and nonwhites. Younger women and nonwhites under 50 years of age are nearly twice as likely to be released as older women and older nonwhites. While the relationship is consistent across race and sex the same cannot be said for arrest charge. For some charges there are virtually no police dispositional differences (for example, assault, vehicle theft, forgery), for other offenses older people are much more likely to be released (kidnapping and sexual assault), and for still other offenses older suspects are less likely to be released (for example, homicide, arson, drug offenses).

In an effort to treat the arrest charge differential in a summary manner, younger suspect arrest charge police disposition percentages were regressed on older suspect arrest charge police disposition percentages. This procedure permits an interpretation of the significance of the disposition

Table 7.2.
Percent of Felony Arrests of Persons Under 50 Years of Age and Over 50 Years of Age Released by the Police, by Sex, Race, and Arrest Charge, California, 1981

	Under 50 %	Over 50 %
Total	10.2	6.6
Sex:		
Male	10.2	6.8
Female	10.0	5.4
Race:		
White	9.4	6.6
Not white	12.1	6.8
Arrest charge:[a]		
Homicide	14.8	7.5
Kidnapping	3.5	9.5
Sexual assault	8.7	12.0
Robbery	15.6	12.2
Assault	7.9	8.4
Arson	7.4	3.9
Burglary	10.1	7.6
Larceny	10.9	7.6
Vehicle theft	16.8	15.8
Forgery/counterfeiting	6.2	6.7
Fraud	2.2	2.3
Drug offenses	11.4	5.1
Sexual offenses	4.9	4.3
Family offenses	9.8	10.2
Gambling	0.0 [b]	1.3
Obstructing justice	0.0	0.0
Weapons offenses	5.5	3.3
Traffic offenses	4.6	1.8
Public order	5.9	6.2

[a]This list of felony arrest charges is not exhaustive. Only those offenses that had 40 or more arrests for either the older offenders or the sample of younger offenders were listed.
[b]There were only 11 arrests in the under 50 sample, all of whom were eventually convicted.
Source: Compiled by authors.

differentials by examining the resulting regression equation and residuals. Figure 7.1 presents the scatterplot of the relationship between older suspect arrest charge police disposition percentages and younger suspect arrest charge police disposition percentages and the regression equation that predicts younger suspect percentages from older suspect percentages. Evaluation of the regression equation is fairly straightforward; if older suspects and younger suspects are treated the same one would expect the intercept to be zero and the slope to be 1. Indeed that is what was found.

Figure 7.1.
Scatterplot and Regression Equation Depicting the Relationship between Older and Younger Police Disposition Percentages by Arrest Charge, California, 1981

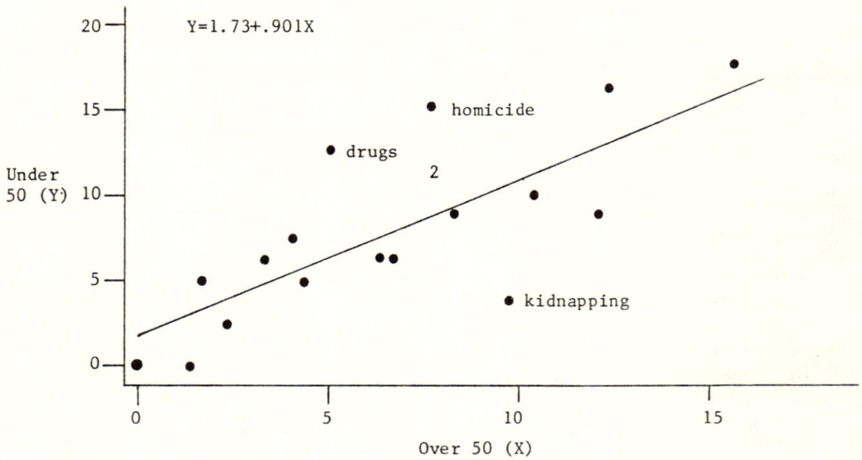

Source: Compiled by authors.

The intercept (equal to 1.73) is just 1.2 standard errors above zero and the slope (0.901) is just .55 standard errors below 1, neither of which is statistically different than our expectation if both groups are treated the same. The same treatment conclusion is further suggested when the residuals from regression are examined. It was found that even in those cases where one might suspect the residuals to be extreme—homicide, kidnapping, and to a lesser degree drug offenses—the differentials are not beyond chance.[4]

The second stage of the analysis focuses on a comparison of models to predict the likelihood of police disposing of an arrested suspect. The models compared are of older suspects and younger suspects. The purpose of the analysis is to see if the two models are the same. If the models are the same or similar one can assume that the same or similar processes are at work with respect to the disposition of both older and younger suspects. However, if it is found that the models are different one would have to conclude that different processes are operating in the decision to release the different classes of suspects. This analysis is of a dichotomous dependent variable, the police either do or do not dispose of the arrest; therefore, logistic regression was employed. The logistic regression model predicts the log of the odds of one particular outcome, in this case police disposition (release), rather than another outcome (nolle pros, dismissal, conviction, etc.).

Table 7.3 presents the two models and diagnostic statistics that predict the log of the odds that the police will dispose of arrested suspects rather than pass the arrest along further into the criminal justice system for disposition. The model to predict the log of the odds that police will release someone they have arrested who is under 50 years of age includes three significant variables—race, age, and arrest charge. Being younger, not white, and arrested for a more serious felony[5] improves the odds of a person being released by the police rather than forwarded for prosecution. A somewhat different model emerges with the examination of the prediction of the log of the odds that police will release someone they have arrested who is over 50 years of age. Only one variable, arrest charge, proves to be a statistically significant predictor of police disposition of older suspects. However, even this predictor acts in the same manner for older suspects as it did for younger suspects. Older suspects arrested for more serious offenses are more likely to be released by the police than older suspects arrested for less serious charges.

While the data presented in Table 7.3 suggest support for the idea that

Table 7.3
Logistic Regression Models Predicting the Log of the Odds that Police Will Release Persons Arrested for Felonies Who Are Under 50 Years of Age and Over 50 Years of Age, California, 1981

Variable	Under 50	Over 50	T-test for difference[a]
Race	.286 * (.086)	.023 (.106)	2.77
Sex	.018 (.120)	-.203 (.162)	1.57
Age	-.015 * (.006)	-.003 (.008)	-1.71
Arrest charge	-.009 * (.003)	-.029 * (.004)	5.68
Constant	-1.962 * (.250)	-1.520 * (.543)	-1.05
-2(log likelihood ratio)	24.7	51.8	

Standard errors are in parentheses.
*Estimate is more than twice its standard error.
[a]The test for equality of coefficients across equations generates t-values that are interpreted the same as z-values (see Visher, 1983:16, 17, 25).
Source: Compiled by authors.

different processes are at work for older and younger suspects, the last column in the table must condition the conclusion somewhat. The test for equality of coefficients across equations isolates just two differences—race and arrest charge. Race is a predictor of police disposition for those younger than 50 years but not for those older than 50 years of age. Arrest charge while a significant predictor for both groups is a much stronger predictor of police disposition of those over 50 years who are arrested than for those under 50. The coefficients of age, however, are not different from each other even though the under-50 coefficient is a significant predictor while the over-50 coefficient is not significant. Thus, while the age coefficient for those under 50 years is different from zero, it is not statistically different than $-.003$, the age coefficient for those over 50 years of age. One final caveat needs to be attached to these findings. Both of the models presented in Table 7.3 appear to be very weak. "Pseudo R^2" computed for both models are less than .01,[6] thus, while the models isolate statistically significant predictors of the log of the odds that police will release rather than forward for prosecution, the models do not appear to fit the data very well. This suggests that we may not realistically be able to compare the models as predictors of police disposition. Nevertheless, it appears that, however weak, the variables in the models are more alike than different. That is, the relationships between the exogenous variables and police disposition seem quite similar in both the under- and over-50-years-of-age models.

DISCUSSION

The intent of the analysis above has been to do an exploratory comparison of police dispositions of younger and older felony arrestees. At the outset of the analysis it was noted that it would not be possible to fully determine from this analysis whether police treat older suspects differently or not because the structure of the arrest decision process with respect to older suspects was not known. However, some light has been shed on what police do with older persons they have arrested. Older suspects are somewhat more likely to be held for further prosecution than younger offenders and race and sex seem not to alter that generalization. In addition, while it appears that there may be disposition percentage differences across arrest charges, analysis of the differentials leads to the conclusion that one could predict the police disposition percentages of younger suspects from police disposition percentages of older suspects with a model containing a 0 intercept and a 1 for the regression coefficient. This latter finding suggests that charges for one group are handled in much the same manner as are charges for the other group, that is, police seem to use the same process and decision criteria for their felony arrest disposition decision of older and younger suspects. Reconciliation of the apparently divergent findings is reasdonable if one notes that though the release percentage for older suspects is just two-thirds that of younger suspects the fact remains that 90 percent of persons under 50 who are arrested are forwarded for prosecution as compared to 93 percent of older suspects—hardly a major difference.

The second stage of the analysis compares models composed of the same variables that ostensibly predict police release of older and younger suspects. Again, considerably more similarity than differences were found. Additionally, the model did not do a very good job of predicting police disposition of felony arrests. This finding leads to a number of concerns for future research.

Weakness of the models was expected at the outset because the data set does not contain a number of important variables—most notably police agency arrest policies and prior record of suspects. Recently, arrest policies of police agencies have been identified as a prime consideration in explaining rates of police release of suspects (Feeney, Dill, and Weir, 1983:Chapter 22). The present analysis did not undertake an agency level analysis but focused instead on a more global statewide examination of police dispositions, but it seems very likely that comparative agency analyses, with associated organizational and environmental variables, could produce very interesting insight into the nature of the police release decision, generally, as well as the nature of the decision as it related to older suspects. The agency comparative form of research into the police treatment of older suspects should be encouraged in the future.

Another variable missing from the OBTIS data set used was prior record of the suspect.[7] There is considerable evidence that prior record is a significant predictor of other criminal justice system decisions regarding the disposition of suspects/defendants. Furthermore, there is evidence that older offenders are more likely to have extensive prior criminal records than are younger offenders (McCarthy and Langworthy, 1987:20). If police are aware of prior records of suspects then it seems likely that police will treat those with prior records more harshly (hold for prosecution) than those without prior records. If police do indeed have this information and if older offenders, as a group, do indeed have more extensive prior criminal records then one should expect to see a lower police release rate for older suspects than for younger suspects. While the initial decision to arrest may not be influenced by prior record there is every reason to believe that a suspect's prior record may well influence the more deliberate subsequent decision to release or hold a suspect for prosecution. Future research into police disposition of older suspects should make every effort to control for prior record of suspects.

While the concerns above apply more generally to research on police disposition of arrests, the remaining issues are more directly related to police treatment of older suspects. In the discussion of the limitations of the study it was noted that the best one could do with the present data was an exploratory research. This limitation is not imposed because of a lack of theory for testing, but because the data presently available are simply not up to the task. Simply put, not enough is known about the structure of the decision to arrest older offenders to know how to interpret the police disposition data. The lack of information is of two sorts: it is not known if the citizen's decision to call the police into a situation is conditioned by the age of the suspect; second, it is not known if the officer's decision to arrest is conditioned by the age of the suspect. Research on the treatment of older suspects by police needs to be focused on gaining insight into the determinants of citizen's reporting of victimizations when older suspects are involved and into the determinants of the police officer's arrest decision when older suspects are involved. While the concerns are somewhat easy to isolate,the solutions to the problems are considerably more difficult.

The easiest of the problems is the citizen's decision to report. Considerable insight has been gained regarding the nature of the citizen's decision to report to police from victimization surveys. Victimization surveys show that the citizen's decision to report a victimization to the police is correlated with characteristics of the offense (complete versus attempt, method of entry, amount of loss, weapon use) and with characteristics of the victim and the victim offender relationship (Hindelang, 1976:Chapter 14; Harlow, 1985). It is also possible to know from these data if being a juvenile offender as opposed to an adult offender conditions the victim's decision to report to the police.[8] What is not presently available is information concerning whether the victim's decision to report is conditioned by the victim's assessment of their assailant as an older person. This deficiency in the data set can be remedied rather simply by expanding age categories to the victim's description of their assailant to include characterizations of older offenders. While modification of the instrument is relatively straightforward it is not at all clear how large the sample would have to be to isolate a significant number of victimizations by older offenders to make an analysis reasonable. The apparent infrequency of older offending (something in the neighborhood of 3 percent of the felony arrests in the 1981 California OBTIS data file are of older offenders) suggests that the approximately 130,000 individuals participating annually in the NCS victimization surveys would generate just 135 victimizations in which the victim would identify their assailant as an older person.[9]

The problem of detailing the police officers arrest decision when the suspect is an older person is even more vexing than the citizen's decision to report because no established vehicle exists for collecting this kind of information. The observational studies by Reiss and Black, and Sykes, Brent, and Clark, and more recently by Smith and colleagues have offered considerable insight into an officer decision to arrest. Demeanor, complainant preference, and seriousness of offense all influence the likelihood that a police officer will make an arrest (Black, 1971; Reiss, 1971; Sykes, Fox, and Clark, 1976; and Smith and Visher, 1981) but it is not known if the suspect's being older matters.[10] It is unlikely, however, that any information will be available about the police officer's decision to arrest older suspects from observational studies for the same reason that it will be difficult to learn about victim's reporting decisions—rarity of events in which the suspect is older. While rarity was not totally damning where the concern is with victim behavior regarding older offenders, it is critical when the focus shifts to police, because there is no vehicle in place to do the massive collection of police-citizen encounter data that would be required to gain insight into this rare event. This last missing link in the police treatment of older suspects data is the most troublesome because it conditions the utility of other criminal justice system processing data that are readily available. As noted above, theories of police behavior (as institutions not as individuals) could not be tested without information concerning intake. Thus it is not known if being older means that one is less likely to be reported to police or, if reported, less likely to be arrested. If information of this sort is lacking, it is not possible to determine whether the "system" is treating older people differently or not because it is not known what the gatekeepers of the system are allowing through the gate. Future research efforts concerned with the disposition of older suspects/defendants/ offenders by the criminal justice system should remain cognizant of the limitations imposed on their efforts by a lack of insight into the determinants of the gatekeepers' decisions. A concerted effort should be made to estimate the effect of suspect age on criminal justice system intake.

NOTES

1. See, for example, Sherman (1980), Smith (1986), and Visher (1983).

2. Communication with Christy Visher concerning the data set she used in examining preferential treatment of women by police (1983) revealed that only 3 out of 785 police suspect encounters involved suspects 65 years or older. This is all the more disconcerting when we realize that one of the data collection sites used to compile this data set was the Tampa-St. Petersburg, Florida SMSA, a community with a large population of senior citizens.

3. Neither do the data reflect the citizen's reaction to victimization by older persons.

4. This conclusion is based on an analysis of studentized residuals. Studentized residuals are computed by dividing each residual by its estimated standard deviation. The "normed residuals" can then be compared to critical table values for studentized residuals and probability decisions can be made regarding their chance occurrence. In the present analysis the most discrepant observation is kidnapping where a much smaller proportion of younger people are released than would be predicted from the release rate of older people. However, even in this case the studentized residual is just -2.56, $p > .25$. See Fox, 1984:164-170 for a discussion of studentized residuals.

5. Recall that arrest charges are coded in an inverse order of their seriousness. Thus the negative coefficient signifies that as arrest charges become less serious (higher codes) police release becomes less likely.

6. Aldrich and Nelson propose a measure of goodness of fit that they call pseudo R^2. The measure is computed by dividing the chi-square statistic for overall fit (-2 times the log likelihood ratio) by the sum of the chi-square statistic and the number of observations. They note that their pseudo R^2 statistic approaches 0 as the quality of the fit diminishes and 1 as it improves (1984:54-59).

7. The 1980 California OBTIS data file contains a prior record variable for felony defendants disposed of at the Superior Court level but this information is not available in the OBTIS data file for suspects/defendants disposed of prior to adjudication in Superior Court.

8. Question 139 on the incident report of the NCS victimization survey instrument asked crime victims to estimate the age of their assailant. Respondents were asked to classify their offender as either under 12, 12-14, 15-17, 18-20, or 21 and older.

9. This estimate is computed from a victimization rate of approximately 35 per 1,000 for personal crimes with contact which yields about 4,500 victimizations of which it is assumed that approximately 3 percent would be victimizations by older offenders.

10. Smith and Visher (1981) note that suspect age (coded as under 19, 19-35, and over 35) is not directly related to the decision to arrest. However, Visher (1983) notes that age (again coded as under 19, 19-35, and over 35) is marginally related to the police officer's decision to arrest women but not men.

8

The Role of the Elderly Defendant in the Criminal Court: Full-Dress Adversary or Reluctant Penitant?

Gary Feinberg

INTRODUCTION

Approximately 200,000 persons ages 60 and older are arrested annually in the United States. Of these, 17 percent involve serious felonies (for example, murder, forcible rape, robbery, aggravated assault, burglary, larceny, motor vehicle theft, and arson). The remaining 83 percent include the full range of lesser felonies and misdemeanors, but especially common are drunkenness, disorderly conduct, driving while intoxicated, petit theft (shoplifting), and simple assault (see Table 8.1).

Based upon current criminal case mortality rates statistics, this translates into over 50,000 elderly individuals who are formally accused of a crime each year. Of these, at least 36,500 (73 percent) plead guilty, 7,000 (14 percent) request a bench trail, and 3,500 (7 percent) request a jury trial. Only a nominal 6 percent are dismissed (President's Commission, 1967). However, although sizeable numbers of elderly offenders are judicially processed, few become subjects of empirical research. Even with the assistance of a computerized search, an archivist will unearth only a handful of studies relating to elderly defendants.

REVIEW OF LITERATURE

One such title is Bachand's (1983) "The Elderly Offender: A Question

Table 8.1
A Comparison of the Most Common Crimes For Which Those 60 Years of Age and Older Are Arrested

Crime	Year		
	1974	1979	1984
Drunkenness	74,892	62,946	45,389
DWI	28,329	44,530	49,020
Larceny	9,854	21,138	26,139
Disorderly Conduct	11,469	12,976	13,666
Simple Assault	3,988	5,948	7,040
Total UCR Arrests, Parts 1 and 2	160,315	198,771	201,678

Source: Based on data provided in the *Uniform Crime Report*, 1974, 1979, 1984.

of Leniency in Criminal Processing.'' This creative work disproves numerous popular myths about the behavior of elderly criminals. Of special interest, he finds that elderly defendants, contrary to common belief, are not only more likely to be convicted than comparably accused younger defendants, but they also are more severely sanctioned. In a related study, Feinberg and Khosla (1985) observe that of the 97 judges they surveyed: (1) almost 50 percent are not especially sympathetic toward the elderly; (2) most sanction elderly shoplifters with fines despite beliefs that their thefts are motivated by economic need; and (3) older judges are not more likely than younger colleagues to favor special treatment for elderly defendants. The few additional articles available on elderly defendants tend to be more concerned with their mental competency and related legal policy issues than with behavioral aspects of their courtroom confrontation (Cohen, 1984).

If there is a poverty of scholarly research on elderly defendants, any belief that one may learn about them from the myriad of actuarial tables in annual state court reports is quickly dispelled. Such basic descriptive data as the number of elderly defendants processed by state courts, the charges against them, the proportion represented by an attorney, the frequency of jury trials, and sanctions imposed are neither readily nor reliably available. Information regarding variance by sex, race, and chronological period in how these cases are adjudicated is virtually unreported.

None of this is to deny the literature regarding the legal and extra-legal factors that affect the decision to obtain legal counsel (for example,

Landinsky, 1976; Lochner, 1975). Similarly, one must acknowledge the wealth of scholarship invested in unraveling the process by which plea decisions are reached (for example, Blumberg, 1979; Feeley, 1982; Newman, 1956), the consequences of pleading not guilty in terms of sanction severity (Brereton and Casper, 1981), and abrogated due process rights (for example, Uviller, 1977). The decision to go to trial, its impact and value have also been the subject of extensive empirical research and critical debate (Kalven and Zeisel, 1966). However, even though research has been done regarding the possible influence of the defendant's sex or race on final decisions (Armstrong, 1977; Greenwood et al., 1976; Jendrek, 1983; Mather, 1979), advanced age, for the most part, has not been conceptualized as relevant.

PROBLEM STATEMENT

This exploratory study introduces the elderly as consumers of criminal justice services. In particular, the purpose of this study is to chart patterns and trends in the use elderly misdemeanant defendants are making of three basic and traditional due process protections: (1) the right to plead not guilty; (2) the right to be represented by an attorney; and (3) the right to a jury trial. Although no formally derived and theoretically based hypotheses are generated and tested, three empirical questions guide our research: (1) are elderly misdemeanant defendants likely to avail themselves of their rights to plead not guilty, be represented by an attorney, and have a jury trial? (2) are elderly misdemeanant defendants more likely to plead not guilty, be represented by an attorney, or request a jury trial today than they were in years past? and (3) are significantly larger proportions of elderly misdemeanant defendants as compared to younger misdemeanant defendants relinquishing their rights to plead not guilty, be represented by an attorney, and have a jury trial? Concomitantly, variances by sex, race, and over time are traced and tested for statistical significance.

A number of justifications may be offered for undertaking this research. This study will provide a basic description of a little known but growing group of role players and consumers in the criminal justice system, that is, elderly misdemeanant defendants. It will also contribute to our knowledge about abrogated due process protections and related allegations of discrimination with respect to minority groups caught up in the criminal justice system. This research should prove valuable to communities seeking to improve their ability to deliver legal services to elderly residents, and it has important implications for improving lawyer-client relationships, especially where strains may be due to age-related stereotypes, prejudices, role reversals, and related dilemmas. From a more theoretical perspective, this study may be revealed as a logical correlative to addressing popular myths that the elderly are less likely to be convicted and/or severely sanctioned than similarly accused younger defendants. Also it contributes to the continuing debate about whether we are witnessing the twilight of the adversary system as Blumberg (1970) contends, or the full-flowering of professionalism within the criminal justice enterprise as Feeley (1982) avers.

METHOD

The findings of this study are based upon an analysis of 4,976 elderly defendants (ages 60 and over) who have been charged with committing a misdemeanor and whose names have been entered onto the dockets of the Dade County Court, Eleventh Judicial District, Miami, Florida. This figure constitutes an aggregate of three separate populations of elderly misdemeanant defendants as follows: 1974, N = 1,545; 1979, N = 1,754; 1984, N = 1,677. Of these, 81 percent are males and 19 percent are females. By race, 84 percent are white, 15 percent are black, and the remainder are either American Indian, (N = 2) or Unknown, (N = 7). Observed frequencies in the use of the not guilty plea, presence of an attorney, and requests for jury trial are calculated for each annual population as well as for the aggregated sample. Using a series of two-by-two and two-by-three tables, variances by sex, race, and over time (1974-1984) are then described and tested for statistical significance with the help of standard chi-square procedures. Since the size of our test group occasionally becomes very large, and since large sample size alone can generate statistically significant chi-squares, further statistical controls in the form of a phi-square test of association is introduced. The .05 level of significance is the predetermined critical cut-off score in all these analyses. Last, we selected out a sample of 12,675 misdemeanants under 60 years of age. Each of these has been accused of at least one of the following four violations: (1) disorderly intoxication; (2) disorderly conduct; (3) petit theft, and (4) simple assault. We subsampled 1,225 of our elderly misdemeanant defendants, all of whom had been similarly charged. Age-based differentials in the use of the not guilty plea, attorney representation, and jury as compared to bench trials are then explored and tested for significance with respect to each of these misdemeanors. This procedure was employed also as a control for the fact that younger defendants generally reflect a different profile of misdemeanor involvement than older defendants, and also because certain misdemeanor data for younger defendants was inaccessible. It is to be noted, however, that these are exactly the kinds of misdemeanors for which the elderly are typically arrested. The one major omission, driving while intoxicated, is due to the absence of available data.

DATA PROBLEMS, LIMITATIONS, AND AMELIORATIVE STRATEGIES

Several conceptual and technical problems were encountered in securing the data for this study. The most significant conceptual problems—and related ameliorative strategies—are discussed below.

The first and most important difficulty is conceptual: We cannot be certain that the court strategies described and the variances analyzed reflect the behavior of elderly defendants, their attorneys, or some unspecified and possibly complex combination of the two. While the decision to retain counsel especially seems to be controlled by the defendant, an abundance of empirical research suggests the plea decision and the type of trial chosen are strongly influenced or even determined by the attorney (Mather, 1979; Rosenthal, 1974). While this dilemma is not resolved, it is ameliorated. Regardless of whose behavior they represent, the findings still carry heuristic value and important policy implications.

Second, in conceptualizing whether or not elderly defendants are adversarial one tends to ignore the fact that there is variance in the meaning as well as the intensity of such behavior. When a defendant pleads guilty, for example, it may be with great remorse, a public and personal acknowledgment of culpability and a powerful yearning to make amends. Alternatively, the plea may be a perfunctory statement, uttered only for its efficiency in obviating the often painful and costly process of a trial (including more severe sanctions), reflecting a cavalier disregard for the nature of the violation and the significance of the victim (Blumberg, 1979). Similar points might be made about the decision to retain an attorney, or to request a jury trial. Are these strategies vigorously sought and applied, or are they only half-hearted efforts at a defense? Indeed, they might even be foisted upon an otherwise passive, contrite, and remorseful defendant by a more aggressive, avaricious, and adversarily-oriented defense counsel.

Third, the possibility is not addressed that some elderly misdemeanants may begin as avid adversaries (professing their innocence, demanding due process, retaining legal counsel, and threatening repeated appeals until vindicated), but end as complaisant defendants (in time the desire for closure, the social and psychological effects of the judicial process, and fiscal costs often quell such adversarial fervor). Even the most vivid not guilty plea has been known to wane into a colorless but terminal guilty plea. These "converts" to a guilty plea, both the more and the less reluctant among them, are otherwise ignored in this study.

Fourth, whether or not a defendant assumes an adversarial posture in responding to formal charges leveled against him is greatly influenced by the nature and severity of the anticipated sanction. The decision to focus upon elderly misdemeanants is partially an acknowledgment of this reality. The adversarial propensity of elderly felons reflects not so much a special psychosocial disposition associated with aging as much as an ubiquitous concern to avoid potentially catastrophic sanctions. Threatened with significant encroachments upon his life, liberty, or property, even the more passive defendant, or those most cynical about the chances of "fighting the system," will assume an adversarial posture. Misdemeanors, on the other hand, typically carry only nominal sanctions. Indeed, the process of enlisting one's constitutional protections is said to be more punitive than any sanction that may be applied to the convicted misdemeanant (Feeley, 1979). Under such circumstances, misdemeanors appear more sensitive than felonies to extra-sanction considerations, including any psychosocially based predilection by defendants to assume an adversarial posture in court. However, even misdemeanors vary among themselves in their prescribed sanctions. They also vary from one historical period to the next, and from one age, sex, or racial group to the next (Chesney-Lind, 1977; Hagan, 1974; Holmes and Daudistel, 1984). Regrettably, none of this variance is controlled. Nor are the more social-psychological dimensions of this issue addressed, including the defendant's awareness of the prescribed sanctions, predictions about the probable sanctions they will receive, and subjective estimations of the severity of those sanctions. Mitigating these deficiencies, the range of sanction severity for misdemeanors is limited. In this particular jurisdiction, misdemeanor sanctions range from a nominal fine to a maximum of one year in jail and a $1,000 fine.

Finally, although the illumination of courtroom strategy of elderly misdemeanant defendants is sought, it is not known for certain if the original charge is a misdemeanor, or a felony that has been plea bargained down to a misdemeanor. While most felony pleas are products of some type of plea bargaining, it rarely involves transforming the felony down to a misdemeanor. More typically, it means that other closely related felony charges are dropped, or there is a promise of concurrent sentences, or the assurance of a reduced sentence (Newman, 1956).

As well as conceptual problems, several technical difficulties were encountered when securing data for this study from the Dade County Court, Eleventh Judicial District, Miami, Florida. These, along with related ameliorative strategies, are discussed below.

Where elderly misdemeanant defendants had multiple charges against them only the first—and typically the most serious—was used. Thus, an individual charged with both simple assault and drunkenness entered the computations solely as one instance of simple assault. The drunkenness incident was not entered. This difficulty was minimized, however, by several considerations. First, when charging a defendant with misdemeanors the strategy of "overcharging" (that is, adding extra charges to the violation of immediate concern so as to increase the prosecutor's plea bargaining power) is less relevant—unlike felonies. Second, the analyses and discussions are couched in terms of elderly misdemeanants in general. That additional misdemeanor charges are lost for certain defendants is less relevant. They are misdemeanants regardless of whether they commit one misdemeanor or a multitude of them. Third, neither multiple counts of the same misdemeanor nor multiple charges for a variety of misdemeanors is common, at least not in this court. When either situation occurs, how defendants respond to the first charge (that is, the plea, presence or absence of counsel, type of trial requested), typically repeats itself with respect to the other charges.

Another difficulty encountered was elderly misdemeanant defendants charged on two or more separate occasions within the same year were counted as "new misdemeanants" each time they were charged. No effort was made to control for recidivism. Consequently, an increase in not guilty pleas, for example, may not necessarily mean that more individual elderly misdemeanant defendants are pleading not guilty. It may simply reflect greater recidivism among those who do plead not guilty.

Also, the defendant's original plea may change. There is evidence, however, of administrative negligence in recording these changes. This would have been a significant dilemma had this study entailed felons. Felons typically plead not guilty initially but usually plea bargain into guilty pleas. Unlike felons, misdemeanants usually plead guilty *ab initio* and never change that plea. Thus, while failures to record changes in the original plea do occur, they are rare and unlikely to bias our results.

FINDINGS

The Plea (Guilty vs. Not Guilty)

Plea information is available for 3,978 elderly misdemeanant defendants; of these approximately 92 percent (3,665) plead guilty (including *nolo contendere* pleas), and only 8 percent (313) plead not guilty. Elderly females are slightly more likely than elderly male misdemeanant defendants to plead not guilty, 16 percent (112/702) as compared to 6 percent (204/3,276) respectively. *Prima facia*, this difference is statistically significant (X^2 = 68.96). However, controlling for the influence of sample size reveals only a weak association between sex and plea among elderly misdemeanant defendants (phi-square = 0.017). Elderly black and elderly white misdemeanant defendants are about equally likely to plead guilty, 93 percent and 92 percent respectively. The difference is not statistically significant (X^2 = 1.02). Essentially similar patterns emerge for each annual population studied (Table 8.2).

Generally speaking, older misdemeanant defenders are less likely to plead not guilty than similarly accused younger defendants, 13.68 percent versus 17.37 percent. The difference is not statistically significant (X^2 = 7.92). This pattern repeats itself when comparing older and younger male as well as older and younger female misdemeanant defendants. It also occurs when holding race constant, that is, both older white and older black misdemeanant defendants are less likely to plead not guilty than their younger counterparts (Figure 8.1). Measuring the significance of these variances results in the following X^2 relationships: older versus younger

Table 8.2
Elderly Misdemeanant Defendants: Percent Pleading not Guilty by Sex, Race, and Year

Sex	Year 1974	1979	1984
Female	6.10 (5/82)	13.06 (41/314)	20.59 (63/306)
Male	2.07 (29/1400)	4.88 (60/1230)	17.80 (115/646)
Total	2.29 (34/1482)	6.54 (101/1544)	18.70 (178/952)
Correlating Sex and Plea			
X^2 =	5.60	27.37	1.06
Phi^2 =	0.004	0.018	0.001

Race	Year 1974	1979	1984
Black	1.51 (4/265)	5.26 (14/266)	21.95 (27/123)
White	2.47 (30/1217)	6.81 (87/1277)	18.16 (150/826)
Total	2.29 (24/1482)	6.55 (101/1543)	18.61 (177/951)
Correlating Race and Plea			
X^2 =	0.89	0.86	1.47
Phi^2 =	0.0006	0.0006	0.0015

Source: Compiled by author.

males, X^2 = 13.85; older versus younger females, X^2 = .026; older versus younger whites, X^2 = 8.77; older versus younger blacks, X^2 = 0.38. Admittedly, only the variance between older and younger males proves to be statistically significant, and even this disappears when sample size is controlled, phi-square = .002. At the same time, it is impressive to realize that regardless of the offense, the direction of the variance is consistently

Figure 8.1
Percent Pleading not Guilty

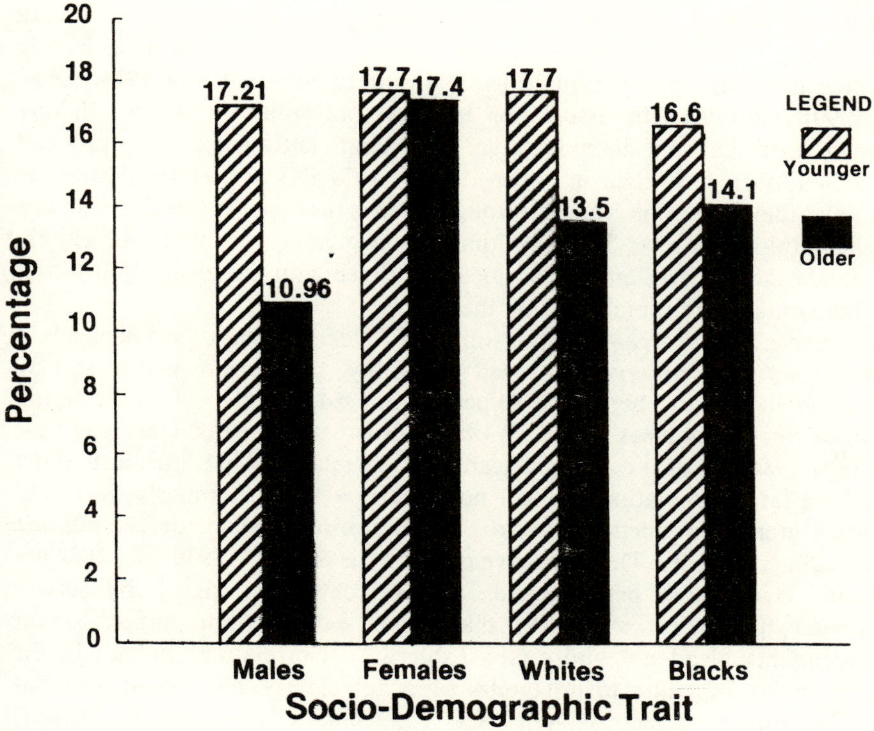

Source: Compiled by author.

the same: Older misdemeanant defendants always lag behind younger defendants in entering not guilty pleas. For example, only 6.5 percent of the older disorderly intoxication defendants as compared to 9 percent of the younger ones plead not guilty.

Over the past ten years the proportion of elderly misdemeanant defendants pleading not guilty has increased. It went from only 2 percent in 1974 to 7 percent in 1979, to a high of 19 percent in 1984. Correlatively the rate of increase in not guilty pleas is also increasing, especially between 1979 and 1984. Approximately equal increases are manifest for elderly male and elderly female misdemeanant defendants. More specifically, the proportion of elderly female misdemeanant defendants who plead not guilty increased by 100 percent between 1974 and 1979, going from 6.10 percent to 13.06 percent. It almost doubles again during the next five years, reaching a high of 20.59 percent in 1984. Similarly, only 2.06 percent of the elderly male misdemeanant defendants plead not guilty in 1974. By 1979, though still rare among elderly male misdemeanant defendants, not guilty pleas had more than doubled to 4.88 percent. Over the next five years it dramatically rises, reaching a high of 17.8 percent in 1984. Although a statistically significant X^2 = 221.27 results when exploring changes in the ratio of not guilty to guilty pleas during this decade, further statistical analysis reveals that this relationship is only a function of large population size (phi-square = 0.06). Controlling for sex reveals that elderly females are significantly more likely to plead not guilty in 1984 than in either 1979 or 1974 (X^2 = 12.99). However, the association is weak (phi-square = 0.136). Elderly male misdemeanant defendants are also significantly more likely to plead not guilty in 1984 than in either 1979 or 1974 (X^2 = 193.45). However, again, the association, though stronger than is the case for females, remains slight (phi-square = 0.243). Ultimately, a greater proportion of elderly female than elderly male misdemeanant defendants plead not guilty, but elderly males are rapidly closing the gap.

Increasingly larger proportions of elderly black misdemeanant defendants are observed to plead not guilty, going from a low of 1.51 percent in 1974 to a high of 21.95 percent in 1984. The X^2 = 56.61 emerging when correlating pleas for elderly black misdemeanant defendants over time (1974-1984) is statistically significant, but the relationship is only a function of the large populations tallied, phi-square = 0.294. Similarly, in recent years greater proportions of elderly white misdemeanant defendants are pleading not guilty. The respective proportions for 1974, 1979, and 1984 are 2.47 percent, 6.81 percent, and 18.16 percent. Interestingly, by 1984 a greater proportion of elderly black than elderly white misdemeanant defendants plead not guilty (see Table 8.2). Correlating changes in the proportion of guilty to not guilty pleas for elderly white misdemeanant defendants over the past ten years results in a X^2 = 168.13. This is statistically significant, but the association is weak, phi-square = 0.225.

In sum, the vast majority of elderly misdemeanant defendants like most other misdemeanant defendants plead guilty. Indeed, there is evidence to suggest that older misdemeanant defendants are actually somewhat more likely to plead guilty than similarly accused younger defendants. Elderly female are slightly more likely than elderly male misdemeanant defendants to plead not guilty, but the difference is not statistically significant. Also, no statistically significant difference is observed between elderly black and elderly white misdemeanant defendants in their likelihood of pleading guilty (or not guilty). Last, from 1974 to 1984 the proportion of elderly misdemeanant defendants pleading not guilty has increased. This is true for males and females alike, and for blacks as well as whites, and by approximately the same proportions. However, these increases are not statistically significant.

Legal Representation

Attorneys are rarely present in cases involving elderly misdemeanant defendants. Of the 4,971 elderly misdemeanant defendants for whom the relevant data is available, only 7 percent are represented by an attorney. Males are slightly less likely than female elderly misdemeanant defendants to be represented by an attorney, 6.5 percent as compared to 10.1 percent. Correlating elderly misdemeanant defendants by sex and presence or absence of an attorney results in a $X^2 = 14.91$. While statistically significant, it is only a function of the sample size. Appropriate controls reveal that these variables are only weakly associated (phi-square = .003). In sum, elderly male and female misdemeanant defendants are about equally rare in their likelihood of being represented by an attorney.

Black and white elderly misdemeanant defendants are also about equally likely, or unlikely, to be represented by an attorney, 6.5 percent and 7.3 percent respectively. The difference is not statistically significant, $X^2 = 0.55$.

Interestingly, our data suggest that older misdemeanant defendants are only half as likely as a comparative group of younger misdemeanant defendants to be represented by an attorney, 12 percent versus 23 percent. This difference is statistically significant, $X^2 = 72.69$, but the association between defendants' age and the likelihood of being represented by an attorney is weak, phi-square = .003. Similarly, older males and females, and older whites and blacks are each less likely to be represented by an attorney than their respective younger counterparts (Figure 8.2). Variance by age is much stronger in distinguishing those who are likely to be represented by an attorney than is observed for the not guilty plea. Indeed, in each instance it proves to be statistically significant. In no instance, however, is there a strong association between age and the likelihood that a misdemeanant defendant will be represented by an attorney. The respective chi-squares and their corresponding phi-squares are as follows: older versus younger males, $X^2 = 20.33$, phi-square = .001; older versus younger females, $X^2 = 38.32$, phi-square = .006; older versus younger whites, $X^2 = 53.06$, phi-square = .002; older versus younger blacks, $X^2 = 15.45$, phi-square = .004.

These patterns are essentially replicated when each of our populations is independently analyzed. More significant, however, are several interesting trends that emerge when comparing patterns over the past decade. First, the proportion of elderly misdemeanor defendants represented by an attorney has steadily increased. It was less than 1 percent in 1974, but over 13 percent in 1984. This increase is observed for both elderly male and elderly female misdemeanant defendants. However, it is accelerating more rapidly for elderly males. This is especially evident for the 1979-1984 quinquennium. During this period, the rate of representation by attorneys in misdemeanor cases doubled for males but only increased by 50 percent (from 9 percent to 13 percent) for females. We also observe an increase in the proportion of both elderly black and elderly white misdemeanant defendants who retain legal representation in these cases. In 1974 less than 1 percent of either racial group are represented by attorneys. Five years later, 9.6 percent of elderly black and 6.5 percent of elderly white misdemeanant defendants are so

Figure 8.2
Percent Represented by an Attorney

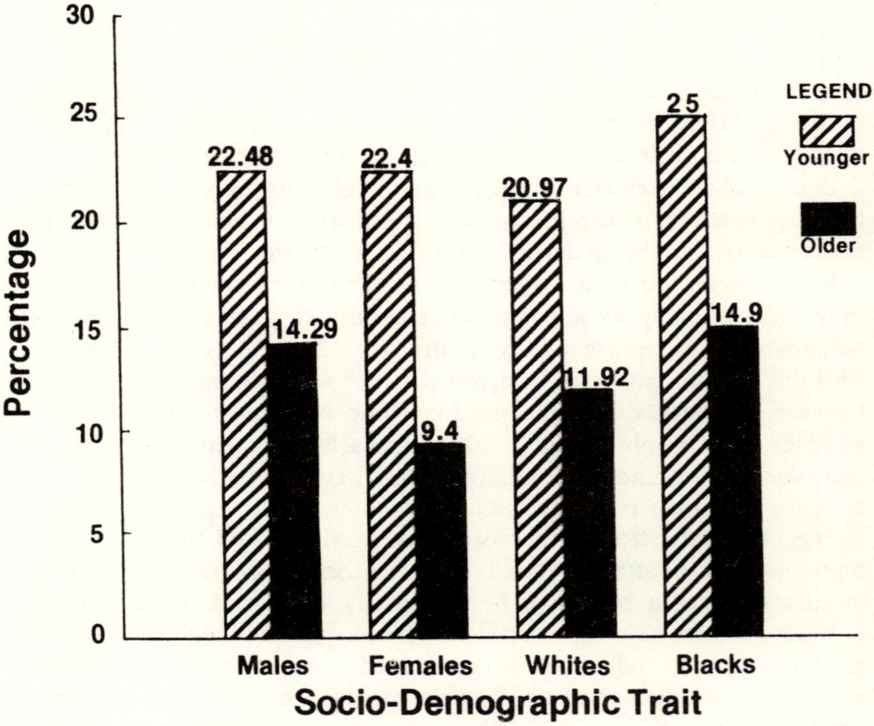

Source: Compiled by author.

represented. While the difference is not statistically significant in either instance (X^2 = .001 and X^2 = 3.50 respectively), it does appear that elderly black misdemeanant defendants are moving more rapidly toward an adversarial posture by retaining attorneys to represent their interests than is true for their elderly white counterparts. Admittedly, however, the rate of increase for elderly black misdemeanant defendants then decelerates during the subsequent quinquennium, that is, 1979-1984, while the comparable figure for elderly whites more than doubles (Table 8.3).

In sum, attorneys are rarely retained by elderly misdemeanant defendants, males or females, blacks or whites. Males are slightly less likely than females to have an attorney but ultimately the defendant's sex is a poor predictor of the likelihood of their retaining an attorney. Race is also a poor predictor. Neither elderly black nor elderly white misdemeanant defendants are especially likely to be represented by an attorney. Nor do we observe any statistically significant difference in this attribute by race. In addition, older

Table 8.3.
Elderly Misdemeanant Defendants: Percent Represented by an Attorney by Sex, Race, and Year

Sex	Year 1974	1979	1984
Female	3.26 (3/92)	8.88 (39/439)	12.79 (55/430)
Male	0.55 (8/1453)	6.32 (83/1314)	13.68 (170/1243)
Total	0.71 (11/1545)	6.96 (122/1753)	13.45 (225/1673)
Correlating Sex and Presence of an Attorney			
X^2 =	8.99	3.35	0.22
Phi^2 =	0.006	0.002	0.0001

Race	Year 1974	1979	1984
Black	0.73 (2/275)	9.63 (26/270)	10.09 (22/218)
White	0.71 (9/1270)	6.48 (96/1482)	13.91 (202/1452)
Total	0.71 (11/1545)	6.96 (122/1752)	13.46 (225/1672)
Correlating Race and Presence of an Attorney			
X^2 =	0.887	3.50	4.67
Phi^2 =	0.0006	0.002	0.003

Source: Compiled by author.

misdemeanant defendants are much less likely than younger misdemeanant defendants to be represented by an attorney. This is true for both males and females, blacks and whites. Finally, the proportion of elderly misdemeanant defendants who are represented by an attorney considerably increases between 1974 and 1984. This trend is about equally true for elderly male and female misdemeanant defendants. It is also true for both blacks and whites, although the pattern is slightly stronger for whites than blacks (Table 8.3). Regardless, despite the consistency of these increases, in no instance are they statistically significant.

Type of Trial (Jury vs. Bench)

Jury trials are very rare events in the life of the misdemeanor court, and elderly misdemeanant defendants are among those least likely to request one. Of the 313 elderly misdemeanant defendants in our aggregated sample who plead not guilty, only 45 (14.4 percent) request a jury trail. The vast majority (85.6 percent) request a bench trial. Elderly male and female misdemeanant defendants are about equally likely to request jury trials. The respective proportions are 14.7 percent (30/204) and 13.8 percent (15/109). Correlating the type of trial requested by sex of the elderly misdemeanant defendant results in a statistically significant $X^2 = 33.10$. However, further statistical testing indicates that the association between these two variables is weak (phi-square = 0.11). In sum, the defendant's sex is a poor predictor of the type of trial elderly misdemeanants request when pleading not guilty (Table 8.4). Interestingly, elderly black are much more likely than elderly white misdemeanant defendants to request a jury trial. Forty percent (18/45) of the former but only 10.1 percent (27/267) of the latter request such trials. The difference is statistically significant ($X^2 = 27.87$). However, controlling for sample size reveals only a weak association between an elderly misdemeanant defendant's race and the type of trial requested, phi-square = 0.09 (Table 8.4). Last, older misdemeanant defendants are only half as likely as younger misdemeanant defendants to request a jury trial, 2.3 percent versus 5.6 percent. The difference is statistically significant, $X^2 = 15.48$, but the association between age and the type of trial requested ultimately proves to be almost nonexistent, phi-square = 0.0001. Essentially this same pattern holds for older as compared with younger males (2.5 percent versus 5.2 percent) and older as compared with younger females (2.0 percent versus 5.5 percent). Moreover, the variance within each sex group is statistically significant, $X^2 = 7.44$ and $X^2 = 14.62$ respectively. In neither case, however, is there a strong association between the misdemeanant defendant's age and the type of trial requested, chi-square = .002 and phi-square = .003 respectively.

Younger male misdemeanant defendants are significantly more likely than older white misdemeanant defendants to seek a jury trial, 5.25 percent versus 1.92 percent respectively. In keeping with what is now a familiar pattern, the difference is statistically significant, $X^2 = 16.92$, but controlling for sample size reveals only a weak association between age of the defendant and the type of trial requested, phi-square = .001. Quite unexpected, however, is the finding that older and younger black

Table 8.4
Elderly Misdemeanant Defendants: Percent of Those Pleading not Guilty Who Request a Jury Trial by Sex, Race, and Year

Sex	Year 1974	1979	1984
Female	0.0 (0/5)	10.0 (4/41)	17.4 (11/63)
Male	3.4 (1/29)	13.3 (8/60)	18.3 (21/115)
Total	2.9 (1/34)	11.9 (12/101)	18.0 (32/178)
Correlating Sex and Type of Trial			
X^2 =	---	0.33	0.02
Phi^2 =	---	0.003	0.0001

Race	Year 1974	1979	1984
Black	0.0 (0/4)	42.9 (6/14)	44.0 (12/27)
White	3.3 (1/30)	6.9 (6/87)	13.3 (20/150)
Total	2.9 (1/34)	11.9 (12/101)	18.1 (32/177)
Correlating Race and Type of Trial			
X^2 =	---	13.13	14.96
Phi^2 =	---	0.130	0.084

Source: Compiled by author.

misdemeanant defendants are about equally likely to request a jury trial, 6.0 percent and 5.3 percent respectively. Indeed, this is the first instance where elderly misdemeanant defendants are actually more likely than those who are younger to take an adversarial stand (Figure 8.3).

From 1974 to 1984, elderly female misdemeanor defendants requesting a

Figure 8.3
Percent Requesting a Jury Trial

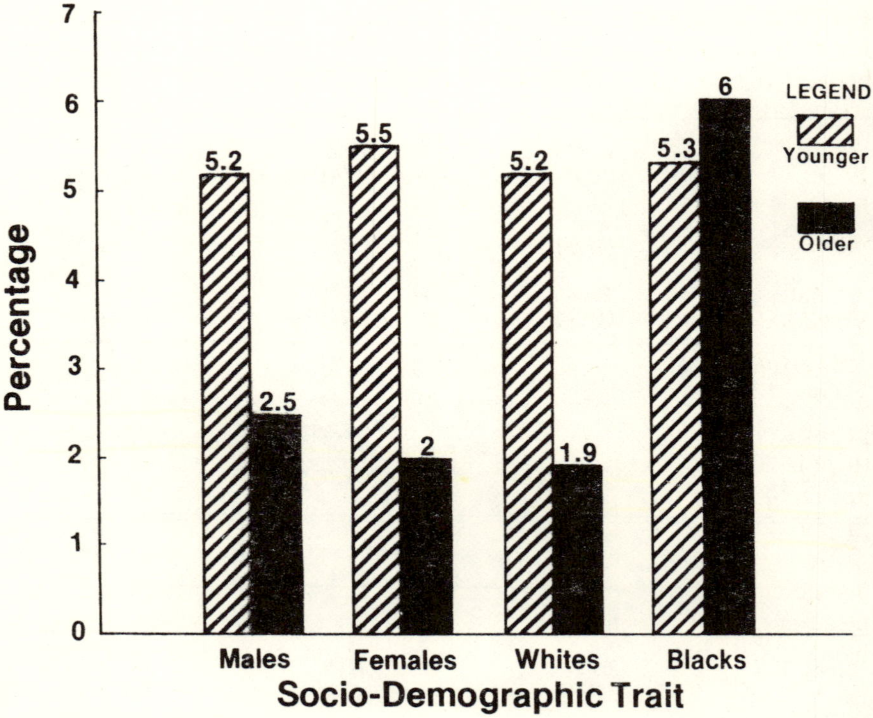

Source: Compiled by author.

jury trial increased from zero to 17.4 percent. Comparable figures for elderly male misdemeanor defendants indicate a parallel increase, from a low of 3.4 percent in 1974 to a high of 18.4 percent in 1984. Essentially, both elderly male and female misdemeanor defendants are growing increasingly likely to request a jury trial. There is some slight indication, however, that elderly female misdemeanor defendants, though behind elderly male misdemeanor defendants in this dimension of adversarial propensity, are closing the gap between them. The reader is cautioned that these percentages are unstable due to the small absolute numbers. They therefore only suggest rather than predict the direction of any anticipated changes (Table 8.4).

The proportion of elderly black misdemeanant defendants who plead not guilty and request a jury trial is also steadily increasing. None request such a trial in 1974. By 1979, 43 percent (6/14) request one, followed by 44 percent (12/27) in 1984. Elderly white misdemeanant defendants exhibit a similar though less dramatic increase. Only 3 percent of this group request a jury trial in 1974. By 1979 it rose to 6.9 percent and in 1984 it reaches a high of 13 percent (Table 8.4).

Tracing and comparing the adversarial profiles of our three separate populations reveals a number of interesting continuities and variances. Use of jury trials was so rare in 1974 for either males (N = 1) or females (N = 0) as to disallow testing for statistical significance. However, chi-square tests for 1979 and 1984 suggest there is no statistically significant relationship between the sex of the elderly misdemeanant defendant and the type of trial requested ($X^2 = 0.33$ and $X^2 = 0.02$ for each year respectively). Race, on the other hand, is significantly related to the type of trial requested in both 1979 ($X^2 = 13.13$) and 1984 ($X^2 = 14.96$). (Jury trials in 1974 were so rare for white (N = 1) and black (N = 0) misdemeanant defendants alike that a stable statistical test of significant differences could not be generated.)

SUMMARY OF FINDINGS

The central thrust of these findings is that the vast majority of elderly misdemeanant defendants do not partake in the advantages of basic due process protections. *Prima facia*, their response to charges leveled against them in court is nonadversarial: they typically plead guilty (92 percent), are not represented by an attorney (93 percent), and only occasionally request jury trials (14 percent).

Elderly female are more likely than elderly male misdemeanant defendants to be adversarial, as measured by two of our criteria, that is, pleading not guilty and being represented by an attorney. On the other hand, elderly black and elderly white misdemeanant defendants are about equally likely to be adversarial as measured by these same criteria. The one possible exception is that elderly black misdemeanant defendants are somewhat more likely to go to jury trial. In no instance, however, does either sex or race prove statistically significant in predicting the elderly misdemeanant's adversarial propensity.

While this essentially describes the posture of most misdemeanant defendants, it is also important to note that older misdemeanant defendants are consistently less likely to be adversarial as measured by each of our indexes than younger misdemeanant defendants. This is especially important to keep in mind as it calls into question any notion that the nominal nature of the misdemeanant violation and its limited consequences is the source of any arrested truth-seeking behavior within the criminal justice system. Even more impressive is the realization that in recent years the elderly are growing increasingly adversarial as misdemeanant defendants. Indeed, we appear to be witnessing their metamorphosis into a new breed of elderly misdemeanant defendants, one which is a less reluctant adversary in the criminal courts. Correlatively, they are more likely to make use of due process protections today than a decade ago. Moreover, this is true of elderly male and elderly female misdemeanant defendants, blacks as well as whites, and by approximately equal proportions. This makes for an especially interesting paradox: at a time when most criminal and civil cases are moving away from adversarial resolutions and toward justice by negotiation, our elderly misdemeanant defendants are pressing for full-dress adversarial courtroom confrontations.

DISCUSSION AND IMPLICATIONS

A major advantage of undertaking exploratory research is that it licenses considerable intellectual speculation. When that research concerns a subject about which there is limited scientific knowledge but extensive public curiosity, one is almost conscripted into making some speculations about a plethora of alternative data interpretations, possible causal relationships, and policy implications. The foregoing statements are offered as reasonable possibilities, and as areas for future empirical research.

Why elderly misdemeanant defendants do not partake in these basic due process protections remains an open question, one not directly addressed in the course of conducting our research. Potentially relevant independent variables include: (1) fear of escalating an otherwise already difficult and embarrassing situation; (2) feelings of powerlessness; (3) fear of incurring a more severe sanction; (4) the desire for closure and resolving the matter as quickly as possible; (5) inadequate psychic, fiscal, and social coping resources, especially with respect to negotiating the bureaucracy of the justice setting; and, (6) the mundane inconveniences related to maintaining a strong defense (for example, extra trips to the court, special filing fees, language limitations, and transportation problems).

Concomitantly, explaining why elderly misdemeanant defendants are not as likely to be adversarial as younger misdemeanant defendants brings to the fore such ideas as: (1) age-based discrimination; (2) alternative, historically based and culturally learned beliefs regarding the proper role of an elderly misdemeanant defendant; and (3) differences caused by the aging process. The fact that elderly females are slightly more likely to be adversarial than elderly male misdemeanant defendants could be a function of the greater likelihood that females in general are more inclined to engage in help-seeking behavior. This is likely maximized in situations where males are traditionally viewed by females as having expertise, for example, automobile repairs, stocks and bonds, business management, and, very possibly, the law and its related bureaucracy. From a somewhat different perspective, one might also predict that elderly females are more likely to have lived a law-abiding existence than males. This, in turn, could steel them against accepting their own criminal culpability when it does occur.

Last, a combination of developments may prove viable when seeking possible causes for recent increases in the adversarial propensity of elderly misdemeanant defendants. Among these are: (1) a better educated, more affluent, socially integrated and involved population of elderly; (2) a greater sense of power, self-confidence, and autonomy among the elderly, and, (3) changing role expectations for the elderly, including greater aggressiveness, increased familiarity with bureaucracies, and improved physical mobility. Possibly, we are encountering a variation on a common theme: the civil rights movement translated in terms of elderly needs and interests. One might also draw an interesting parallel between the elderly's increasing use of the not guilty plea, attorney representation, and jury trial, their awakening concern about age-based discrimination in housing and at the workplace, and related civil actions brought at their initiative. The status position of the elderly in our society is in flux, perhaps more so today than ever before. Their orientation toward the law and other forms of social control may also be changing.

THE ADMINISTRATION OF JUSTICE AND THE ELDERLY

A number of practical suggestions for improving the administration of justice with respect to the elderly emerge from this study. First, judges, prosecutors, public defenders, private attorneys, law professors, and related supportive personnel, especially those serving the legal needs of communities with large elderly populations, would profit from a diversified education program designed to provide the skills, insights,and rationales necessary for mediating justice in elderly offender cases. This could be achieved using several pedagogic formats. For example, education workshops are urged to provide legal practitioners with special skills in such areas as: (1) interrogating the elderly; (2) coping with fears and concerns of elderly clients in criminal and civil cases; (3) plea negotiating in elderly offender cases; (4) developing sanction guidelines for convicted elderly offenders; and, (5) jury selection in elderly defendant cases. In addition, seminars may be organized so that legal scholars, practitioners, and those responsible for planning and administrating legal services at various political levels may share ideas about the most appropriate and efficient way to process elderly offenders. Court diversionary programs, filtering certain elderly offenders through the family or probate court, the preventive education of potential elderly criminals, and even the creation of an elderly justice system parallel to the juvenile justice system are among the kinds of issues and policy matters which lend themselves to such seminars.

Second, whether the elderly in fact enjoy ready access to the legal services they want must be empirically evaluated. Where access is poor—and we suspect that it is especially poor in retirement communities where residents are recent migrants and lack the indigenous family and friendship ties through whom attorneys are typically located and retained (Landinsky, 1976)—remedial strategies need to be organized and implemented. Legal out-reach services for the elderly are not nearly as well developed in most places as comparable services by the medical profession. Shopping mall locations, periodic volunteer work at senior centers, and provision of legal directories to relocating elderly residents are just three of the more creative strategies the legal profession could use to improve the dissemination of information about its practitioners and to popularize community-based legal clinics and related legal aid services. Venue flexibility to allow "face saving," and similar strategies to protect the elderly from the often catastrophic and irreparable loss of reputation which frequently accompanies the public display of an aggressive adversarial defense also deserve further consideration.

Third, public administrators responsible for selecting judges and hiring public defenders and assistant prosecutors should consider the candidate's ability to relate with the community's elderly and to carry out their role requirements when cases involve the elderly as defendants, witnesses, and victims. Just as some practitioners work better with juvenile offenders, others with female offenders, and still others with various minorities, and just as these abilities are articulated where possible for the benefit of all parties, so too should similar considerations be made in meeting the criminal justice needs of the elderly.

Finally, further research into elderly offenders in general, and their behavior at various stages of the criminal justice process is strongly prescribed. Concomitantly, more needs to be known about the beliefs, attitudes, and responses of the various role-players who implement that process with respect to elderly offenders. How, for instance, does an attorney's relative youthfulness affect his ability to plea bargain with an elderly client? Are public defenders especially sympathetic toward their elderly clients? Do prosecutors curry disfavor among voters for pursuing elderly offender cases? Does a criminal conviction impact upon the elderly in significantly different ways as compared to similarly convicted younger defendants? Hopefully, scholarly inquiry into such questions will continue to find interest and support, not only among gerontologists and sociologists who have pioneered the study of elderly criminality, but also among those who can bring to it a strong legal education and policy-oriented perspective.

9

The Severity of Sentencing: Do Federal Judges Really Go Easier on Elderly Felons in Plea-Bargaining Negotiations Compared with Their Younger Counterparts?

Dean J. Champion

INTRODUCTION

The present research examines plea-bargaining agreements and sentencing decisions and the extent to which they are influenced by offender age. In 1980, the U.S. Bureau of the Census reported that there were 25.5 million Americans age 65 and over, or approximately 11 percent of our population. By the year 2000, this figure will have grown to 32 million according to the bureau's best projection. Every day, about 5,000 persons turn 65, and about 3,400 persons age 65 and over die (Harris and Cole, 1980).

As the proportion of elderly persons increases in our population, there also is a corresponding increase in the frequency of crimes committed by the elderly (Newman, Newman, and Gewirtz, 1984; Shichor, 1985; Wilbanks

My appreciation is extended to Raymond Katz, Brian L. Ingram, F. Grant Buttram, Jeffrey A. Stahl, Maurey Miesner, Efrem P. Moser, Geri A. Newman, and Myron Schindler for their assistance in providing portions of information utilized here pertaining to federal cases for the years 1983-85. LeRoy Baker and Michael F. Rainier are thanked as well for their thoughtful comments on earlier drafts of this paper. Court clerks Julia Adams, Betty Purvis, Mae E. Reynolds, Agnes R. Lombard, Rebecca Dreyfuss, and John Milhouse are also thanked for their kind assistance in furnishing access to plea-bargain documents and other pertinent information in the jurisdictions selected for investigation.

and Kim, 1984). Estimates of the actual number of persons age 65 and over who commit crimes range from 300,000 to 500,000. This accounts for less than 1 percent of all victimizations in the United States. But while the elderly currently exert no significant impact on the amount of crime in the United States, there is evidence that crime committed by elderly persons is increasing rather rapidly (Wilbanks and Kim, 1984).

Currently, the criminal justice system makes no distinction between adults of different ages who commit similar offenses. If anything, judges appear to be more lenient with elderly offenders compared with their younger counterparts. For instance, in 1986 a judge in Kentucky administered widely disparate sentences to an 80-year-old woman and a 22-year-old man for growing marijuana. The woman was arrested and charged with growing 100 marijuana plants (supposedly for her glaucoma condition). The man was arrested and charged similarly for growing 30 marijuana plants. Neither of these persons had prior records, but the judge sentenced the man to three years in prison and gave the woman a suspended sentence, lecture, and fine.

The present research is designed to explore variations in sentencing severity that may be attributable to one's age. Specifically examined are court records of a sample of federal judges in several different ages, and the sentences imposed following conviction.

Decision Making in the Federal Courts

Comparatively little is known about the sentencing dispositions of federal judges in district courts compared with state and local judiciary. Few studies have examined patterns of sentencing among federal judges, and fewer still have investigated sentencing disparities pertaining to socioeconomic factors, ethnic and racial variables, and age/sex attributes (Alschuler, 1979; Cook, 1973; Sutton, 1978a; 1978b).

Contrasted with their local and state counterparts, federal judges in each district court are scrupulously insulated from external contacts with the press, the public, and, of course, criminal justice researchers (Mather, 1979). With Howard Hughes-like privacy, these judges are seldom seen outside of their courtrooms, have unlisted telephones and anonymous addresses, and it is often difficult to gain access to public information relating to dispositions of cases handled within their jurisdictions.

Procedurally, cases heard in federal courts are initiated by the U.S. Attorney's Office stemming from civil and criminal complaints and violations of the laws of the United States (Cramer, 1981; Haller, 1979; Nagel, 1982). Prior to a case being aired in court, however, attorneys for the government conduct extensive background research with their investigative arm, the FBI, and submit all cases to periodic review by teams of Assistant U.S. Attorneys. Cases are scanned and only those possessing "prosecutive merit'' are retained in the screening process. Of these remaining cases having prosecutive merit, discussions are held and determinations are made that permit the development of a list of case priorities.

Each case is assigned to one or more Assistant U.S. Attorneys who make further ''prosecutive merit'' investigations (Feeley, 1983). If a potential defendant is aware of an ongoing investigation and has contacted an attorney, informal negotiations are usually conducted between the U.S. Attorney's Office and defense counsel as a means of determining the nature of offenses alleged, some measure of the strength of the government's evidence against the person, and a proposal from the government seeking an out-of-court settlement (that is, a plea bargain) of the matter (Alschuler, 1975, 1976; Brereton and Casper, 1981; Cavender, 1984; Champion, 1987; Cramer, 1981; Farr, 1984).

The more routine pattern is for the U.S. Attorney's Office to proceed with its investigation of alleged offenses and obtain an indictment or indictments against various persons through the federal grand jury process (LaFave, 1970; Lagoy, Senna, and Siegel, 1976; Miller, Cramer, and McDonald, 1978). Then, after an indictment has been obtained, negotiations referred to above are conducted with the defendant and defendant's counsel. These negotiations are popularly and collectively known as plea bargaining (Alschuler, 1979; Maynard, 1982; Myers and Hagan, 1979; Nagel, 1982; Rhodes, 1979).

Over 90 percent of all criminal convictions in federal courts are obtained through plea bargaining (Church, 1976; Friedman, 1979; Gertz and Price, 1985; Maynard, 1982; Stitt and Siegel, 1986). Plea-bargain agreements are routinely submitted to the district judge for approval. Almost all plea-bargain agreements submitted are approved and the cases are concluded to the mutual satisfaction of prosecution and defense (Green, 1961; Hagan, 1975; Hagan and Albonetti, 1980; Hyman, 1979; Jaros and Mendelsohn, 1967; Kipnis, 1976).

Plea Bargaining: A Controversial Issue

Plea bargaining is not without its critics. It is regarded as a time-saving device by its supporters (Rhodes, 1979; Utz, 1978; Wheatley, 1974). It is viewed as a denial of due process by its opponents. Some states prohibit its use in the settlement of criminal cases, while most others condone it. The federal government endorses plea bargaining as an effective means of case disposition as well (Alschuler, 1979; Church, 1979; Rubenstein and White, 1979; Stitt and Siegel, 1986).

Plea bargaining is the process of obtaining a plea of guilty from a criminal defendant in exchange for a reduction in the severity of a sentence and/or dropping or reducing various charges that ultimately mitigate the penalties otherwise accruing to the accused. Regardless of its relative merits, it is pervasive in the American criminal justice system (Heumann, 1975; Heumann and Loftin, 1979; McDonald, 1985; Meeker, 1984).

A coterie of critics has focused upon several conspicuous inequities of this process, however. These inequities pertain to sentencing disparities apparently attributable to factors unrelated to the offenses alleged, including age of offender, race of offender, sex of offender, and socioeconomic status of offender (Spohn, Gruhl, and Welch, 1981; Thomson and Zingraff, 1981; Unnever, Frazier, and Henretta, 1980; Welch, Gruhl, and Spohn, 1984; Zatz, 1984; Zatz and Lizotte, 1982). Persons incurring more severe sentences or less favorable plea-bargain agreements have typically consisted of members of lower socioeconomic strata, ethnic and racial minorities, and males (Hopkins, 1977; Maynard, 1982; Peterson and Hagan, 1984; Tiffany, Avichai, and Peters, 1975; Wheeler, Weisburd, and Bode, 1982).

METHODS AND DATA

Six circuit court jurisdictions were randomly selected from the 13 judicial circuits of the United States. Table 9.1 shows a distribution of these circuits and the states included within each.

The six jurisdictions selected for analysis included the Fourth, Sixth, Seventh, Ninth, Tenth, and Eleventh Circuits. In each of these circuits, 20 federal judges were selected at random for a total of 120 district judges. Records of criminal convictions for each of these judges during the years 1983-85 were subjected to content analysis to determine the numbers of felony convictions, ages of offenders, and subsequent punishment. Only criminal convictions were included in the present research.

Subsequent examination of each of the criminal conviction records revealed considerable background information including age of offender, offenses alleged, prior offenses, if any, the disposition of the case, and the severity of the sentence imposed. Table 9.2 shows the number of criminal convictions processed by the 120 judges in the six circuit court jurisdictions including the proportion of convictions obtained through plea bargaining.

ANALYSIS

Table 9.2 shows that on the average, 85 percent of the criminal convictions in the six jurisdictions examined were obtained through plea bargaining. These proportions were observed to vary from one jurisdiction to the next, and this variation was perhaps attributable to factors such as variable caseloads of judges, court procedures followed, the resources of the various U.S. Attorney's Offices involved, and the types of crimes committed. The jurisdiction appearing to use plea bargaining the least was the Eleventh Circuit (78 percent), while the Ninth Circuit (which includes

Table 9.1.
The Thirteen Judicial Circuits of the United States

CIRCUITS	COMPOSITION
District of Columbia	District of Columbia
First	Maine, Massachusetts, New Hampshire, Puerto Rico, Rhode Island
Second	Connecticut, New York, Vermont
Third	Delaware, New Jersey, Pennsylvania, Virgin Islands
Fourth	Maryland, North Carolina, South Carolina, Virginia, West Virginia
Fifth	Canal Zone, Louisiana, Mississippi, Texas
Sixth	Kentucky, Michigan, Ohio, Tennessee
Seventh	Illinois, Indiana, Wisconsin
Eighth	Arkansas, Iowa, Minnesota, Missouri, Nebraska, North Dakota, South Dakota
Ninth	Alaska, Arizona, California, Idaho, Montana, Nevada, Guam, Oregon, Washington, Hawaii
Tenth	Colorado, Kansas, New Mexico, Oklahoma, Utah, Wyoming
Eleventh	Alabama, Florida, Georgia
Federal	All Federal judicial districts

Source: Compiled by author.

California, Oregon, and Washington) had the most cases and the greatest use of plea bargaining of 92 percent.

Further analysis of the data divided the criminal convictions resolved through plea bargaining or trial according to age of offenders. Using the standard "65-and-over" category yielded so few cases that it was decided to reduce the age distinction to 60 and over. This permitted a more reasonable comparison for drawing inferences concerning sentencing disparities according to age differences. Of the 2,365 criminal convictions examined, 2,009 were plea bargained and 279 were obtained through trial proceedings. Offenders age 60 and over accounted for 56 of the plea-bargained convictions (3 percent) and for 32 (11 percent) of the 279 trial convictions.

Table 9.2.
Criminal Convictions in Six Circuits of the United States and the Proportion of Convictions Obtained Through Plea Bargaining, 1983-85

Circuit Court	Number of Criminal Convictions N	Number of Plea-Bargained Convictions N	%
Fourth	298	261	87
Sixth	375	302	81
Seventh	329	271	82
Ninth	748	686	92
Tenth	259	210	81
Eleventh	356	279	78
TOTALS	2,365	2,009	85

Source: Compiled by author.

Comparatively more offenders age 60 and over resorted to trial proceedings as opposed to plea-bargain negotiations with prosecutors.

In order for sentencing disparities to be charted with some measure of accuracy, a ratio was determined by taking the actual sentence imposed (AS) and contrasting that figure with the maximum sentence (MS) provided by federal statutes for the crime(s) alleged. This AS/MS ratio permitted a comparison of the average sentencing severity for the judges in each of the six jurisdictions. For instance, if an offender were charged with a robbery of a federally insured bank, the maximum sentence could be ten years. Calculating this AS/MS ratio in terms of months, it becomes an AS/MS ratio of 24/120 = .20, and so on. In this study, the AS/MS ratio functioned as the measure of sentencing severity. Because of the large number of convictions involved, the .001 level of significance was selected for assessing subsequent AS/MS ratio differences. The Z test for differences between proportions was utilized (Champion, 1981).

Table 9.3 shows AS/MS ratios (sentencing severity) for each of the six circuit courts for the years 1983-85 involving offenders under 60 and 60 and over. Plea-bargained convictions are included together with those convictions resulting from trial. Using the Z test for differences between proportions to determine the significance of difference between AS/MS ratios in all instances, observed Z values were statistically significant at $P < .001$.

Table 9.3 clearly reveals sentencing disparities both for offenders negotiating guilty pleas and those convicted through trial proceedings. On the average, offenders under 60 years of age had AS/MS ratios of .17 compared with .08 for those age 60 and over in convictions obtained through plea bargaining (P < .001). Furthermore, for those defendants convicted through trial proceedings, convicts under age 60 received AS/MS ratios averaging .34 compared with .13 for convicts 60 and over (P < .001). It might be concluded tentatively from these figures that convictions secured through trial lead to somewhat harsher sentences compared with sentences imposed as the results of a plea bargain agreement.

Table 9.3.
Sentence Severity for Plea-Bargained Convictions and Convictions Through Trials, 1983-85, Comparing Older and Younger Offenders*

	Sentencing Severity**			
	Plea-Bargained Convictions		Trial Convictions	
Circuit Courts	(Under 60)	(60 & Over)	(Under 60)	(60 & Over)
Fourth	.17	.08	.33	.13
Sixth	.18	.09	.35	.15
Seventh	.15	.07	.28	.10
Ninth	.20	.09	.44	.16
Tenth	.18	.10	.35	.14
Eleventh	.15	.06	.28	.09
AVERAGES	.17	.08	.34	.13

*All proportion differences AS/MS ratios for younger and older offenders for both plea-bargained and trial cases significant at P < .001, *Z* test for significance of difference between proportions (Champion, 1981).

**AS/MS Ratio = Actual Sentence Imposed/Maximum Sentence.

Source: Compiled by author.

One interesting proportionate distinction involving offenders age 60 and over deserves further analysis. It will be recalled that for the entire aggregate of criminal convictions examined, persons age 60 and over accounted for 3 percent of all convictions obtained through plea bargaining. But 11 percent of those convictions from trial proceedings involved persons age 60 and over. In other words, over three times as many persons age 60 and over were convicted through trial proceedings rather than through the plea-bargaining alternative. What factors might account for this?

Prior Record

First of all, prior records of offenders of both age groups were examined. For the 2,277 offenders under age 60, 81 percent or 1,844 had prior records. Proportionately, there were no significant differences between those persons under age 60 convicted through trial and those convicted through plea-bargaining agreements ($P < .001$). But for offenders age 60 and over, a different pattern emerged. Table 9.4 shows the proportion of offenders age 60 and over who had prior records and who either were convicted through trial or through a plea-bargain agreement.

An examination of Table 9.4 shows that of those offenders age 60 and over who were convicted through plea bargaining, approximately 75 percent had prior records, whereas 25 percent did not have prior convictions. In the case of those persons who went to trial and were convicted, however, 78 percent did not have prior records. The distribution of table frequencies was significant at the .001 level (1 df) utilizing chi square (Chi square observed = 24.318). While the table frequencies are not particularly large, it must be remembered that persons age 60 and over made up a relatively small portion of cases dealt with in these six federal jurisdictions.

One interpretation of this finding is that persons without prior records do not want to admit guilt in a plea agreement and will take their case to trial, if necessary. At the very least, if a person has no prior record, he or she does not want to acquire one, especially at this stage of life.

Table 9.4
Offenders Age 60 and Over With and Without Prior Records Who Were Convicted Through Trial or from Plea Bargaining

Type of Conviction	Prior Record		No Prior Record	
	N	Prop.	N	Prop.
Plea-Bargained Conviction	42	.75	14	.25
Trial Conviction	7	.22	25	.78

Chi square observed = 24.318; 1 df; P .001.

Source: Compiled by author.

The statistics associated with federal court convictions are somewhat depressing for a person facing trial, however. For instance, in the Federal Court in the Eastern District of Tennessee, 85 percent of the cases resulting in trial are civil and 15 percent are criminal. Of the 15 percent resulting in trial, *convictions are secured in over 95 percent of those cases*. The laws of probability operate to make a criminal defendant give serious consideration to a plea-bargain agreement, unless, of course, there are strong grounds supportive of one's innocence.

For the older offenders who obtained plea-bargain agreements, it might be argued that these persons are "career criminals," and therefore, they are more inclined to go along with system inducements to plead guilty and take a chance on felony probation. Prison overcrowding and judicial propensities in sentencing older offenders place these persons in an advantageous position in this regard.

Plea bargaining appears to make a difference in the severity of sentencing, at least in the jurisdictions examined in the present research. Also, the age factor appears to be prominent in affecting sentencing severity. This finding holds both for plea bargain situations and those cases concluded by trial convictions.

Offense Type

One possible explanation for the disparity in sentencing severity between older and younger offenders might be that the younger offenders engage in more violent crimes compared with their older counterparts. For example, 1985 Uniform Crime Report figures indicate that while the frequency of both violent crime and property crime arrests systematically decreases for the age categories of 21 and beyond, there are significantly greater proportions of violent crime arrests compared with property crime arrests for persons between the ages of 25 and 49.

In the present study, records of all convictions were examined and classified according to *violent crimes* (including robbery, murder, rape, and assault) and *property crimes* (including stolen property offenses, burglary, vehicular theft, forgery, and embezzlement). Table 9.5 shows sentencing severity according to violent crimes and property crimes by age of offender. On the average, violent crimes draw harsher sentences from judges compared with property crimes. AS/MS ratios were .19 and .13 for violent and property crimes respectively.

Table 9.5 reveals that 67 out of 88 or 76 percent of the offenders age 60 and over were convicted of property crimes. A substantial difference in sentence severity exists for elderly offenders convicted of violent crimes (AS/MS Ratio = .10) compared with those convicted of property crimes (AS/MS Ratio = .05). Approximately 69 percent of all convictions involved property offenses. For violent offenses, persons age 60 and over

Table 9.5.
Sentencing Severity and Type of Crime According to Age of Offender

Age	Violent Crimes			Property Crimes			Total	
	N	(%)	AS/MS Ratio	N	(%)	AS/MS Ratio	N	%
18-29	256	(34.5)	.23	582	(35.8)	.14	838	34.4
30-39	201	(27.2)	.21	470	(28.9)	.16	671	28.4
40-49	186	(25.1)	.17	356	(21.9)	.13	542	22.9
50-59	76	(10.3)	.15	150	(9.2)	.05	226	9.6
60+	21	(2.9)	.10	67	(4.2)	.05	88	3.7
TOTALS	740	(100)		1,625	(100)		2,365	100.0
AVERAGE			.19			.13		

Source: Compiled by author.

accounted for about 3 percent of these compared with slightly over 4 percent of the total property offenses.

Sentencing severity is greatest for persons age 18-29 who have committed violent crimes (AS/MS Ratio = .23). Sentencing severity declines for offenders in advancing age categories for both violent and property crimes, although the severity of sentencing is substantially lower for property crimes in all age categories. It is interesting to note that sentencing severity drops dramatically from the 40-49 to the 50-and-over age categories for persons convicted of property offenses (AS/MS Ratio = .13 for persons age 40-49, AS/MS Ratio = .05 for persons 50 and over). There is an especially sharp reduction in sentencing severity between the 50-59 and 60-and-over age categories relating to violent crimes (for example, in the 50-59 age category, sentencing severity is .15, but it drops to .10 for the category 60 and over).

Older offenders in the sample of convictions investigated here are involved mostly in nonviolent property offenses. This could be a significant factor in accounting for disparities in sentencing severity when different age categories are examined. But Table 9.5 shows clearly that sentencing severity decreases systematically for persons in older age categories generally. With one minor exception, this observation holds for both violent and property crimes.

SUMMARY AND DISCUSSION

An examination of 2,365 criminal convictions in the courts of 120 federal judges selected randomly in six of the thirteen United States Circuit Court jurisdictions revealed that 2,009 of these convictions or 85 percent were resolved through plea-bargain agreements. Furthermore, of the remaining 356 convictions, 279 resulted from trial proceedings for an overall trial conviction rate of 78 percent. Both plea-bargaining rates and trial conviction rates varied from one circuit court jurisdiction to the next.

When offenders were categorized according to age, some sentencing discrepancies were observed. All persons convicted (either through plea bargaining or trial verdicts) were divided according to under age 60 or age 60 and over. Ratios of sentencing severity were calculated on the basis of the actual sentence (AS) imposed against the maximum possible sentence (MS). Thus, AS/MS ratios were used as measures of sentencing severity in each and every case.

It is difficult to equate the seriousness of similar offenses committed by both old and young alike. There are many mitigating and aggravating circumstances that are considered before a final disposition of a case is made by a judge when a conviction is secured. The AS/MS ratio, the measure of sentencing severity, was designed to overcome partially some of these limitations. Regardless of whether the crime involved robbery, burglary, or interstate transportation of stolen property, the actual sentence imposed against the maximum possible sentence for the offenses as prescribed by statute seemed to level such offense differences that might otherwise account for sentencing disparities.

Age and Sentence Leniency

It was found that older offenders age 60 and over receive sentences in plea-bargaining agreements that are less than half the severity of their younger counterparts. In cases where trials are conducted and convictions are obtained, the discrepancies are even greater. Persons under age 60 receive sentences that are almost three times as severe as offenders age 60 and over. While these findings in and of themselves are not conclusive regarding the mitigating function of age in sentencing severity, they nevertheless raise some serious questions concerning the ethics and inequities of the sentencing process which might be attributable to age differences.

Under similar circumstances where similar crimes have been committed, older and younger offenders should logically receive similar sentences, especially where presumptive sentencing is practiced. Under the presumptive sentencing alternative, a judge is obligated to impose a sentence length that is set by law for each offense or class of offense in all "unexceptional cases" (Cunniff, 1985; Koppel, 1984). However, judges may exercise discretion by shortening or lengthening sentences in those instances where there are especially aggravating or mitigating circumstances prevalent.

Federal judges have extraordinarily broad sentencing powers compared with many of their state and local trial judge counterparts. It is apparent from this study that for the judges examined, sentencing severity is greater for younger offenders. It is also clear that sentencing severity is greater where violent crimes have been committed compared with nonviolent property crimes. But even for violent crimes, older offenders, especially those 60 and over, draw considerably less harsh sentences compared with more youthful offenders.

One interpretation is that judges perceive one's age to be a mitigating factor in determining an appropriate sentence. In a 1983 New Jersey case, for instance, an Assistant U.S. Attorney offered a 63-year-old defendant a three-year probation in exchange for pleading guilty to one count of mail fraud. The defendant declined the offer, went to trial, and was convicted of mail fraud. The judge was obviously reluctant to impose a sentence involving incarceration, but such a sentence was imposed anyway. The offender served six months in a minimum-security federal prison facility. For a much younger offender convicted of mail fraud, the sentence undoubtedly would have been more severe.

Compared with younger offenders, older felons, especially those 60 and over, probably adapt less to prison conditions and pose special problems for their custodians (for example, special diets, medications, and an assortment of health problems). An important question is whether or not incarceration has much deterrent value for the older offender compared with younger offenders. Certainly these are factors that federal judges consider when approving plea agreements or when imposing sentences in trial proceedings.

Plea Bargaining and the Older Offender

While most convictions examined in this research were obtained through plea bargaining, 279 of these were obtained through trial verdicts. Persons age 60 and over were disproportionately convicted through trial proceedings (36 percent) compared with younger offenders who went to trial and were convicted (8 percent). Acquittal figures for the federal jurisdictions examined here reveal no significant differences between older and younger offenders regarding the proportion of "not guilty" verdicts. Therefore, taking one's case to trial occurs more frequently for older offenders than for younger ones.

When an examination of the prior records of offenders was made, offenders under age 60 exhibited no significant proportionate differences in plea bargained or trial convictions concerning their prior records. For older offenders, however, a majority of older offenders without prior records went to trial, while a majority of those with prior records opted for a plea-bargain agreement. A likely reason for such a finding is that those without criminal records simply wanted to keep things that way at any cost, including an expensive trial proceeding.

U.S. Attorneys and their staffs are obligated by rules not to disclose the nature and contents of any investigation, when it commences, when it terminates, and/or the ultimate disposition of it. Thus, it is difficult to formulate any accurate picture of the true function of age insofar as it serves to modify plea-bargain agreements. But secondary source and content analysis of convictions, either through trial or plea agreements which are a matter of public record, enables researchers to draw some tentative inferences about the nature of sentencing and any observable disparities which may be attributable to one or more variables.

This research has focused primarily on age differences as they may influence the configuration of plea-bargain agreements and the resulting sentence severity as outlined in those agreements and/or imposed by judges in the sentencing process following a trial. Not only are there less severe punishments outlined in plea-bargain agreements for persons age 60 and over compared with younger offenders, there are also less severe sentencing penalties associated with older offenders who have taken their cases to court and have been convicted of one or more of the offenses alleged.

It is particularly interesting to note that for both plea-bargained convictions and for convictions resulting from trial, offenders age 60 and over received probation or probation recommendations in 68 percent of the cases, in spite of the AS/MS ratios observed. In other words, a sentence was imposed, but probation was included in lieu of formal incarceration in 68 percent of these cases involving older offenders. For younger offenders, the overall probation recommendation and usage was only 16 percent. Again, age does appear to influence incarceration decisions.

Violent offenses draw consistently more severe punishment compared with property offenses across all age categories. But from the data presented here, it appears that sentencing severity decreases with advancing age, regardless of the type of crime committed. It is clear that further study is needed to understand more fully the functions of age and other factors in the plea-bargaining process, as well as in sentencing decisions.

10

Care for Elderly Inmates: Conflicting Concerns and Purposes in Prisons

Elmer H. Johnson

INTRODUCTION

Usually crime is conceived as the transgressions of individuals against social institutions. Following the lead of many criminologists, Hahn turns the limelight of public scrutiny on the transgressions of social institutions. While addressing "the aging as victims in the institutions," Hahn (1976:85-92) describes the "crimes" of nursing homes, boarding homes, and mental hospitals. He suggests that the conditions in these institutions for the aged should meet standards for physical and emotional security, safeguards against fire and serious accident, medical care, fiscal responsibility, security of belongings, good nutrition, hygiene and housekeeping, constructive leisure, and emotional atmosphere respecting human dignity.

In a related vein, gerontologists have recently become concerned about the treatment of those aged individuals who have been committed to prisons. Only recently empirical literature on the elderly offender has begun to appear, its development slowed by the stereotypical image of the aged as frail, passive, and dependent individuals opposes the general concept of career criminals. Although the image runs counter to that of the typical notion of the criminal, some of the elderly do commit crimes and do go to prison.

"When society removes people from its midst, it assumes the responsibility for their care and well-being," Rubenstein says. "The older prisoner's care and well-being depends on society's degree of caring and capacity for understanding" (Rubenstein, 1984:154). Three popular interpretations of "caring" for the elderly prisoner are: (1) humanitarian care, (2) therapeutic care, and (3) custodial care. Humanitarian care is charged with compassion for residents. Therapeutic care is oriented toward improving their capacity to cope with their personal-social problems. Custodial care carries the obligation to provide for their basic needs as physical organisms and human beings. This chapter raises the question: What can the prison reasonably be expected to do in meeting the demands of caring for the older prisoner?

THE PRISON AS A DOMICILIARY INSTITUTION

Prison is one type of domiciliary institution where the residents live together around the clock within a circumscribed space under a scheduled sequence of activities implemented by a staff and administered in a bureaucratic style. In advancing the concept of a total institution, Goffman expanded on this by noting that prisons share some of the qualities characteristic of military bases, mental hospitals, monasteries, and certain kinds of schools (Goffman 1961:1-8). One might add to this list nursing homes and some residential complexes for the elderly. Regardless of the purposes—stated or implied—of incarceration, the prison is responsible for the *care* of its inmates.

Of all domiciliary institutions, the prison is unique in that its functions center on control of residents who have been convicted as criminals. The perception of prison inmates as "enemies of society" lingers in spite of increasing concern for their living conditions. This perception stems from the fact that, of all a prison's goals, its first priority is to protect society, a view which no doubt partially explains the reluctance to perceive the prison as a caring institution.

The quality of care for prisoners pivots ultimately on the public's concern for the human being experiencing captivity (Rubenstein, 1984:153-154). Penal reform has been promoted in the past by the public's special concerns for juvenile and female prisoners. Mitigating the pains of confinement and developing alternatives to incarceration for those two status groups have won general acceptance and have opened the way later to extend the reform agenda to adult males. The elderly prisoners may serve in this way as a third status group.

HUMANITARIAN CARE: EXPRESSION OF COMPASSION

The concept of "care" is subject to differing interpretations. Humanitarian care is charged with compassion for the underprivileged who lack power to press authorities to correct deficiencies that are perceived to produce miseries for the underprivileged. For residents of domiciliary institutions those miseries may be attributed to bureaucratic indifference, inhumane living conditions, inadequate diet, and medical neglect. Nursing homes have been subjected to particular criticism on the latter account.

Elderly prisoners are among the primary targets for humanitarian concern because the elderly are expected to be relatively free of criminality and, when imprisoned, to suffer undue harassment. Official arrest and imprisonment statistics appear to confirm the expectation, but criminologists have established that those statistics do not capture the full quantity and quality of crime and that the data are more representative of the administrative actions of criminal justice agencies than of criminal behavior. We may suspect that their particular involvement in nonpredatory offenses insulates a portion of elderly criminals from apprehension and sentencing because predatory offenses are more subject to criminal justice processing.

Since there are old persons among prisoners, that insulation does not safeguard all the elderly offenders from incarceration. The factors involved in differential insulation include type of crime and circumstances of the offense, but further research is required. Although the humanitarian concern for the elderly in general is not extended in full measure to elderly prisoners, they attract more concern than the younger inmates. Since they suffer the deprivations of being both old and prisoners, the elderly inmates have been described as "the forgotten minority" (Ham, 1976b).

A common view is that aged prisoners deteriorate rapidly because they are supposed to be vulnerable to the aggression of younger prisoners and to be typically depressed, anxious, and dependent on their keepers (Adams and Vedder, 1981; Baier, 1961; Bergman and Amir, 1973). Similarly, since age becomes advanced with long-term incarceration, they are believed to become especially fearful about being released into the community. Both of those expectations are related to the gerontological hypothesis that, as older persons become disengaged from adult roles in the family, work, and the community, they withdraw from usual social relationships.

Humanitarian concern is encouraged by those views, but their validity for all elderly prisoners is subject to the criticism of unwarranted stereotyping and untested assumptions about the universal effects of incarceration. Some studies suggest the need for more rigorous testing. Gillespie and Galliher (1972) found that young inmates were optimistic that aging would "mature" or "preserve" them, whereas the oldest prisoners were convinced that prison life increased the pace of aging. But Reed and Glamser (1979) report that most prisoners in their study group of older offenders felt younger than persons of similar age on the outside, were interested in politics, and held a job in prison. Nevertheless, friendships in prison were avoided and contacts with family members were atypical. An Israeli investigation of how aged prisoners cope with incarceration discovered that some draw primarily on resources internal to their personality and others require outside intervention (Silfen, 1977).

The differential effects of penal incarceration on elderly prisoners involves the distinction between those who have aged in prison and those who have received their first conviction and incarceration in their senior years. Humanitarian concern focuses on the shock of abrupt confinement for the aged first offender. Although incarceration has impact on the long-term prisoner as well as the newly arrived first offender, humanitarian evaluation of the confinement experience tends to overlook the existence among elderly inmates of those who gradually have become adjusted to the inmate subculture through a long process of institutionalization and thereby do not qualify necessarily as vulnerable personalities.

THERAPEUTIC CARE: EFFECTING CHANGE

The concept of care intersects that of treatment in the sense of doing things for people who have problems they cannot handle without the help of others. Unlike the sentimental solicitude of humanitarian care, therapeutic care gives priority to correction of attitudes, aptitudes, and capacities of the client that are believed to be part of the explanation for the undesirable behavior. The feelings of the client are pertinent, but avoidance of pain is secondary to stimulating behavioral change deemed essential to solving the client's difficulties. Achieving rapport between the client and the therapeutic environment is essential to a favorable outcome, but rapport is the means rather than an end in itself.

Are elderly prisoners proper candidates for prison treatment programs? If the answer pivots on the idea that released prisoners are to be better prepared for gaining access to the job opportunity structure, there appears to be little point to vocational training and formal education for those without future work careers. Yet, counseling, medical care, recreational activities, and other forms of therapeutic intervention are relevant to assisting them in understanding the offense etiology, adjusting to the circumstances of confinement, and preparation for postrelease conditions.

In light of the disengagement hypothesis, will older offenders participate actively in those modes of treatment appropriate to their needs? Rubenstein's review of relevant studies unearthed mixed conclusions on this issue (Rubenstein, 1984:161-162). The disengagement hypothesis identifies aging with the loss of family, work, and other roles in the adult social system and the withdrawal of senior citizens from previous relationships. As for elders in society at large, the older prisoners bring their peculiar personality qualities and previous experiences to the disengagement situation. The physiological effects of aging also have differential impact. Prisoners who have aged while serving long sentences probably differ in their accommodation to the conditions of confinement than those entering prison for the first time at an advanced age.

CUSTODIAL CARE: MEETING BASIC NEEDS

The legal and ethical obligation of domiciliary institutions to care for their residents also involves the provision of the necessities for physical survival—food, clothing, shelter, and medical services. "Custodial care" as a term centers attention on the obligation of the management of domiciliary institutions to meet ordinary needs of their residents as physical organisms and human beings. Since the elements of custodial care are prerequisites to survival of the physical organism, they are of overwhelming importance to inmates and color the quality of their lives under confinement. Further, control of the delivery system can possibly subvert humanitarian and therapeutic care. In that sense, the quality of custodial care is the foundation upon which all forms of care are implemented.

As the domiciliary institution charged with the responsibility for managing the convicted criminal, the prison is unique in that its obligation for custodial care is matched with an obligation to prevent the inmates from endangering the public, one another, or the prison employees. The latter obligation has caused the word "custody" to be identified in prison language with the portion of the staff engaged in maintaining surveillance and control of inmates. The distinction between "control custody" and "care custody" is further confused by the heavy dependence on the surveillant division of the prison staff for monitoring the delivery of goods and services.

Correctional officials carry a public trust that is defined in terms of conventional beliefs about criminals in the society at large. As an instrument of the coercive authority of criminal law, the prison must be legitimate in that its activities receive the moral support of constituencies holding political power. In the lack of general agreement on general goals, the specific goals of the correctional leadership must find a balance between custodial security, productivity of prison labor, humanitarianism, and therapeutic objectives.

WHAT CAN THE PRISONS DO?

What can prison executives and their staffs do to respond to the demands placed upon them for the care of elderly prisoners? The question rests on several premises.

First, prisons *should* be among the caring institutions. Three versions of "care" and the responsibilities they mandate have been considered. By including the prison among hospitals, schools, and other caring institutions, concerns about conditions of penal confinement and the needs of prisoners can be identified. Policies and practices can be developed in a context that assumes respect for the individual and his future destiny.

Second, the question implies that the senior-age status of elderly prisoners justifies particularized response to their unique needs in experiencing incarceration. As for all prisoners, they have been committed to prisons after conviction for crimes, but the second premise is that they should be singled out for special attention. Presumably, the justifications reflect the physiological, psychological, and sociological effects of the aging process. The premise is strongly supported by the humanitarian judgment that the elderly are especially vulnerable and dependent in trying to cope with consequences of deterioration. The elderly inmate appears to be a dramatic exception to the stereotype of "the criminal" as an aggressive and dangerous enemy of society. The categorical images of *the* senior citizen and of *the* young adult criminal are in conflict. Both stereotypes are exaggerations that distort the great variety of characteristics found among members of both groups, but the conflict works to the advantage of aged inmates when compared with the imagery applied to younger peers.

Third, the qualifications of the prison as a caring institution should be assessed in terms of the societal functions assigned to it. The fundamental justification is that convicted criminals should be removed from the community under a legalized mandate. The justification may be expressed variously in the rationales of punishment for deterrence, incapacitation for protection of the outside community, treatment to reduce criminalistic tendencies, or restoration of inmates to the free community as effective and socially constructive individuals. The function of legalized control differentiates the prison from other domiciliary institutions and complicates its observance of the mandate for humanitarian and therapeutic care.

Another inhibition stems from the restrictions on resources available to a prison management endeavoring to address the conflicting rationales that are supposed to justify forced confinement. In competing for public funds, prisons are at a disadvantage when compared with other types of domiciliary institutions. The additional costs of therapeutic programs receive low priority when increasing numbers of prisoners require additional resources simply to meet basic human needs. Many prisons were built before contemporary standards for providing care were accepted; modernization and provision of proper therapeutic settings exact costs beyond maintenance alone.

These inhibitions help explain the failure of prison classification to live up to its promise that inmates will receive individualized attention appropriate to their particular needs. Classification outcomes are weakened by the shortages of meaningful work assignments, housing alternatives, and choices among appropriate treatment programs. The usual outcome is that prisoners are assigned to quarters, work positions, and treatment programs as generalized categories, rather than according to their peculiar needs and qualities.

American prisons have adopted two policies in trying to implement authentic classification plans: the age segregation of the elderly in a special facility or their distribution throughout the prison system. Separate housing may increase self-respect, diminish feelings of loneliness, stimulate social interaction, encourage identification with peers, and, if available, generate treatment programs oriented to the age group. Conversely, segregation may deny assignments to appropriate work assignments, may deny access to treatment programs provided more numerous younger prisoners, and may violate the preferences of those older inmates who do not identify with other members of their age group. Prison officials frequently argue that the distribution of older inmates throughout the prison system enables the more mature prisoners to stabilize and counter the aggressive tendencies of the younger prisoners, but in speaking of older prisoners in this regard, prison officials are referring mostly to those with ages from 35 to 50 years. The inmates older than 65 years are generally seen as too passive and dependent to influence younger peers significantly.

These policies pit the advantages of age-segregated housing against the conditions of incarceration in general custody. Both forms of housing raise questions in regard to the concern for elderly prisoners in all three versions of care. The exploration of these issues calls for collaboration among gerontologists and criminologists. By placing these issues within the context of the realities of prison administration, this study is intended to encourage further collaborative research on what all domiciliary institutions for the elderly can be expected to accomplish in meeting the obligations for care.

11

The Concerns of Older Inmates in a Minimum Prison Setting

Lincoln J. Fry

INTRODUCTION

When older persons are sentenced to prison, they enter a system predicated on the assumption that those it processes and incarcerates for the length of their sentences will be relatively young. Commenting on that issue, Cain (1979:2) observed that the neglect of age as a crucial variable has led to acceptance of the proposition that "aging and age differentials are irrelevant to understanding social processes within or administering a prison." Recent literature reviews have made essentially the same point and have stressed the need to overcome several major weaknesses in the research devoted to older convicts. This chapter addresses one of those weaknesses by providing a means to begin to assess the institutional concerns of older inmates.

THE ELDERLY IN PRISON

As the reviews of the elderly prisoner have indicated, there is no

This study resulted from a larger study of prison overcrowding funded by the John Randolph Haynes and Dora Haynes Foundation of Los Angeles. That support is gratefully acknowledged and deeply appreciated. I would like to express my appreciation for comments and suggestions provided by Belinda R. McCarthy.

concensus on how to define older or elderly inmates. For instance, Rubenstein (1984) noted that he found varying ages at which inmates are classified as older, from as young as 25 to as old as 82; however, the majority of studies adopted either 50 or 55 as the age used to define older convicts.

Another major question in reviews devoted to elderly inmates is whether they should be integrated or segregated into the general prison population (Goetting, 1983; Rubenstein, 1984). One group of researchers has stressed the need to provide separate facilities for older prisoners (Krajick, 1979a; Roberg and Webb, 1981; Weigand and Burger, 1979). They argue that special programs should be implemented to meet the needs of older prisoners and that age segregation contributes to positive mental health and social adjustment. In the same vein, Reed and Glamser (1979) and others advocate special facilities for older prisoners based on the notion that such an arrangement would provide them protection from younger, aggressive inmates.

Others have stressed the opposite view and have argued that the elderly should be integrated into the general prison population. Straus and Sherwin (1975) indicated that older inmates have a stabilizing influence on the inmate population, a view supported in more general works devoted to the prison environment (Jacobs, 1977; Irwin, 1980). As Goetting (1984) has noted, other researchers (Silfen, 1977; Wooden and Parker, 1980) found no need or justification to provide special programming for older offenders. During the course of her work, Goetting found that some prison administrators believed that special consideration extended to the older inmate was a form of discrimination. They indicated that convicts should be assigned to housing and work assignments based on their custody levels and only then should their health, family, and community status be considered. This group of administrators suggested that placing an inmate in a special unit could be detrimental to his overall needs, including security, family and occupational interests.

One reason the segregated versus integrated issue remains an open question is because it is unclear how older inmates are affected by their prison experiences. In his review, Rubenstein (1984) pointed to the great diversity of opinion regarding the reactions of older persons to prison environments. He cited a study by Reed and Glamser (1979) which reported that 15 of 19 older inmates indicated they felt younger in prison. Their research concluded that older convicts were better off than their counterparts of similar social status on the outside in that they ate regularly, rested often, had access to medical care, and were not exposed to hard labor and excessive drinking. By way of contrast, a study conducted in Israel by Bergman and Amir (1973) found the physical and mental conditions of older prisoners deteriorated rapidly once they were sentenced to prison.

Rubenstein's (1984) review of the effects of prison on older prisoners included both psychological and sociological factors. In summarizing studies that reported on the results of psychological testing, he found the following: (1) older inmates had higher introversion scores and higher neuroticism scores than younger inmates (Eysenck et al., 1977); (2) based on their MMPI scores, older inmates were reported to be more neurotic and less psychotic in their responses than the general population (Panton, 1976-77; McCreary and Mensh, 1977). Panton also reported older inmates to exhibit greater anxiety, despondency, apprehension, and concern with physical functioning; (3) using a Bi-Polar Psychological Inventory, Teller and Howell (1979) found that older inmates exhibited less psychic pain, but were depressed, impulsive, and hostile, while less socially deviant.

Some of the sociological factors cited in Rubenstein's (1984) review included social control, socialization, and institutionalization. In this context, social control referred to the ability of the elderly to supposedly maintain the prison order. Socialization and institutionalization referred to the processes all inmates undergo when they are sentenced to prison. Aday and Webster (1979) pointed to the way prison destroys ties with the family, friends, and the community, losses that force the inmate to turn to the prison environment for support. For some inmates, this can result in what Ham (1976a) has described as an institutional neurosis that manifests itself in not wanting to leave the prison. Researchers are likely to see older inmates as most vulnerable to that process, especially because prison environments provide them with fewer means to counteract that effect. Krajick (1979a) reported that older inmates are not easy to motivate regarding programming, which reduces their chances for parole. Wiegand and Burger (1979) found that educational and vocational programs were of no value to older inmates, which reduces their chances of postinstitutional success. They noted that older inmates were not active in prison organizations, had no support systems, no place to live, had health problems, and were unemployable.

AN ECOLOGICAL PERSPECTIVE

As suggested above, one of the problems that plagues the older inmate literature is inability to specify how elderly inmates are affected by prison. Toch (1977a) has proposed a way to look at the adjustment of inmates that may explain some of the divergent findings related to any age group. He noted that similar inmates survive in one setting and break down in others, and that situations that are stressful to some inmates have no impact on others. Toch argued that the effect of prison cannot be understood until we understand the personal impact of prison, and he suggested that one way to begin to approach these issues is to examine the person-environmental fit; that is, the congruence between a person's needs and how well the environment meets those needs.

Based on interviews conducted with 2,650 inmates in five different prison systems, Toch (1977a) identified certain environmental concerns. Out of this work, the Prison Preference Inventory (PPI) was developed and this 56-item instrument was included in the questionnaire administered to the inmates in this study. The eight environmental concerns identified by the PPI include: (1) privacy—a concern with social and physical overstimulation; a preference for isolation, peace and quiet, absence of environmental irritants such as noise and crowding; (2) safety—a concern about one's physical safety; a preference for social and physical settings that provide protection and that minimize the chances of being attacked; (3) structure—a concern about environmental stability and predictability; a preference for consistency, clear cut rules, orderly and scheduled events and impingements; (4) support—a concern about reliable tangible assistance from persons and settings and about services that facilitate self-advancement and self-improvement; (5) emotional feedback—a concern about being loved, appreciated, and cared for; a desire for intimate relationships that provide emotional sustenance and empathy; (6) social stimulation—a concern with congeniality and a preference for settings which provide an opportunity for social interaction, companionship, and gregariousness; (7) activity—a concern about understimulation; a need for distraction; and (8) freedom—a concern about circumspection of one's autonomy; a need for minimal restriction and for maximum opportunity to govern one's own conduct (Toch, 1977a: 16-17).

Toch (1977a:246-283) developed preference profiles out of his preliminary work on the PPI, and age was one of these. (However, older inmates in his study ranged from 28 to 35 years of age in the various subsamples.) Toch reported older inmates were less concerned with freedom and support and more concerned with emotional feedback when compared to younger inmates. The most striking finding was on structure dimension, where the concern with structure increased dramatically with age. Toch commented that overall these results made sense, based on the way persons are perceived to change as they grow older. As a result, he presented two age profiles. The first he defined as "middle age," a profile that featured low freedom, low support, high structure, and high emotional feedback concerns. The second, defined as the "model youth profile," featured high freedom, high support, low structure, and low emotional feedback concerns.

Toch's (1977a) findings are important for our purposes here because they provide a way to identify inmate concerns and examine the way they are affected by age differences. One of the contributions of this research is that it includes a sufficient number of inmates that meet the commonly accepted age standard to be classified as older offenders. However, the scope of the present study is narrow in that it is restricted to inmates in special housing, which is exclusively dorm housing. Consequently, the results cannot be generalized to inmates found in the entire range of inmate housing. This issue will become clear as the study is described in more detail.

THE STUDY

This research was part of a larger prison overcrowding study conducted in California. The largest prison system in the United States, it had over 33,000 inmates when the research began in 1983 and the population grew to over 47,000 inmates in the fall of 1985, when the research ended. The data reported here were collected from inmates at the California Institution for Men (CIM), located at Chino, about 30 miles east of Los Angeles. CIM serves as the major gateway into the prison system for Southern California. It consists of four distinct units, including two reception centers, a Level 3 (medium security) facility, and a minimum custody unit.

THE SETTING AND THE ELDERLY OFFENDER UNIT

The minimum facility was an excellent place to study overcrowding. Its rated capacity was 976 and it had 1,564 inmates when the research began in June 1983, and 1,673 when it ended in June 1985. Minimum had seven different housing units. Three dorm housing units offered mainline housing for inmates completing their sentences in the minimum facility and another unit offered exclusively dorm housing which served as the new arrival unit for those either newly admitted from the reception centers or about to leave on parole or work furlough. One unit was completely double-celled and another was mixed, half dorm housing and half double-celled in an upper and lower arrangement. Known as Elm Hall, the final unit was the primary reason this study focused on the minimum facility in that it was an elderly offender unit which also offered only dorm housing. This 156 bed unit will be described in detail below.

METHOD

The research consisted of two phases, a fieldwork component and a survey phase. Out of the fieldwork phase, a 155-item inmate survey was developed, pretested, and administered to inmates at CIM minimum. As indicated above, this questionnaire contained the PPI, a paired comparison instrument which asks respondents to circle one of two choices. The number of pairs, 56, allows the eight dimensions to be paired with each other twice. Respondents received scores on each dimension, which can range from 0 to 14. Examples of the types of items included as paired indicators of the eight dimensions are as follows: I would prefer "being by myself" (privacy) versus "learning something" (support). I would prefer "housing in which no one can harm me" (safety) versus "staying away from guards" (freedom). I would prefer "having consistent rules" (structure) versus "being busy all day" (activity). I would prefer "housing where people rap" (social stimulation) versus "a friend who shares my problems" (emotional feedback).

At the time of the voluntary survey in November 1984, there were 1,538 inmates at the minimum facility and 538 of these returned useable questionnaires, a response rate of 35 percent. Useable questionnaires were returned by 62 inmates who were at least 50 years of age. Older inmates were actually overrepresented among survey respondents, based on their numbers in the total population. The ages of 481 respondents were known and the 62 known to be 50 years of age or over accounted for about 13 percent of the total sample. At the time of the survey, institutional statistics indicated that this age group made up about seven percent of the total minimum facility population.

Fifty was chosen as the age that defined older inmates for several reasons. One was the fact that it was the age chosen to define those eligible for Elm Hall, and 50 was the age used by McCain et al. (1980) in their study of the effects of overcrowding and the research reported here was designed to replicate some of their findings. Also, the California Department of Corrections used 50 to 59 as one of the age breakdowns in its reports.

When the responses of older inmates were examined in detail, it was found that 50 of the 62 respondents were residents of Elm Hall, and that only two of the older inmates had double cells. As a result, the analysis presented below is restricted to Elm Hall. Since that unit only offered dorm housing, comparisons with other inmate age groups were restricted to only those in similar housing. The analysis replicated Toch's procedures, which meant that average dimension scores were calculated and then scores were trichotomized into low, medium, and high categories and then cross-tabulated by age.

FINDINGS

Direct observation and staff interviews of Elm Hall confirmed Goetting's (1984) assertions regarding the way older offender units have changed in recent years in most state prison systems. Her admonitions about referring to such units as elderly offender units were supported as were her claims that most had become what she defined as medical/geriatric units. Her point was that they no longer housed exclusively elderly offenders and offered programs specifically tailored to their needs.

Previous visits had been made to Elm Hall in 1979 and 1980 when it had been considered "the old folk's home" of the California prison system. Direct involvement in the unit and the staff interviews indicated that Elm Hall's priorities and admission policies had changed from the earlier period. It had become a medical/geriatric unit with severe medical cases now receiving top priority and age considerations secondary. Staff indicated this was due to overcrowding. While all elderly inmates transferred to the minimum facility were still eligible for Elm Hall, they were sometimes forced to wait up to a month before bed space became available.

The primary change from the earlier period was that older inmates now had to share space with younger, infirmed inmates. When queried about the unit and these changes, most residents indicated that Elm Hall was the best housing in the minimum facility. Follow-up interviews held as the fieldwork was terminating, in November and December of 1985, revealed that only a handful of residents were still in the unit who had completed the questionnaire the year before. None of these inmates had been in the unit when Elm Hall was considered to be an elderly offender unit, which meant that this new arrangement was all the respondents had known; simply, they were unable to assess what the policy change had meant to older offenders.

Two groups of staff were interviewed regarding Elm Hall, namely, those who had worked there under the old system and those currently assigned. The former group expressed relief at being gone and complained primarily about how the unit had changed. Overcrowding was seen as the source of those problems. Staff indicated that as population pressures rose, there was less time to work with inmates. The increased number of medical cases meant more time had to be spent keeping track of, sending, and/or escorting inmates to the hospital to keep their numerous medical appointments. Also, a new work incentive program had resulted in a shortage of work assignments, which reduced the opportunity for older inmates to be involved outside the unit. Consequently, idleness was more of a problem.

Those currently assigned pointed to the way other correctional officers perceived their duty in Elm Hall. Some suggested that other correctional officers saw the assignment as a gravy train, a kind of retirement for C.O.s. Yet, staff argued that Elm Hall had the "heaviest" offenders in the institution, especially violent offenders. Elsewhere (Fry, 1987), these assertions were confirmed when it was reported that 52 percent (26 of 50 Elm Hall respondents) were sentenced to prison for violent offenses, compared to about 40 percent of the remaining respondents. These 26 violent offenses included 14 for murder or manslaughter, and four others for assaults with deadly weapons.

Elm Hall was arranged differently than the other dorm housing units in the minimum facility. While the other dorm units were primarily double-bunked, Elm Hall had only single beds. This was because of the composition of the inmate population, aged and infirmed. This made Elm Hall seem more crowded than some of the other units due to the fact that the beds were side to side around the walls of the unit and very close together. This was the reason Elm Hall's population remained almost constant over the two and one half years of the study; simply, there was no room to add additional beds.

There were some other differences between Elm Hall and the other units in the minimum facility that were important in the analysis of the PPI responses. As indicated elsewhere (Fry, 1987), consistent with the literature, whites were overrepresented among older inmates when compared to the rest of the inmate population (54 percent compared to 36 percent for all other inmates). In fact, whites and those with higher levels of education were overrepresented in the inmate sample. Observation of inmates as they completed the questionnaire, and of the completed instruments, revealed that the inability to read and follow directions explained those differences.

This was a concern because Toch (1977a:237) had collected part of what he defined as the California sample at CIM's reception center. The rest of the sample came from the Northern Reception Center at Vacaville. Toch indicated that his sample was nonrandom because 25 percent of the intake population was excluded since they had not been certified as reading at the sixth grade level through the intake testing process. While inmates were not screened due to their reading level, 22 percent (107 of 481 respondents) whose ages were known and who did not provide useable responses were eliminated. Given the fact that there was a literary bias in both samples, the first task in the analysis of the PPI results was to compare the dimension scores in the current survey with those reported in the original Toch study. These results are presented in Table 11.1.

As Table 11.1 shows, the dimension scores in this study were based on the responses of 238 inmates living in dorm housing. The greatest divergence in these scores was on the privacy dimension where the average score was a 6.9 in this study as compared to 5.5 in Toch's (1977a) original California sample, and 5.4 in the overall sample. The other divergence of any note was on the activity dimension where the average score was 6.9 in this study as compared to 8.1 in the original California sample, and 7.8 in the combined sample. With those two exceptions, the other dimension scores were quite similar.

The next task was to determine whether the dimensions identified by Toch (1977a) as crucial to his age preference profiles would be supported when the PPI dimension scores calculated for this research were broken down by age. That data appears in Table 11.2.

Table 11.2 revealed that significant differences by age were found on three of the four dimensions identified by Toch (1977a) as central to the PPI age profiles, namely, structure, support, and freedom. A significant difference was not found on the emotional feedback dimension, but a significant difference did appear on the activity dimension.

The data presented in Table 11.2 generally support Toch's findings. Older inmates did show greater concern with structure, with 46 percent of those 50 and over in the high category. The percentage of those in the high category declined with age and only 11 of those under 25 were in that group. As Toch suggested, older inmates were less concerned with freedom than younger inmates, with 8 percent of the older inmates in the high concern category as compared to 50 percent of the inmates under 25. While Toch (1977a) reported a U-shaped relationship in terms of the support dimension,

Table 11.1.
Comparisons between CIM Average, PPI Dimension Scores, and the Toch* Study

Dimension	CIM (n=238)	California (n=327)	New York (n=299)	Connecticut (n=201)	Pennsylvania (n=314)	Federal (n=512)	Combined Toch Sample (n=471)
Privacy	6.9	5.5	5.8	5.4	4.7	5.5	5.4
Safety	7.1	7.6	7.4	6.0	7.3	7.5	7.3
Structure	6.4	5.4	6.1	6.1	6.4	6.9	6.3
Support	9.4	10.1	10.2	9.9	10.2	9.3	9.9
Emotional Feedback	7.9	7.9	7.8	8.8	8.4	8.7	8.3
Social Stimulation	6.3	7.0	6.5	6.7	7.3	6.6	6.8
Activity	6.9	8.1	8.7	7.4	8.6	6.7	7.8
Freedom	5.1	4.5	3.7	5.9	3.3	5.0	4.5

*Partially reproduced from *Living in Prison: The Ecology of Survival* by Hans Toch. Copyright © 1977 by Hans Toch. Reproduced by permission of The Free Press, a division of Macmillan, Inc.

Table 11.2.
Cross-tabulation of PPI Scores by Age (n = 238)

PPI Dimension	Age: Under 25 (n=38) n	(%)	25–34 (n=97) n	(%)	35–49 (n=53) n	(%)	50+ (n=50) n	(%)	Total (n=238) n
Privacy									
Low (0–5)	15	(40)	30	(31)	18	(34)	23	(46)	86
Medium (6–8)	10	(26)	39	(40)	21	(40)	14	(28)	84
High (9+)	13	(34)	28	(29)	14	(26)	13	(26)	68
x^2=5.45 N/S									
Safety									
Low (0–5)	16	(42)	24	(25)	15	(28)	14	(28)	69
Medium (6–8)	12	(32)	37	(38)	17	(32)	15	(30)	81
High (9+)	10	(26)	36	(37)	21	(40)	21	(42)	88
x^2=5.34 N/S									
Structure									
Low (0–5)	18	(47)	44	(45)	19	(36)	11	(22)	92
Medium (6–7)	16	(42)	28	(29)	16	(30)	16	(32)	76
High (8+)	4	(11)	25	(26)	18	(34)	23	(46)	70
x=17.23 P=.01									

Table 11.2. (continued)

PPI Dimension	Age: Under 25 (n=38) n	(%)	25-34 (n=97) n	(%)	35-49 (n=53) n	(%)	50+ (n=50) n	(%)	Total (n=238) n
Support									
Low (0-8)	9	(24)	34	(35)	18	(34)	29	(58)	90
Medium (9-10)	11	(29)	30	(31)	23	(43)	11	(22)	75
High (11+)	18	(47)	33	(34)	12	(23)	10	(20)	73
x=18.48 P=.01									
Emotional Feedback									
Low (0-6)	14	(37)	30	(31)	13	(25)	20	(40)	77
Medium (7-9)	14	(37)	36	(37)	29	(55)	20	(40)	99
High (10+)	10	(26)	31	(32)	11	(21)	10	(20)	62
x=7.68 N/S									
Social Stimulation									
Low (0-4)	8	(21)	26	(27)	11	(21)	18	(36)	63
Medium (5-7)	18	(45)	39	(40)	26	(49)	23	(46)	105
High (8+)	13	(34)	32	(33)	16	(30)	9	(18)	70
x=6.41 N/S									
Activity									
Low (0-5)	12	(32)	31	(32)	11	(21)	19	(38)	73
Medium (6-7)	16	(42)	38	(39)	16	(30)	9	(18)	79
High (8+)	10	(26)	28	(29)	26	(49)	22	(44)	86
x=13.95 P=.05									

Table 11.2. (continued)

PPI Dimension	Age: Under 25 (n=38) n	(%)	25-34 (n=97) n	(%)	35-49 (n=53) n	(%)	50+ (n=50) n	(%)	Total (n=238) n
Freedom									
Low (0-3)	5	(13)	26	(27)	24	(45)	29	(58)	84
Medium (4-6)	14	(37)	47	(49)	17	(32)	17	(34)	95
High (7+)	19	(50)	24	(25)	12	(23)	4	(8)	59
x=34.70 P=.001									

Source: Toch (1977a) and author.

Table 11.2 showed that the percentages of those in the high support category decreased with age. Twenty-four percent of those under 25 were in the low support category, compared to 58 percent of those over 50.

As for the significant difference on the activity dimension, a fairly large percentage of older inmates were found in the low or higher categories, 38 and 44 percent, respectively. However, it was the 35 to 49 year age category that had the largest percentage of respondents in the high category, 49 percent, and the least in the low category, 21 percent.

SUMMARY AND CONCLUSIONS

Based on a sample that contained 50 respondents that met the commonly accepted definition of older inmate, this chapter has re-examined the age profiles generated by Toch's (1977a) PPI Inventory. The purpose was to identify the concerns of older offenders and to compare them to other inmates. When the PPI dimension scores were compared to Toch's original study, the greatest divergence was found on the privacy dimension, followed by the activity scale score. The other dimension scores were all in the range of Toch's original study.

These results appear to be interpretable based on what the privacy and activity dimensions purport to measure and the impressions gathered through direct observation. Since privacy refers to an absence of environmental irritants, including crowding, a concern with this dimension should have been expected. As far as the increased concern with activity, the description of the changes in Elm Hall brought about by overcrowding, the work incentive program, and the influx of severe medical cases would seem to explain why older inmates would become more concerned with their understimulation. Idleness in Elm Hall was described as a problem, and speaks to the need to provide stimulation in age-segregated housing, especially when faced with severely overcrowded conditions.

From the description of the kinds of offenses that sent this group of older inmates to prison, it was apparent that a large percentage were "overrides"; that is, convicts whose crimes and sentences mandate that they serve their time in higher security level institutions. Instead, their classification scores are "overridden" and they are allowed to serve their time in a lower custody level prison. One implication of this study is that older inmates can be sent to, and will adjust in, minimum facilities, and perhaps hospital settings as well.

Another implication of this research relates to the issue of determining the age used to define "old in prison." The findings essentially replicated Toch's (1977a) original study with a sample who were 50 years of age and older. There was a great deal of similarity with Toch's study where the older inmate group was 35 and over, which in turn provides support for those earlier studies which used a relativistic approach in defining the older inmate. Clearly, there is the need to extend the study of older inmates to those included in different kinds of housing and prisons, especially maximum security institutions. Unfortunately, given the present difficulty in securing access to inmates in these institutions, there will most likely be a long wait before any such study becomes available.

12

Factors Affecting the Adjustment of Elderly Inmates to Prison

Michael J. Sabath
Ernest L. Cowles

INTRODUCTION

All prison inmates experience some weakening or breakdown of their customary support systems upon being incarcerated. Removed from familiar situations and relationships, they are pressed to compensate for social and psychological losses and acclimate to the prison setting. Research suggests that there is a constellation of personal and environmental factors shaping this adjustment process and that special subgroups of inmates like the elderly, handicapped, and first offenders may rely on different adjustment strategies. Unfortunately, much of what is known about the adjustment of offenders to imprisonment is based on descriptive studies or anecdotal accounts (Gibbs, 1982; Parisi, 1982; Toch, 1977b). These offer useful insights into the adjustment process, but they do not lend themselves to the development of policy-relevant models which might be of use to correctional administrators looking for better ways of managing the prison population.

This study was supported by the Handling Long-Term Offender Project, funded by the National Institute of Justice, Grant Number 84-IJ-CX-0043. Opinions expressed in this article do not necessarily represent the official position or views of the U.S. Department of Justice, National Institute of Justice, or those of the Missouri Department of Corrections and Human Resources.

FOCUS ON ADJUSTMENT OF ELDERLY INMATES

In this study, we examine patterns of adjustment for elderly inmates in Missouri's correctional system. By modeling the interrelationships among several background, institutional, and other variables used to explain adjustment to imprisonment, we attempt to identify sources of variation in elderly adjustment and to explore the implication of these relationships for managing the adjustment process.

The elderly have posed unique problems for corrections management because they typically make up only a small percentage of the prison population and have needs that are substantially different from those of the average inmate. Often they are more vulnerable to victimization and require special attention when it comes to medical treatment, nutrition, housing, and institutional activities. These problems are likely to persist into the future and may grow in importance as the effects of more restrictive correctional policies become felt in our correctional systems. The prevalence of determinant sentences, mandatory minimum periods of imprisonment and extended prison terms without benefit of parole are among forces combining to produce a group of inmates who will spend a significant portion of their adult lives in a correctional institution. At the upper end of this group are elderly individuals who are likely to live out the remainder of their lives in a correctional setting.

FACTORS RELATED TO ELDERLY INMATE ADJUSTMENT

There is little evidence relating to the effects of institutional and personal factors on the adjustment of the elderly to prison, or to the effects of their adjustment on correctional management. Much of the existing research tends to support the notion that there may be differences in adjustment patterns for the elderly and other subgroups of inmates, or identifies some of the factors believed to have an important bearing on adjustment. There are no systematic investigations of how personal and environmental factors or coping strategies affect the adjustment of elderly inmates to imprisonment.

Research findings on the adjustment of elderly inmates, while not unanimous, do seem to support the idea of different adjustment patterns for older inmates and for subgroups of older inmates. For example, Panton (1976-1977) in comparing Minnesota Multiphasic Personality Inventory (MMPI) scores of older inmates with a sample of the male general population found significant differences between the groups on several of the instrument's scales and subscales. He concluded that while both inmate groups demonstrated patterns indicative of a behavior disorder, the aged inmates showed greater anxiety, despondency, apprehension, concern with physical functioning, were somewhat naive and demanding of attention and support, and appeared to want to avoid responsibility. He also found older inmates to have feelings of inadequacy and insecurity, and to be more easily influenced and intimidated by younger, more aggressive inmates. Panton observed that older inmates seemed to show a lessening of psychopathy which he speculated might imply less antisocial hostility and, therefore, less acting out behavior. Supporting these personality differences, Bergman and Amir (1973) described older inmates as more depressed and dependent in their relationships with guards.

Other research suggests that elderly inmates may be better adjusted than younger inmates (Silfen, 1977; Teller and Howell, 1981). Using the Bipolar Psychological Inventory (BPI), Teller and Howell found the older inmate to be "less likely to experience psychic pain," "less depressed," and "less socially deviant." Still other research indicates there may be differences in adjustment within the elderly population. There is general agreement that the "new" first-time elderly inmate shows better prison adjustment than the "chronic" repeat offender (Aday and Webster, 1979; Adams and Vedder, 1961; Bergman and Amir, 1973; Silfen, 1977; Teller and Howell, 1981).

Little specific attention has been given to the prisonization or institutional socialization of older inmates. Even more isolated are attempts at developing conceptual frameworks through which we can study adaptation or adjustment. An exception is the research of Aday and Webster (1979) who offer the concept of institutional dependency. These investigators maintain that there are important personal and background characteristics that influence the process of prisonization for older inmates and, eventually, their dependence upon the institution. Those inmates who come to prison without prior institutional orientation and with extra-institutional support systems are better able to withstand the inmate socialization process. Accompanying this concept is the idea that the length of time spent in the prison environment negatively impacts the older inmate's ties with significant others in the outside community. Faced by a continuing loss of free world relationships, the problems associated with advancing age, and the loss of major self-identity roles, the elderly inmate turns to the institutional environment for support, nurturance, and replacement role identity.

In testing their framework, Aday and Webster (1979) found unmarried elderly inmates displaying a greater level of institutional dependency than their married counterparts. Those imprisoned earlier in their lives revealed significantly more institutional dependency than those imprisoned later in life. They did not find any significant differences when examining the influence of length of incarceration on institutional dependency, although a measure of association was positive and supported the hypothesized direction of the relationship. They also found that chronic offenders demonstrated greater institutional dependency, and were much less likely to be married or to receive community visits than were the other offenders in the study.

MODEL OF ELDERLY ADJUSTMENT

The primary objective of this study was to explore the institutional coping strategies of elderly inmates by specifying and testing a model of their adjustment process. The model is based on the assumption that adjustment can usefully be viewed as how an inmate's personal characteristics influence his response to or participation in the prison environment. The notion is similar to the proposition, "behavior is a function of individual characteristics and the environment," advanced by Lewin (1951) and follows the line of reasoning represented by the interaction or combinational perspective on prisonization.

The model includes three major concepts: (1) involvement: the frequency with which elderly inmates participate in personal, social, work, and treatment program activities; (2) morale: an inmate's general attitude and outlook in prison; and (3) adjustment: the degree to which elderly inmates do not perceive difficulties getting along with institutional staff and other inmates, or difficulties in coping with aspects of the prison environment. The hypothesized relationships among the concepts in the model are depicted in Figure 12.1. The model proposes that the three concepts are linked together in a temporal order where involvement in various types of activities precedes morale which, in turn, precedes the dependent concept of adjustment.

As indicated in the figure, a number of background variables are presumed to condition the relationships among involvement, morale, and adjustment. These variables, or characteristics, are: chronic offender (inmates who had previous incarcerations versus those imprisoned for the first time), frequency of family contacts, health status, education, financial position, current marital status, and time served on present sentence, and have been included in the model either because they have been associated with elderly inmate adjustment in previous research or because it was believed that they were particularly important factors in terms of fostering or inhibiting the use of different coping strategies by elderly inmates.

Generally, the model proposes that elderly inmates who demonstrate higher levels of involvement will have a more positive attitude and outlook on life, the concept termed "morale," than will inmates with lower levels of involvement. The final linkage in the model assumes that those inmates with high morale will be better adjusted to the institutional environment than inmates with low morale. Thus, morale and involvement are seen as the most important predictors of elderly adjustment with the background variables being of secondary importance and influence.

METHODOLOGY

The study is based on survey and secondary data gathered for a sample of

Figure 12.1
Model Depicting the Hypothesized Relationships Among Factors Leading to Elderly Inmate Adjustment

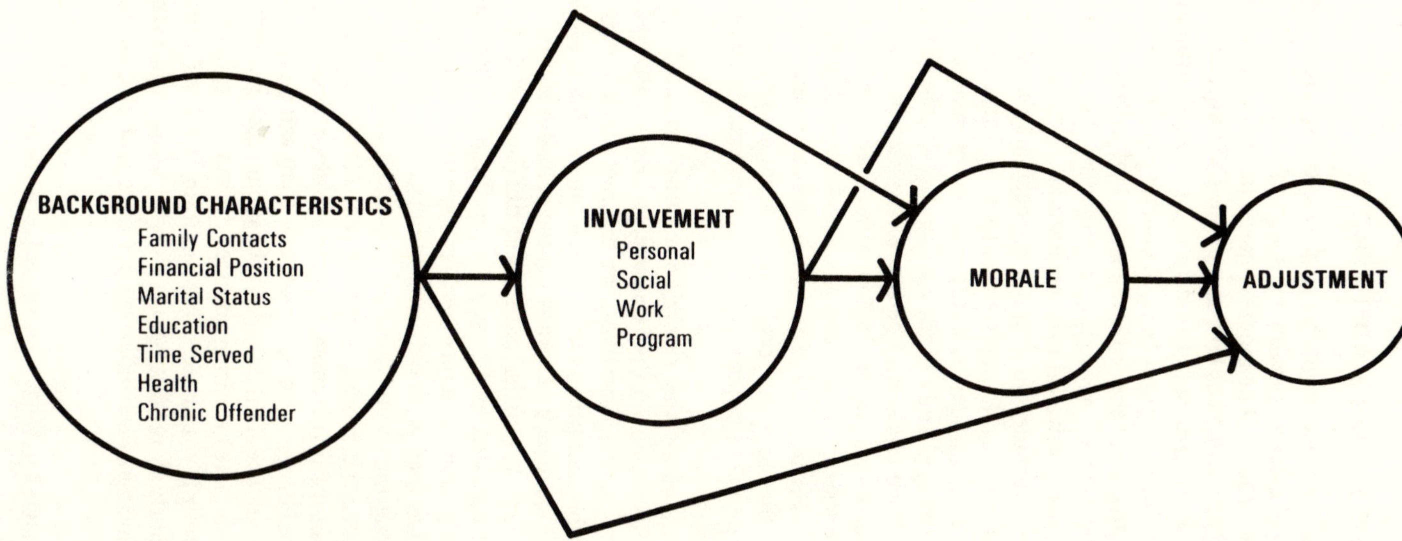

111 inmates aged 55 years and older in Missouri's correctional system. The data were obtained through mail surveys of elderly inmates and their caseworkers administered during the summer of 1986, and through the Department of Corrections and Human Resources' Offender Management Information System (OMIS). The sample ranged in age from 55 to 78 years; more than half had spent at least five years in Missouri's prisons.

Aside from the marital status, all background variables in the model were operationalized at ordinal or interval levels of measurement. Current marital status was treated as a dummy variable with a value of 0 representing not married and a value of 1 representing married. Inmates provided subjective assessments of their health status and self-reported information about the frequency of their contacts with family members and their ability to cover basic needs in prison (financial position). Educational level and total time served in prison were measured in actual years. The variable, chronic offender, was coded into two categories with one category representing first offender and the other repeat offender.

Involvement was operationalized using four additive indexes measuring how frequently elderly inmates engaged in: (1) activities requiring low levels of interaction with others, such as reading and watching television (personal involvement index), (2) group and organizational activities, for example, inmate club meetings (social involvement index), (3) part-time or full-time work (work involvement index), and (4) institutional programs, such as vocational training and psychological counseling (program involvement index). A list of 24 activity and program areas was included in the mail survey. Respondents were asked to indicate how frequently they had been involved in each area over the past two years using a five-point scale ranging from "never" to "very often or on a regular basis." Of the responses received and calculated, index scores ranged from 0 to 30 for personal involvement, from 0 to 35 for social involvement, from 0 to 15 for work involvement and from 0 to 40 for program involvement. Higher scores represented greater involvement in each of the areas.

Morale was measured by asking caseworkers to rate the general attitude and outlook on life of each elderly inmate in their charge. Ratings could range from 1 to 7, with a higher score indicating high morale.

The dependent variable, adjustment, was operationalized in three ways. A set of nine items drawn from Clark's (1968) personality and social network adjustment scale formed the basis for constructing an inmate self-reported index of adjustment. Higher scores on the index indicated better adjustment. Caseworker perceptions of inmate adjustment were measured on a seven-point scale of adjustment to living in the institution. This scale is a modified version of one employed by Carp (1966) to assess the adjustment of elderly persons to a residential living environment. Last, the number of conduct violations received over the last two years was employed as an indicator of inmate adjustment. Each of these three measures provides a different perspective of the individual's adjustment to the prison environment. The first is a reflection of the individual's own perspective on how he is adjusting to the environment. The second provides a subjective evaluation of the individual's adjustment as perceived by a caseworker who is familiar with the personal characteristics and events shaping adjustment. Finally, the third provides a standard: the institutional rules, against which to measure the individual's behavior. However, this measure also reflects a subjective evaluation of the inmate's adjustment in that the conduct violation is based on the evaluation of a particular behavior by a staff member.

Path analysis was employed to test the relationships suggested by the model and to determine whether or not the hypothesized structure was operating. Basically, the existence of hypothesized relationships is tested by examining the significance of the standardized partial regression coefficients resulting from a variable being regressed on all variables causally preceding it. The coefficients provide an estimate of the direct effect between variables controlling for all other variables in the regression. In all, three path analyses were performed, one for each of the three measures of adjustment used in the study.

ELDERLY INVOLVEMENT IN PRISON ACTIVITIES

Information about the types of activities in which elderly inmates choose to be involved offers some clue as to the strategies they employ in dealing with prison. Data presented in Table 12.1 shows what the elderly inmates in the study reported as to how they spent their time. Overall, the data indicate that the elderly prefer to spend their time in personal involvements and working given the range of activity options that are available to them. The majority report that they read books and newspapers, watch television, and exercise frequently. A substantial number work at a paid job in the institution for more than 20 hours per week and socialize with their fellow inmate workers.

In marked contrast to these involvements, few elderly inmates report participating in socially oriented activities such as inmate clubs/organizations, or doing volunteer work. Even more striking is that the vast majority of elderly inmates are not involved in any of the formal programs (such as psychological counseling, academic education, and vocational training) offered at their institutions.

RESULTS OF THE PATH ANALYSIS

Zero-order correlations among all of the variables in the model are shown in Table 12.2. The table indicates that, for the most part, the three measures of adjustment (conduct violations, inmate reported, and caseworker

Table 12.1.
Elderly Inmate Involvement in Prison Activities: Affirmative Responses (N = 111)

Activity	Percent Responding			
	Rarely	Occasionally	Fairly Often	Very Often/ Regular Basis
1. Read books or newspapers (PI)	4	14	21	53
2. Watch television (PI)	6	23	23	40
3. Sit alone and think (PI)	11	39	23	18
4. Work on a hobby (woodwork, painting, knitting, leather) (PI)	10	16	5	11
5. Exercise such as walking or running (PI)	7	24	21	38
6. Sleep or lay in bed during the day (PI)	31	23	8	7
7. Play cards or other board games (SI)	15	28	14	12
8. Visit or have informal discussions (bull sessions) (SI)	15	37	19	16
9. Participate in inmate clubs/organizations as a member (SI)	12	5	7	8
10. Hold office in inmate clubs/organization (SI)	5	6	6	6
11. Participate in organized recreational sport (SI)	9	5	3	5
12. Volunteer to help other inmates or do volunteer work for some group or organization (SI)	13	27	10	14
13. Attend church or other religious meeting (SI)	8	23	11	30
14. Work at a paid job for more than 20 hours per week in the institution (WI)	2	7	5	62

Table 12.1. (continued)

Activity	Percent Responding			
	Rarely	Occasionally	Fairly Often	Very Often/ Regular Basis
15. Make suggestions to your boss for improving how your job is done (WI)	7	25	18	12
16. Socialize with fellow inmate workers during non-working hours (WI)	12	36	17	23
17. Attend(ed) a GED or ABE program (PROG)	3	5	2	9
18. Attend(ed) college classes or college programs (PROG)	2	2	1	9
19. Attend(ed) substance abuse programs (i.e., AA, Narcotics Anonymous) (PROG)	1	7	6	6
20. Meet with your caseworker or psychologist to discuss problems you were having (PROG)	18	23	5	4
21. Attend(ed) a counseling program like "One-on-One", Transactional Analysis, Reality Therapy (PROG)	6	6	3	3
22. Attend(ed) a vocational program such as electronics, cosmetology, nurses aide, data entry (PROG)	1	6	3	7
23. Attend(ed) Positive Mental Attitude or Silva Mind Control groups (PROG)	5	7	1	6
24. Attend(ed) Missouri Sexual Offender Program (PROG)	1	4	2	8

The respondents were asked to think back over the last two years and to indicate how often they spent their time doing each activity. Letters noted in parentheses designate the involvement index in which the item was used: Personal Involvement (PI), Social Involvement (SI), Work Involvement (WI), and Program Involvement (PROG).

Source: Compiled by authors.

reported) are weakly associated with one another. The correlations appear to reflect differences in perceptions of adjustment between inmates and corrections staff. The strongest correlation is between staff and caseworker measures of adjustment (−.29) and is in the expected direction, while associations between staff-related measures and inmate self-reported adjustment are near zero. None of the variables in the study are highly intercorrelated, thus discounting the problem of multicollinearity.

Only the significant paths among the background variables, involvement variables, morale, and inmate self-reported adjustment are depicted in the path diagram shown in Figure 12.2. With the exception of those paths leading to inmate self-reported adjustment, the paths are the same for the other two operationalizations of adjustment. Table 12.3 summarizes the significant paths leading to caseworker reported adjustment and to adjustment measured by conduct violations.

Relationships Among Background Variables

The significant bivariate relationships found among the background variables seem to follow intuitive logic. That is, elderly offenders who have a history of incarceration appear to have fewer ties to the outside world as is seen in the negative relationships between being a chronic offender and family contacts (−.34), marital status (−.30), and financial position (−.40). Similarly, married inmates enjoy more frequent family contact (.33), and those with more frequent contacts are in a better financial position (.50), probably due to money provided to them by relatives; although interestingly, there was no significant relationship between marital status and financial position. Health concerns, which appear to be significant problems for elderly inmates, show little relationship to the other background variables investigated.

Background Variables, Involvement, and Inmate-Reported Adjustment

Examination of the path diagram (Figure 12.2) and the summary of significant effects of the model's explanatory variables (Table 12.3) reveals that five of the seven background variables have a significant impact on one of the four independent "involvement" variable concepts. However, only two forms of involvement as measured appear to have a significant impact on the inmate's reported adjustment. Social involvement would appear to have a significant direct positive (.33) relationship to adjustment in this model. Work involvement, on the other hand, would appear to influence adjustment through morale. That is, work involvement has a significant positive relationship with morale (.34) and morale, in turn, displays a significant positive relationship (.24) with adjustment. In this regard, only this "path," of those assessed, would seem to support the model for

Table 12.2.
Zero-Order Correlations for All Study Variables

Variable	Mean	Standard Deviation	1	2	3	4	5	6	7	8	9	10	11	12	13	14	15
1. Conduct Violations — staff reported	.35	.96	1.00														
2. Adjustment — self reported	39.11	4.06	.09	1.00													
3. Adjustment — caseworker reported	5.38	1.72	–.29	.11	1.00												
4. Morale	4.91	1.48	–.06	.23	.36	1.00											
5. Program Involvement	12.15	4.09	.24	.17	.05	.11	1.00										
6. Personal Involvement	21.06	3.41	.11	.14	–.03	.14	.32	1.00									
7. Work Involvement	9.88	3.19	.07	.24	.15	.29	.19	.56	1.00								
8. Social Involvement	16.74	5.31	.31	.30	.06	.07	.47	.38	.34	1.00							
9. Family Contacts	3.11	1.00	–.40	.14	.18	.29	.02	–.03	–.02	.05	1.00						
10. Financial Position	2.46	1.11	–.27	.17	.18	.20	–.15	.03	–.07	.07	.50	1.00					
11. Marital Status	—	—	-.08	.11	–.02	.03	–.19	–.23	–.02	–.20	.33	.08	1.00				
12. Education	10.78	4.32	.11	–.21	–.17	.16	.27	.28	.11	.37	.14	.15	.04	1.00			
13. Time Served	5.85	5.20	.03	.22	–.01	–.02	.09	.32	.28	.18	–.09	–.23	.00	–.07	1.00		
14. Health	2.52	1.40	.06	.24	–.05	.09	.01	.11	.27	.38	–.10	.05	–.22	.06	.13	1.00	
15. Chronic Offender	1.35	.48	.10	.04	–.20	–.28	.05	.22	.13	.06	–.34	–.40	–.30	–.11	.25	.23	1.00

Source: Compiled by authors.

Figure 12.2
Path Diagram for Inmate Reported Measure of Adjustment: Numerical Values and Paths Presented for Significant Coefficients Only

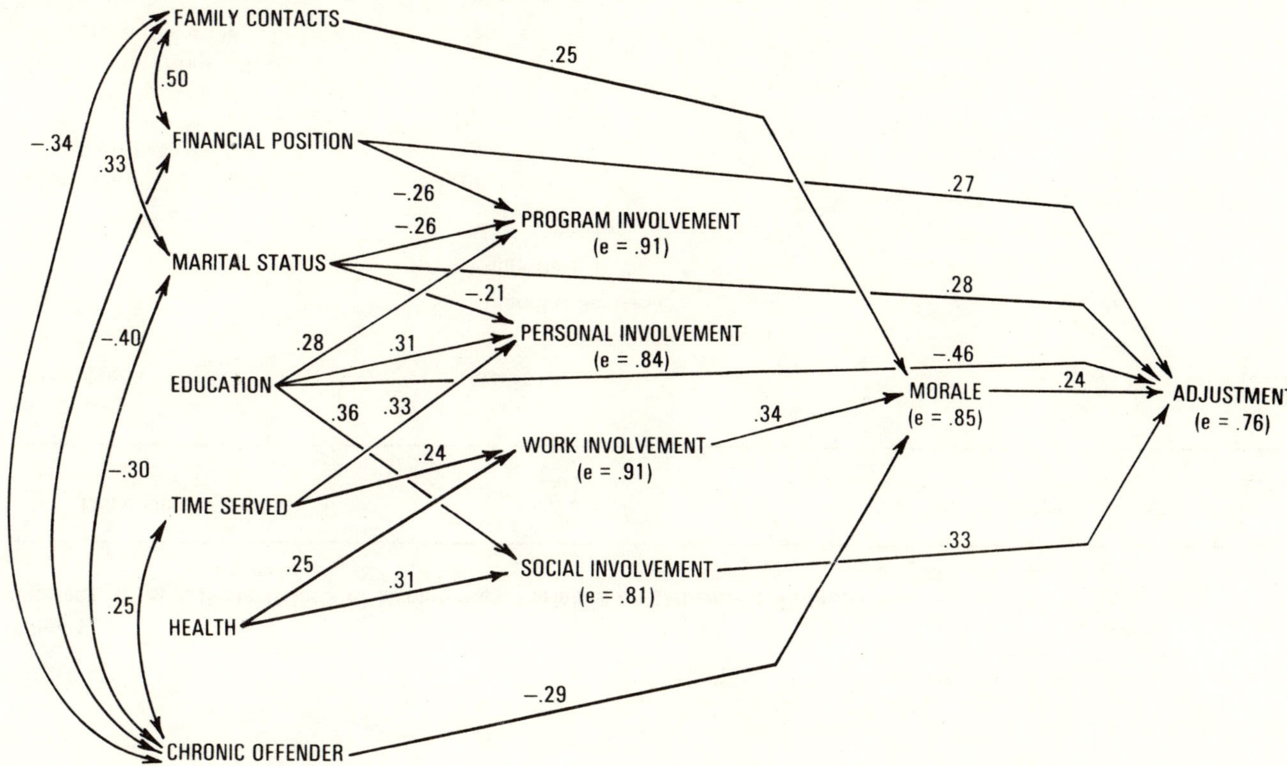

Table 12.3.
Summary of Significant Effects of Explanatory Variables on Dependent Variables

Dependent Variable and R^2	Explanatory Variable	Total Effect (r)	Direct Effect (B)	Total Indirect Effects
Adjustment - Inmate Reported (R^2 = .42)	Morale	.23	.24	-.01
	Social Involvement	.30	.33	-.03
	Financial Position	.17	.27	-.10
	Education	-.21	-.46	.25
	Marital Status	.11	.28	-.17
Adjustment - Caseworker Perception (R^2 = .27)	Morale	.36	.31	.05
	Education	-.17	-.28	.11
Conduct Violations - Staff Reported (R^2 = .32)	Social Involvement	.31	.37	-.06
	Family Contacts	-.40	-.45	.05
Morale (R^2 = .27)	Work Involvement	.29	.34	-.05
	Family Contacts	.29	.25	.04
	Chronic Offender	-.28	-.29	.01

Table 12.3. (continued)

Dependent Variable and R^2	Explanatory Variable	Total Effect (r)	Direct Effect (B)	Total Indirect Effects
Program Involvement (R^2 = .17)	Financial Position	-.15	-.25	.11
	Education	.27	.28	-.01
Personal Involvement (R^2 = .28)	Education	.28	.31	-.03
	Marital Status	-.23	-.21	-.02
	Time Served	.32	.33	-.01
Work Involvement (R^2 = .16)	Time Served	.28	.24	.04
	Health	.27	.25	.02
Social Involvement (R^2 = .33)	Education	.37	.36	.01
	Health	.38	.31	.07

Source: Compiled by authors.

adjustment as originally proposed, that is, certain background variables impact involvement, greater involvement leads to higher morale, and higher morale positively impacts adjustment.

Further examination of these relationships reveals that the two background variables which display significant associations with work involvement are health and time served. The positive relationship (.25) between health and work involvement seems fairly straightforward, in that older, healthier inmates are more likely to be involved in work than those with health problems. The work involvement leads to higher morale, which in turn positively impacts adjustment. The positive relationship between time served and work involvement is probably not as straightforward although the previous research on elderly inmates and prisonization provides the framework for understanding it. Here perhaps we are seeing the concept of "institutional dependency" (Aday and Webster, 1979) in operation. The elderly offender who has been incarcerated longer develops an interinstitutional orientation. That is, he develops support systems within the institutional environment to replace those lost from outside. The inmate with longer time on his sentence is more likely to be involved in work as a mechanism for relieving boredom, gaining a measure of self-worth, achieving status, and earning income. Thus, the work involvement positively impacts morale and indirectly impacts adjustment.

Perhaps as significant as the above were those "paths" that did not appear as hypothesized. Three background variables—financial position, marital status, and education—displayed direct impacts on the dependent variable, adjustment. The moderate positive relationships between family contacts (.25) and adjustment and financial position (.27) and adjustment would suggest that both of these areas are important to elderly inmates in terms of adjustment to prison.

The Education Variable

Perhaps one of the most puzzling linkages revealed in the findings was the association between education and adjustment. Education displayed a significant and fairly substantial direct negative relationship (−.46) with adjustment. This would suggest that the better educated the individual (at least in terms of older inmates), the more poorly he sees himself adjusting to the institution. These individuals may see the institution as less able to satisfy their needs and as more unpleasant than those individuals with less education.

In other words, those individuals with more education have higher expectations than those with less education. Adding even more interest to this relationship is the "path" between education, social involvement, and adjustment. Education displays a significant positive relationship (.36) with social involvement; and social involvement similarly reveals a positive association with adjustment (.33). Viewing the two "paths" of influence simultaneously, it would appear that social involvement ameliorates the negative impact of being educated, as to prison adjustment for elderly inmates. If valid, this finding would be of considerable policy interest to those managing prison programs. It should be noted that health also revealed an indirect linkage to adjustment through social involvement. This finding again lends support to the idea that health is important to the older prisoner in terms of his self-reported adjustment as it does impact both forms of involvement (work through morale and social directly) which contribute to adjustment.

Two background variables, family contacts and chronic offender, displayed an indirect influence on adjustment through morale. However, the relationship was not through involvement but rather directly between the two variables and morale. Family contacts appeared to have a direct significant positive impact on morale (.25) while being a chronic offender displayed a significant negative relationship (−.29) with morale.

Paths Involving Caseworker Perception of Adjustment

Turning to the second path analysis in which the dependent variable—adjustment—was operationalized as the caseworkers' assessment of the inmates' adjustment, many of the relationships observed in the first analysis are again apparent (see Table 12.3). However, what is readily apparent is that only one form of involvement appears to directly or indirectly impact older inmate adjustment as perceived through the eyes of the caseworker. The linkage of background variables influencing involvement, in turn impacting morale, which influences adjustment, does remain for the work involvement variable. The direct impact of social involvement, seen with the self-reported measure of adjustment, disappears in this analysis. The association between morale and adjustment is slightly stronger with this measure of adjustment (.31 as opposed to .24) again emphasizing that higher morale leads to better adjustment in inmates.

Of note in this perspective is the fact that only two of the independent variables, education and morale, show a direct influence on adjustment. Once again, the somewhat surprising negative association between education and adjustment is displayed, although it appears weaker (−.28 as opposed to −.46) for the caseworker perception of adjustment than for the inmate's own perception. However, with social involvement displaying no significant impact directly upon adjustment, the ameliorating impact upon adjustment by this type of involvement becomes a moot point. The other background variables, financial position and marital status, which directly impacted adjustment in the first analysis, do not show a significant relationship to adjustment measured in this manner. This would suggest that these variables are more important to the older individual's concept of being "adjusted" than to others' perceptions of his adjustment.

Also interesting in this analysis is the positive relationship between family contacts (.25) and morale, and the negative association between a chronic offender and morale (−.29). Following the arguments presented earlier, these relationships, and the fact that there is a significant negative association between being a chronic offender and having family contacts (−.34), seem to lend credence to the idea that those elderly inmates who are newer to the prison environment and who have ties to a support system external to the institution have better morale which promotes better adjustment.

Paths Involving Conduct Violation Measure of Adjustment

Finally, the third analysis of adjustment took on a slightly different perspective. While the first two measures of adjustment were primarily attitudinal assessments, the third analysis operationalized adjustment as a behavioral measure—conduct violations. Again reviewing the relationships revealed in the "paths," some distinct differences exist between the first two analyses. In this formulation, the hypothesized linkages between background variables, involvement, morale, and adjustment simply do not appear. While there are linkages from the background variables through work and social involvement to morale, a significant association between morale and conduct violations, that is, adjustment, does not exist. Two independent variables do show direct impacts upon conduct violations. Family contacts display a significant negative (−.45) relationship with the dependent variable, arguing that families appear to influence elderly inmates to "behave themselves." On the other hand, older inmates who are more socially involved in the prison milieu are more likely to be involved in disciplinary infractions (.37). Again, this might argue for the existence of different prison adjustment mechanisms for elderly prisoners. One group has not been socialized into the prison culture and maintains a support system external to the institutional environment. The second group, more "experienced" inmates, are involved with the internal prison milieu for a support structure and nurturance. In the last analysis these individuals would be more likely to engage in behavior that was officially sanctioned as inappropriate by the prison administration.

CONCLUSIONS

This study proposed a model to explain why certain elderly prison inmates were better adjusted than others. The model hypothesized temporal ordered variable relationships involving certain individual background characteristics, inmate involvement, morale, and adjustment. Results obtained from path analysis did not entirely support the model, although predicted linkages did appear for work involvement in two of the operationalizations.

The dependent variable, adjustment, was operationalized in three ways: inmate-reported adjustment, caseworker-reported adjustment, and conduct violations. Support was given in each instance to the idea that adjustment results from an interaction of background or "extra-prison" variables and situational or "intra-prison" variables. Depending upon the operationalization of adjustment, all seven of the background variables—family contacts, financial position, marital status, education, time served, health, and chronicity of offender—are important to elderly inmates in terms of their adjustment to prison. Of these variables, three—family contacts, education, and health—seem to directly or indirectly affect all three conceptualizations of adjustment. The positive impact of family contact on morale, which in turn positively impacts adjustment, would suggest the importance of this variable to elderly offenders. In a similar fashion, contact with the family tends to reduce conduct violations. The rather straightforward policy implication of this relationship is that programs which increase family contact and foster outside support mechanisms for the elderly prisoner should be maximized.

As would intuitively be expected, health concerns become a major factor in adjustment for older inmates. The characteristic does not directly impact upon adjustment, but rather has an indirect "path" of influence by increasing or decreasing the inmates' ability to be involved in social or work activities. Again, these involvements directly or indirectly impact "adjustment."

However, two forms of involvement, personal involvement and program involvement, did not impact directly or indirectly upon adjustment in either of the three model versions. Particularly interesting about the lack of impact of personal or program involvement is that despite the fact that elderly offenders engage in some of these activities fairly often, they appear to bear little relationship to adjustment, even when it is measured as a subjective phenomenon by the inmate.

The policy implications of these findings for correctional management run in sharp contrast to current practice. Because elderly inmates are a small and relatively easily "managed" subgroup, they have a low visibility. In this vein, they share commonalities with their free world counterparts. Predominant correctional programs, which are directed toward education, learning a legitimate occupation, and personal development, and which are geared toward returning the offender to mainstream society, have little relevance for this age group. Perhaps the notion of prison "retirement communities," addressing the particular needs of this age group, would be more appropriate for those elderly inmates who spend their final years in an institution. For those older offenders who have the opportunity of returning to society, programs geared toward community adjustment, education about available social agency support, and maintaining family contacts would appear to be more beneficial than those programs now generally available.

Bibliography

Abrams, A. J. 1984. Foreword. In *Elderly Criminals*, edited by E. Newman, D. Newman, and M. Gewirtz, pp. xi-xviii. Cambridge: Oelgeschlager, Gunn and Hain.

Adams, Mark E., and Clyde B. Vedder. 1961. "Aged and Crime: Medical and Sociologic Characteristics of Prisoners over 50." *Geriatrics* 16:177-81.

Aday, Ronald H. 1984. "Criminals." In *Handbook of the Aged in the United States,* edited by Erdman B. Palmore, pp. 295-309. Westport, CT: Greenwood Press.

Aday, R. H., and E. L. Webster. 1979. "Aging in Prison: The Development of a Preliminary Model." *Offender Rehabilitation* 3:271-82.

Adler, Freda. 1975. *Sisters in Crime*. New York: McGraw-Hill.

Agnew, Robert. 1985a. "Social Control Theory and Delinquency: A Longitudinal Test." *Criminology* 23:47-61.

______. 1985b. "A Revised Strain Theory of Delinquency." *Social Forces* 64:151-67.

Akers, Ronald L. 1973. *Deviant Behavior: A Social Learning Approach.* Belmont, CA: Wadsworth.

______. 1977. *Deviant Behavior: A Social Learning Approach.* 2nd ed. Belmont, CA: Wadsworth.

______. 1984. "Delinquent Behavior, Drugs, and Alcohol: What is the Relationship." *Today's Delinquent* 3:19-47.

______. 1985. *Deviant Behavior: A Social Learning Approach.* 3rd ed. Belmont, CA: Wadsworth.

Akers, Ronald L., and John K. Cochran. 1985. "Adolescent Marijuana Use: A Test of Three Theories of Deviant Behavior." *Deviant Behavior* 6:323-46.

Akers, Ronald L., Robert L. Burgess, and Weldon Johnson. 1968. "Opiate Use, Addiction, and Relapse." *Social Problems* 15:459-69.

Akers, R. L., M. D. Krohn, L. Lanza-Kaduce, and M. J. Radosevich. 1979. Social Learning and Deviant Behavior: A Specific Test of a General Theory." *American Sociological Review* 44:636-55.

Akers, Ronald L., Anthony J. La Greca, John Cochran, and Christine Sellers. 1986. "Alcohol Behavior Among the Elderly: A Test of Social Learning Theory." Unpublished manuscript, Gainesville, FL: University of Florida.

Aldrich, J., and F. Nelson. 1984. *Linear Probability, Logit, and Probit Models.* Sage University Paper series on Quantitative Applications in the Social Sciences, series no. 07-045. Beverly Hills: Sage.

Alschuler, Albert W. 1975. "The Prosecutor's Role in Plea Bargaining." *University of Chicago Law Review* 36:50-59.

______. 1976. "The Trial Judge's Role in Plea Bargaining: Part I." *Columbia Law Review* 76:1,059-1,154.

______. 1979. "Plea Bargaining and Its History." *Law and Society Review* 13:211-45.

Alter, J. 1983. "Why Crime Is on the Decline." *Newsweek*, September 26, pp. 37-38.

American Association of Retired Persons. 1985. *A Profile of Older Americans.* Washington, D.C.: American Association of Retired Persons.

American Broadcasting Corporation. 1983. *This Week.* Interview with William Webster, Director, Federal Bureau of Investigation.

American Law Institute. 1962. *Model Penal Code.* Proposed Official Draft.

Ando, Albert, and Franco Modigliani. 1963. "The 'Life-Cycle' Hypothesis of Saving: Aggregate Implications and Tests." *American Economic Review* 53, 1:55-84.

Andrews, D. A. 1980. "Some Experimental Investigation of the Principles of Differential Association Through Deliberate Manipulations of the Structure of Service Systems." *American Sociological Review* 45:448-62.

Apao, William K., and Amy M. Damon. 1982. "Locus of Control and the Quantity-Frequency Index of Alcohol Use." *Journal of Studies on Alcohol* 43:233-39.

Armstrong, Gail. 1977. "Females Under The Law—Protected But Unequal." *Crime and Delinquency* 23:109-20.

Avio, K. L., and C. S. Clark. 1976. *Property Crime in Canada: An Econometric Study.* Ontario Council of Economic Research Studies, Ontario, Canada.

Bachand, Donald J. 1983. "The Elderly Offender: A Question of Leniency in Criminal Processing." Paper presented at the 78th Annual Meeting of the American Sociological Association, Detroit, MI, August 31-September 4.

______. 1984. "The Elderly Offender: An Exploratory Study with Implications for Continuing Education of Law Enforcement Personnel." Ph.D. diss., University of Michigan.

Baier, George F. 1961. "The Aged Inmate." *American Journal of Corrections* 23:4-6, 30, 34.

Baldwin, John D., and Janice I. Baldwin. 1981. *Behavior Principles in Everyday Life.* Englewood Cliffs, NJ: Prentice-Hall.

Barlow, Hugh D. 1984. *Introduction to Criminology.* 3rd ed. Boston: Little, Brown.

Barnes, Grace M. 1979. "Alcohol Use Among Older Persons: Findings from a Western New York State General Population Survey." *Journal of the American Geriatric Society* 17:244-50.

Becker, Gary S. 1968. "Crime and Punishment: An Economic Approach." *Journal of Political Economy* 76, 2:169-217.

______. 1974. "Crime and Punishment: An Economic Approach." In *Essays in the Economics of Crime and Punishment,* edited by Gary S. Becker and William M. Landes, pp. 1-54. New York: Columbia University Press.

Belknap, Michael. 1977. "The Merchants of Repression." *Crime and Social Justice* 7:49-58.

Bergman, Simon, and Menachem Amir. 1973. "Crime and Delinquency Among the Aged in Israel." *Geriatrics* 28:149-57.

Berk, R. A., K. J. Lenihan, and P. H. Rossi. 1980a. "Crime and Poverty: Some Experimental Evidence from Ex-Offenders." *American Sociological Review* 45:766-86.

______. 1980b. *Money, Work and Crime: Experimental Evidence.* New York: Academic.

Best, J., and G. T. Horiuchi. 1985. "The Razor Blade in the Apple: The Social Construction of Urban Legends." *Social Problems* 32:488-99.

Black, D. 1971. "The Social Organization of Arrest." *Stanford Law Review* 23:1,087-1,111.

______. 1976. *The Behavior of Law.* New York: Academic Press.

Blumberg, Abraham. 1970. *The Scales of Justice.* Chicago: Aldine.

______. 1979. *Criminal Justice.* 2nd ed. New York: New Viewpoints.

Blumer, Herbert. 1971. "Social Problems as Collective Behavior." *Social Problems* 18:298-306.

Borgatta, E. F., R. J. W. Montgomery, and M. L. Borgatta. 1982. "Alcohol Use and Abuse, Life Crisis Events, and the Elderly." *Research on Aging* 4:378-408.

Brereton, David, and Jonathan Casper. 1981. "Does It Pay to Plead Guilty? Differential Sentencing and the Functioning of the Criminal Courts." *Law and Society Review* 16:45-70.

Briar, Scott, and Irving Piliavin. 1965. "Delinquency, Situational Inducements, and Commitment to Conformity." *Social Problems* 13:35-45.

Brickfield, Cyril. 1982. "Media Reports on Crime, Elderly Are Sensational and Deceptive." *American Association of Retired Persons News Bulletin* 23:11.

Bureau of the Census. 1966-1985. *Statistical Abstract of the United States: 1967-1986.* Washington, D.C.: U.S. Government Printing Office.

______. 1971. *Population Estimates and Projections* (December 1971). Series P-25, No. 470, pp. 13-14. Washington, D.C.: GPO.

______. 1972. *Population Estimates and Projections* (April 1972). Series P-25, No. 483, p. 3. Washington, D.C.: GPO.

______. 1975. *Historical Statistics of the United States, Colonial Times to 1970.* Bicentennial edition, Part 1. Washington, D.C.: GPO.

Burgess, Robert L., and Ronald L. Akers. 1966. "A Differential Association-Reinforcement Theory of Criminal Behavior." *Social Problems* 14:128-47.

Burnett, C., and S. T. Ortega. 1984. "Elderly Offenders: A Descriptive Analysis." In *Elderly Criminals,* edited by W. Wilbanks and P. Kim, pp. 17-40. New York: University Press of America.

Cain, L. 1979. "Aging Behind Prison Walls." Paper presented at Pacific Sociological Association Meeting, Anaheim, CA.

Carney, F. 1971. "Evaluation of Psychotherapy in a Maximum Security Prison." *Seminars in Psychiatry* 3:363.

Carp, F. M. 1966. *A Future for the Aged: Victoria Plaza and Its Residents.* Austin, TX: University of Texas Press.

Carr-Hill, R. A., and N. H. Stern. 1973. "An Econometric Model of the Supply and Control of Recorded Offences in England and Wales." *Journal of Public Economics* 2:289-318.

Cavender, Gray. 1984. "Justice, Sanctioning, and the Justice Model." *Criminology* 22:203-13.

Champion, Dean J. 1981. *Basic Statistics for Social Research.* New York: Macmillan.

______. 1987. "Felony Offenders, Plea Bargaining, and Probation." *The Justice Professional* (forthcoming, Fall 1987).

Chassin, Laurie, Clark C. Presson, Michell Bensenber, Eric Corty, Richard W. Olshavsky, and Steven J. Sherman. 1981. "Predicting Adolescents' Intentions to Smoke Cigarettes." *Journal of Health and Social Behavior* 22:445-55.

Chein, C. P., B. A. Strotsky, and J. O. Cole. 1973. "Psychiatric Treatment for Nursing Home Patients: Drug, Alcohol and Milieu." *American Journal of Psychiatry* 130:543-48.

Chesney-Lind, Meda. 1977. "Judicial Paternalism and the Female Status Offender: Training Women to Know Their Place." *Crime and Delinquency.* 23:121-30.

Church, Thomas, Jr. 1976. "Plea Bargaining, Concessions, and the Courts: Analysis of a Quasi-Experiment." *Law and Society Review* 10:377-401.

______. 1979. "In Defense of 'Bargain Justice.'" *Law and Society Review* 13:509-25.

Clark, A. W. 1968. "The Personality and Social Network Adjustment Scale: Its Use in the Evaluation of Treatment in a Therapeutic Community." *Human Relations* 31:68-95.

Clemmer, D. [1940] 1958. *The Prison Community.* New York: Holt, Rinehart and Winston.

Cloward, Richard, and Lloyd Ohlin. 1959. "Illegitimate Means, Anomie, and Deviant Behavior." *American Sociological Review* 24:164-77.

______. 1960. *Delinquency and Opportunity: A Theory of Delinquent Gangs.* Glencoe: Free Press.

Cochrane, Donald, and Guy H. Orcutt. 1949. "Application of Least Squares Regression to Relationships Containing Autocorrelated Error Terms." *Journal of the American Statistical Association* 44:32-61.

Cohen, Ben-Zion, G. Fishman, and J. Soroka. 1985. "Judicial Discretion and Sentencing Disparity in Adult Felony Courts in Israel." *Journal of Criminal Justice* 13:99-115.

Cohen, Albert K. 1955. *Delinquent Boys: The Structure of the Gang.* Glencoe: Free Press.

Cohen, Fred. 1984. "Old Age as a Criminal Defense." In *Elderly Criminals,* edited by E. Newman, D. Newman, and M. Gewirtz, pp. 113-41. Cambridge: Oelgeschlager, Gunn and Hain.

Cohen, Lawrence, and Marcus Felson. 1979. "Social Change and Crime Rate Trends: A Routine Approach." *American Sociological Review* 44:588-608.

Cole, Stephen. 1975. "The Growth of Scientific Knowledge: Theories of Deviance as a Case Study." In *The Idea of Social Structure: Papers in Honor of Robert K. Merton*, edited by L. Coser, pp. 175-220. New York: Harcourt, Brace, Jovanovich.

Collins, James J. 1981a. "Alcohol Use and Criminal Behavior: An Empirical, Theoretical, and Methodological Overview." In *Drinking and Crime,* edited by James J. Collins, pp. 288-316. New York: Guilford.

_____. 1981b. "Alcohol Careers and Criminal Careers." In *Drinking and Crime*, edited by James J. Collins, pp. 152-206. New York: Guilford.

Columbia Broadcasting Corporation. 1982. *60 Minutes.*

Conger, Rand. 1976. "Social Control and Social Learning Models of Delinquency: A Synthesis." *Criminology* 14:17-40.

Cook, B. B. 1973. "Sentencing Behavior of Federal Judges, Draft Cases, 1972." *University of Cincinnati Law Review* 42:597-633.

Cotton, Nancy S. 1979. "Familial Incidence of Alcoholism: A Review." *Journal of Studies on Alcohol* 40:89-116.

Cramer, James A. 1981. *Courts and Judges.* Beverly Hills: Sage.

Creecy, R. F., W. Berg, and R. Wright, Jr. 1985. "Loneliness Among the Elderly: A Causal Approach." *Journal of Gerontology* 40, 4:487-93.

Cullen, Francis T., John F. Wozniak, and James Frank. 1985. "The Rise of the Elderly Offender: Will a 'New' Criminal be Invented?" *Crime and Social Justice* 15:151-65.

Cunniff, Mark A. 1985. *Felony Sentencing in 18 Local Jurisdictions.* Washington, D.C.: U.S. Department of Justice, Bureau of Justice Statistics.

Curran, Debra. 1983. "Characteristics of the Elderly Shoplifter and the Effect of Sanctions and Recidivism." Paper presented at the Annual Elderly Offender Conference, Miami, FL., February 23-25.

Curran, D. 1984. "Characteristics of the Elderly Shoplifter and the Effect of Sanctions on Recidivism." In *Elderly Criminals,* edited by W. Wilbanks and P. K. H. Kim, p. 123. New York: University Press of America.

Currie, Elliott P. 1972. "Crimes Without Criminals: Witchcraft and Its Control in Renaissance Europe." *Law and Society Review* 6:7-32.

Cutshall, C., and K. Adams. 1983. "Responding to Older Offenders: Age Selectivity in the Processing of Shoplifters." *Criminal Justice Review* 8:1.

Danziger, Sheldon, and David Wheeler. 1975. "Malevolent Interdependence Income Inequality and Crime." Readings in Correctional Economics, Correctional Economics Center of the American Bar Association, Washington, D.C., pp. 35-66.

Datesman, Susan, and Frank Scarpitti. 1975. "Female Delinquency and Broken Homes." *Criminology* 13:33-55.

Daugherty, J. 1982. "Crime: Old Problem with Old Twist." *Miami Herald,* August 1, p. 1B.

DeFronzo, James. 1983. "Economic Assistance to Impoverished Americans: Relationship to Incidence of Crime." *Criminology* 21, 1:119-36.

Dickinson, George, and Alban Wheeler. 1980. "The Elderly in Prison," *Corrections Today* 42:10.

Dickson, Donald. 1969. "Bureaucracy and Morality: An Organizational Perspective on a Moral Crusade." *Social Problems* 16:143-56.

Dupree, L. W., H. Broskowski, and L. Schonfeld. 1984. "The Gerontology Alcohol Project: A Behavioral Treatment Program for Elderly Alcohol Abusers." *The Gerontologist* 24:510-16.

Durbin, J., and G. S. Watson. 1950. "Testing for Serial Correlation in Least-Squares Regression, I." *Biometrika* 37:409-28.

______. 1951. "Testing for Serial Correlation in Least-Squares Regression, II." *Biometrika* 38:159-78.

Durkheim, Emile. 1951. *Suicide: A Study in Sociology*. Translated by John A. Spaulding and George Simpson. New York: The Free Press.

Ehrlich, Isaac. 1970. "Participation in Illegitimate Activities: An Economic Analysis." Ph.D. diss., Columbia University.

Ehrlich, Isaac. 1973. "Participation in Illegitimate Activities: A Theoretical and Empirical Investigation." *Journal of Political Economy* 81:521-65.

______. 1974. "Participation in Illegitimate Activities: An Economic Analysis." In *Essays in the Economics of Crime and Punishment,* edited by Gary S. Becker and William M. Landes, pp. 68-134. New York: Columbia University Press.

Eisenstein, J., and H. Jacob. 1977. *Felony Justice: An Organizational Analysis of Criminal Courts*. Boston: Little, Brown.

Elliott, Delbert S. 1966. "Delinquency and Perceived Opportunity." *Sociological Quarterly* 32:216-27.

Elliott, Delbert S., David Huizinga, and Suzanne S. Ageton. 1985. *Explaining Delinquency and Drug Use*. Beverly Hills: Sage Publications.

Embree, Scotty. 1977. "The State Department as Moral Entrepreneur: Racism and Imperialism as Factors in the Passage of the Harrison Narcotics Act." In *Corrections and Punishment,* edited by David F. Greenberg, pp. 193-204. Beverly Hills: Sage Publications.

Epstein, K., C. Mills, and A. Simon. 1970. "Antisocial Behavior of the Elderly." *Comprehensive Psychiatry* 11:36.

Eysenck, J. B. G., J. Rust, and H. J. Eysenck. 1977. "Personality and the Classification of Adult Offenders." *British Journal of Criminology* 17:169-79.

Farnworth, M., and P. M. Horan. 1980. "Separate Justice: An Analysis of Race Differences in Court Processes." *Social Science Research* 9:381-99.

Farr, Kathryn Ann. 1984. "Administration and Justice: Maintaining Balance Through an Institutionalized Plea Negotiation Process." *Criminology* 22:291-319.

Federal Bureau of Investigation. 1965-1984. *Crime in the United States*. Washington, D.C.: U.S. Government Printing Office.

______. 1985. *Crime in the United States, 1984*. Washington, D.C.: GPO.

______. 1985. *Uniform Crime Reports, 1974, 1979, 1984*. Washington, D.C.: GPO.

Feeley, Malcolm M. 1983. *Court Reform on Trial: Why Simple Solutions Fail. A Twentieth Century Fund Report*. New York: Basic Books.

______. 1982. "Plea Bargaining and the Structure of Criminal Process." *The Justice System Journal* 7:338-54.

______. 1979. *The Process Is the Punishment: Handling Cases in a Lower Criminal Court*. New York: Russell Sage.

Feeney, R., F. Dill, and A. Weir. 1983. *Arrest Without Conviction: How Often They Occur and Why*. Washington, D.C.: U.S. Department of Justice, National Institute of Justice.

Feinberg, Gary. 1984a. "A Profile of the Elderly Shoplifter." In *Elderly Criminals,* edited by E. Newman, D. Newman, and M. Gewirtz, p. 35-50. Cambridge: Oelgeschlager, Gunn and Hain.

______. 1984b. "White-Haired Offenders: An Emergent Social Problem." In *Elderly Criminals,* edited by William Wilbanks and Paul K. H. Kim, pp. 83-108. New York: University Press of America.

Feinberg, Gary, and Dinesh Khosla. 1985. "Sanctioning Elderly Delinquents." *Trial* 21:46-56.

Feinberg, G., S. Glugover, and I. Zwetchkenbaum. 1984. "The Broward Senior Intervention and Education Program: A Pilot Program." In *Elderly Criminals*, edited by E. Newman, D. Newman and M. Gewirtz, p. 177. Cambridge: Oelgeschlager, Gunn and Hain.

Fishman, Mark. 1978. "Crime Waves as Ideology." *Social Problems* 25:531-43.

Fleisher, B. M. 1963. "The Effects of Unemployment on Juvenile Delinquency." *Journal of Political Economy* 71, 6:543-55.

______. 1966. *The Economics of Delinquency*. Chicago: Quadrangle Books.

Forsyth, Craig, and Neal Shover. 1986. "No Rest for the Weary . . . Constructing a Problem of Elderly Crime." *Sociological Focus* 19: (forthcoming).

Fox, J. 1984. *Linear Statistical Models and Related Methods: With Applications to Social Research.* New York: John Wiley and Sons.

Frazier, C. E., and E. W. Bock. 1982. "Effects of Court Officials on Sentence Severity: Do Judges Make a Difference? *Criminology* 20:257-72.

Friedland, N. S. Maital, and A. Rutenberg. 1978. "A Simulation Study of Income Tax Evasion." *Journal of Public Economics* 10:107-16.

Friedman, Lawrence. 1979. "Plea Bargaining in Historical Perspective." *Law and Society Review* 13:253-60.

Fry, Lincoln. 1984. "The Implications of Diversion for Older Offenders." In *Elderly Criminals,* edited by W. Wilbanks and P. Kim, pp. 143-56. New York: University Press of America.

______. 1987. "The Older Inmate: A Profile." *The Justice Professional.* (In press).

Fyfe, James J. 1984. "Police Dilemmas in Processing Elderly Offenders." In *Elderly Criminals,* edited by E. Newman, D. Newman, and M. Gewirtz, pp. 91-111. Cambridge: Oelgeschlager, Gunn and Hain.

Gertz, Marc G., and Albert C. Price. 1985. "Variables Influencing Sentencing Severity: Intercourt Differences in Connecticut." *Journal of Criminal Justice* 13:131-39.

Gibbs, J. 1982. "Disruption and Distress: Going From the Street to Jail." In *Coping with Imprisonment,* edited by N. Parisi, pp. 27-44. Beverly Hills: Sage Publications.

Gibson, J. L. 1978. "Race as a Determinant of Criminal Sentences: A Methodological Critique and a Case Study." *Law and Society Review* 12:455-77.

Gillespie, Michael W., and John R. Galliher. 1972. "Age, Anomie, and the Inmates Definition of Aging in Prison: An Exploratory Study." In *Research Planning and Action for the Elderly,* edited by Donald F. Kent, Robert Kostenbaun, and Sylvia Sherwood, pp. 465-83. New York: Behavioral Publications.

Glaser, Daniel, and Kent Rice. 1959. "Crime, Age and Employment." *American Sociological Review* 24, 5:679-86.

Glatt, M. M., A. J. Rosin, and P. Jauhar. 1978. "Alcoholic Problems in the Elderly." *Age and Aging* 7:64-71.

Goetting, Ann. 1983. "The Elderly in Prison: Issues and Perspectives." *Journal of Research in Crime and Delinquency* 20:291-309.

______. 1984. "Prison Programs and Facilities for Elderly Inmates." In *Elderly Criminals,* edited by E. S. Newman, D. J. Newman, and M. L. Gewirtz, pp. 169-75. Cambridge: Oelgeschalger, Gunn and Hain.

Goffman, Erving. 1961. *Asylums.* Garden City, NY: Doubleday Anchor.

Golden, D. 1984. "Elderly Offenders in Jail." In *Elderly Criminals,* edited by E. Newman, D. Newman, and M. Gewirtz, p. 143. Cambridge: Oelgeschlager, Gunn and Hain.

Goldsmith, Jack, and Sharon S. Goldsmith. 1976. *Crime and the Elderly.* Lexington, MA: Lexington Books.

Gordon, Margaret, and Linda Heath. 1981. "The News Business, Crime and Fear." In *Reactions to Crime,* edited by Dan A. Lewis, pp. 227-50. Beverly Hills: Sage Publications.

Gouldner, Alvin W. 1968. "The Sociologist as Partisan: Sociology and the Welfare State." *The American Sociologist* 3:103-16.

Green, E. 1961. *Judicial Attitudes in Sentencing.* New York: St. Martin's Press.

Greenberg, David F. 1985. "Age, Crime, and Social Explanation." *American Journal of Sociology* 91:1-21.

Greenwood, Michael J., and Walter J. Wadycki. 1973. "Crime Rates and Public Expenditures for Police Protection: Their Interaction." *Review of Social Economy* 31:138-51.

______. 1976. "Crime Rates and Public Expenditures for Police Protection: Their Interaction." In *The Economics of Crime and Law Enforcement,* edited by Lee R. McPheters and William B. Stronge, pp. 360-75. Springfield, IL: Charles C. Thomas.

Greenwood, Peter W., Sorrell Wildhorn, Eugene C. Poggio, Michael J. Strumweisser, and Peter De Leon. 1976. *Prosecution of Felony Defendants.* MA.: D. C. Heath.

Gutmann, P. M. 1977. "The Subterranean Economy." *Financial Analysts Journal* 33:26-27, 34.

Hagan, Frank E. 1986. *Introduction to Criminology.* Chicago: Nelson-Hall.

Hagan, J. 1973. "Labeling and Deviance: A Case Study in the Sociology of the Interesting." *Social Problems* 20:447-58.

______. 1974. "Extra-Legal Attributes and Criminal Sentencing: An Assessment of a Sociological Viewpoint." *Law and Society Review* 8:357-83.

______. 1975. "The Social and Legal Construction of Criminal Justice: A Study of the Pre-Sentencing Process." *Social Problems* 22:620-37.

Hagan, J., and C. Albonetti. 1980. "The Differential Sentencing of White Collar Offenders in Ten Federal District Courts." *American Sociological Review* 45:802-20.

Hahn, Paul H. 1976. *Crimes Against the Elderly: A Study in Victimology.* Santa Cruz: Davis.

Haller, Mark H. 1979. "Plea Bargaining: The Nineteenth Century Context." *Law and Society Review* 13:273-79.

Ham, Joseph Neal. 1976a. "The Forgotten Minority: An Exploration of Long Term Institutionalized Aged and Aged Male Prison Inmates." Ph.D. diss., University of Michigan.

______. 1976b. *The Forgotten Minority . . . An Exploration of Long-Term Institutionalized Aged and Aging Prison Inmates.* Washington, D.C.: National Institute of Law Enforcement, U.S. Department of Justice.

______. 1980. "Aged and Infirm: Male Prison Inmates." *Aging* (July-August): 24-31.

Harlow, C. 1985. "Reporting Crimes to the Police." Bureau of Justice Statistics Special Report. Washington, D.C.: U.S. Government Printing Office.

Harper, T. 1982. "An Elderly Crime Wave? Aged Offenders Tax Criminal Justice System." *National Law Journal* 4:1.

Harris, Diana K., and William E. Cole. 1980. *Sociology of Aging.* Boston: Houghton Mifflin.

Hendin, Herbert. 1982. *Suicide in America.* New York: Norton.

Henry, James. 1976. "Calling in the Big Bills." *Washington Monthly* (May):27-33.

Hepburn, John R. 1976. "Testing Alternative Models of Delinquency Causation." *Journal of Criminal Law and Criminology* 67:450-60.

Heumann, M. 1975. "A Note on Plea Bargaining and Case Pressure." *Law and Society Review* 9:515-28.

Heumann, M., and Colin Loftin. 1979. "Mandatory Sentencing and the Abolition of Plea Bargaining: The Michigan Felony Firearms Statute." *Law and Society Review* 13:393-431.

Hindelang, Michael J. 1973. "Causes of Delinquency: A Partial Replication and Extension." *Social Problems* 20:471-87.

______. 1976. *Criminal Victimization in Eight American Cities: A Descriptive Analysis of Common Theft and Assault.* Cambridge: Ballinger.

Hirschi, Travis. 1969. *Causes of Delinquency.* Berkeley: University of California Press.

Hirschi, Travis, and Michael Gottfredson. 1983. "Age and the Explanation of Crime." *American Journal of Sociology* 89, 3:552-84.

Holmes, Malcom, and Howard C. Daudistel. 1984. "Ethnicity and Justice in the Southwest: Sentencing of Anglo, Black, and Mexican Origin Defendants." *Social Science Quarterly* 65:265-77.

Holzer, C., L. Robins, J. Meyers, M. Weissman, G. Tischler, P. Leaf, J. Anthony, and P. Bednarski. 1984. "Antecedents and Correlates of Alcohol Abuse and Dependence in the Elderly." In *Nature and Extent of Alcohol Problems Among the Elderly*, edited by George Maddox, Lee Robins, and Nathan Rosenberg, pp. 217-44. DHHS No. 84-1321. Washington, D.C.: U.S. Government Printing Office.

Hopkins, A. 1977. "Is There a Class Bias in Criminal Sentencing?" *American Sociological Review* 42:176-77.

Hubbard, R. W., J. F. Santos, and M. A. Santos. 1979. "Alcohol and Older Adults: Overt and Covert Influences." *Social Casework*. 60:166-70.

Hucker, S. 1984. "Psychiatric Aspects of Crime and Old Age." In *Elderly Criminals*, edited by E. Newman, D. Newman, and M. Gewirtz, p. 67. Cambridge: Oelgeschlager, Gunn and Hain.

Hucker, S. J., and M. H. Ben-Aron. 1984. "Violent Elderly Offenders: A Comparative Study." In *Elderly Criminals,* edited by W. Wilbanks and P. Kim, pp. 69-81. New York: University Press of America.

Humphries, Drew. 1981. "Serious Crime, News Coverage, and Ideology: A Content Analysis of Crime Coverage in a Metropolitcan Paper." *Crime and Delinquency* 27:199-205.

Hyman, J. M. 1979. "Philosophical Implications of Plea Bargaining: Some Comments." *Law and Society Review* 13:565-66.

Irwin, J. 1980. *Prisons in Turmoil.* Boston: Little, Brown.

Jacobs, J. B. 1977. *Stateville: The Penitentiary in Mass Society.* Chicago: University of Chicago Press.

Jaros, D., and R. I. Mendelsohn. 1967. "The Judicial Role and Sentencing Behavior." *Midwest Journal of Political Science* 11:471-88.

Jendrek, Margaret Platt. 1983. "Judge-Jury Options. Factors Involved in Counsel Decisions." *Free Inquiry in Creative Sociology* 11:175-81.

Jensen, Gary F. 1972. "Parents, Peers, and Delinquent Actions: A Test of the Differential Association Perspective." *American Journal of Sociology* 78:68-72.

______. 1977. "Age and Rule Breaking in Prison—A Test of Two Sociocultural Interpretations." *Criminology* 14:555.

Jessor, Richard, and Shirley L. Jessor. 1977. *Problem Behavior and Psychosocial Development: A Longitudinal Study of Youth.* New York: Academic Press.

Johnston, J. 1984. *Econometric Methods.* New York: McGraw-Hill.

Jones, E. Terrence. 1973. "Evaluating Everyday Policies: Police Activity and Crime Incidence." *Urban Affairs Quarterly* 8:267-79.

______. 1974. "The Impact of Crime Rate Changes on Police Protection Expenditures in American Cities." *Criminology* 11:516-24.

Jurik, Nancy C. 1983. "The Economics of Female Recidivism: A Study of TARP Women Ex-Offenders." *Criminology* 21, 4:603-22.

Kalven,Harry, and Hans Zeisel. 1966. *The American Jury.* Boston: Little, Brown.

Keller, O., and C. Vedder. 1968. "Crimes That Old Persons Commit." *Gerontologist* 8:43.

Kelly, H. E. 1976. "Comparison of Defense Strategy and Race as Influences in Differential Sentencing." *Criminology* 14:241-49.

Kelsey, O. W. 1986. "Elderly Inmates: Providing Safe and Humane Care." *Corrections Magazine* 48, 3:56-58.

Kerlinger, F. N., and E. J. Pedhazur. 1973. *Multiple Regression in Behavioral Research.* New York: Holt, Rinehart and Winston, pp. 305-31.

Kipnis, Kenneth. 1976. "Criminal Justice and the Negotiated Plea." *Ethics* 86:93-106.

Kleck, G. 1981. "Racial Discrimination in Criminal Sentencing: A Critical Evaluation of Evidence with Additional Evidence on the Death Penalty." *American Sociological Review* 46:783-805.

Koppel, Herbert. 1984. *Sentencing Practices in 13 States.* Washington, D.C.: U.S. Department of Justice, Bureau of Justice Statistics.

Krajick, Kevin. 1979a. "Growing Old in Prison." *Corrections Magazine* (March):34.

______. 1979b. "Project 60: Dignity and Freedom." *Corrections Magazine* 5:44-46.

Krohn, M. D., L. Lanza-Kaduce, and R. L. Akers. 1984. "Community Context and Theories of Deviant Behavior." *Sociological Quarterly* 25:353-71.

Krohn, Marvin D., and James L. Massey. 1980. "Social Control and Delinquent Behavior: An Examination of the Elements of the Social Bond." *Sociological Quarterly* 21:545-61.

Krohn, Marvin D., James L. Massey, William Skinner, and Ronald M. Lauer. 1983. "Social Bonding Theory and Adolescent Cigarette Smoking: A Longitudinal Analysis." *Journal of Health and Social Behavior* 24:337-49.

Krohn, M. D., W. F. Skinner, J. Massey, and R. L. Akers. 1985. "Social Learning Theory and Adolescent Cigarette Smoking: A Longitudinal Study." *Social Problems* 32:455-71.

LaFave, W. L. 1970. "The Prosecutor's Discretion in the United States." *American Journal of Comparative Law* 18:532-48.

Lagoy, Stephen P., Joseph J. Senna, and Larry J. Siegel. 1976. "An Empirical Study of Information Usage for Prosecutorial Decision-Making in Plea Negotiations." *American Criminal Law Review* 13:435-49.

La Greca, Anthony J., and Silvi Dzegede. 1980. "Residential Segregation and Centrality: A Cross Sectional Study." Presented at the Human Ecology Section of 1980 Meetings of the American Sociological Association, New York.

La Greca, Anthony J., Ronald L. Akers, and Jeffrey W. Dwyer. 1986. "Life Events and Alcohol Behavior Among Older Adults." Presented at the 39th Annual Scientific Meetings of the Gerontological Society of America.

Land, K. C., and M. Felson. 1976. "A General Framework for Building Dynamic Macro Social Indicator Models: Including an Analysis of Changes in Crime Rates and Police Expenditures." *American Journal of Sociology* 82, 3:565-604.

Landinsky, Jack. 1976. "The Traffic in Legal Services: Lawyer-Seeking Behavior and the Channelling of Clients." *Law and Society Review* 11:207-23.

Langbein, John H. 1979. "Understanding the Short History of Plea Bargaining." *Law and Society Review* 13:261-72.

Lanza-Kaduce, Lonn, Ronald L. Akers, Marvin D. Krohn, and Marcia J. Radosevich. 1984. "Cessation of Alcohol and Drug Use Among Adolescents: A Social Learning Model." *Deviant Behavior* 5:79-96.

Lauer, R. M., R. L. Akers, J. Massey, and W. Clarke. 1982. "The Evaluation of Cigarette Smoking Among Adolescents: The Muscatine Study." *Preventive Medicine* 11:417-28.

Leonard, Wilbert M. 1977. "Sociological and Social-Psychological Correlates of Anomia Among a Random Sample of Aged." *Journal of Gerontology* 32:303-10.

Levine, James P., Michael Musheno, and Dennis Palumbo. 1986. *Criminal Justice in America: Law in Action*. New York: John Wiley and Sons.

Lewin, K. 1951. *Field Theory in Social Science.* New York: Harper & Row.

Linden, Rick. 1978. "Myths of Middle-Class Delinquency: A Test of the Generalizability of Social Control Theory." *Youth and Society* 9:407-32.

Lindquist, J., O. White, and C. Chambers. 1986. "Judicial Disposition of Elderly Misdemeanor and Felony Defendants: Bexar County, Texas, 1973-1985."

Unpublished manuscript, San Antonio, TX: Trinity University.

Liska, A. E. 1971. "Aspirations, Expectations, and Delinquency: Stress and Additive Models." *Sociological Quarterly* 12:99-107.

Liska, Allen E., and Mark D. Reed. 1985. "Ties to Conventional Institutions and Delinquency: Estimating Reciprocal Effects." *American Sociological Review* 50:547-60.

Lochner, Philip R., Jr. 1975. "The No Fee and Low Fee Legal Practice of Private Attorneys." *Law and Society Review* 9:431-73.

Long, Judy. 1982. "Serious Crime by the Elderly Is on the Rise." *Wall Street Journal,* June 21, pp. 10, 19.

Long, Sharon, and Ann D. Witte. 1981. "Current Economic Trends: Implications for Crime and Criminal Justice." In *Crime and Criminal Justice in a Declining Economy*, edited by Kevin N. Wright, pp. 69-143. Cambridge: Oelgeschlager, Gunn and Hain.

Lopata, Helen Z. 1984. "Social Construction of Social Problems Over Time." *Social Problems* 31:249-72.

Luckenbill, David F. 1977. "Criminal Homicide as a Situated Transaction." *Social Problems* 25:176-86.

Malinchak, A. 1980. *Crime and Gerontology*. NJ: Prentice-Hall.

Markham, G. R. 1981. "A Community Service for the Elderly." *The Police Journal* 54:325-28.

Mather, L. M. 1979. *Plea Bargaining or Trial? The Process of Criminal Case Disposition*. Lexington, MA: Lexington Books.

Maynard, D. W. 1982. "Defendant Attributes in Plea Bargaining: Notes on the Modeling of Sentencing Decision." *Social Problems* 29:347-60.

McAlister, Alfred, Jon A. Krosnick, and Michael A. Milburn. 1984. "Causes of Adolescent Cigarette Smoking: Tests of a Structural Equation Model." *Social Psychology Quarterly* 47:24-36.

McCain, G., V. Cox, and P. Paulus. 1980. *The Effects of Prison Crowding on Inmate Behavior.* Washington, D.C.: U.S. Department of Justice.

McCarthy, B., and R. Langworthy. 1987. "Older Offenders on Probation and Parole." *Journal of Offender Counseling, Services and Rehabilitation* 11, 3:forthcoming.

McCarthy, Maureen. 1983. "The Health Status of Elderly Inmates." *Corrections Today* 45:64-65, 74.

McCreary, C., and I. Mensh. 1977. "Personality Differences Associated with Age in Law Offenders." *Journal of Gerontology* 32:164-67.

McDonald, William F. 1985. *Plea Bargaining: Critical Issues and Common Practices.* Washington, D.C.: U.S. Department of Justice, National Institute of Justice.

McPheters, Lee R., and William B. Stronge. 1974. "Law Enforcement Expenditures and Urban Crime." *National Tax Journal* 27:633-44.

Meeker, James W. 1984. "Criminal Appeals Over the Last 100 Years: Are the Odds of Winning Increasing?" *Criminology* 22:551-71.

Meier, D. L., and W. Bell. 1959. "Anomia and Differential Access to the Achievement of Life Goals." *American Sociological Review* 24:189-202.

Merton, Robert K. 1938. "Social Structure and Anomie." *American Sociological Review* 3:672-82.

Messner, Steven F., and Kenneth Tardiff. 1985. "The Social Ecology of Urban Homicide: An Application of the 'Routine Activities' Approach." *Criminology* 23, 2:241-67.

Meyers, Allan R. 1984. "Drinking, Problem Drinking, and Alcohol-Related Crime Among Older People." In *Elderly Criminals,* edited by Evelyn S. Newman, Donald J. Newman, and Mindy Gewirtz, pp. 51-65. Cambridge: Oelgeschlager, Gunn and Hain.

Meyers, A. R., E. Goldman, R. Hingson, N. Scotch, and T. Mangione. 1981-82. "Evidence for Cohort or Generational Differences in the Drinking Behavior of Older Adults." *International Journal of Aging and Human Development* 14:37-44.

Meyers, A. R., R. Hingson, M. Mucatel, and E. Goldman. 1982. "Social and Psychological Correlates of Problem Drinking in Old Age." *Journal of the American Geriatrics Society* 30:452-56.

Miller, Herbert S., James A. Cramer, and William F. McDonald. 1978. *Plea Bargaining in the United States: Phase I Report.* Washington, D.C.: U.S. Government Printing Office.

Miller, Marv. 1979. *Suicide After Sixty: The Final Alternative.* New York: Springer.

Minor, W. William. 1977. "A Deterrence-Control Theory of Crime." In *Theory in Criminology: Contemporary Views,* edited by Robert F. Meier, pp. 117-37. Beverly Hills: Sage Publications.

Moberg, D. 1953. "Old Age and Crime." *Journal of Criminal Law Criminology and Police Science* 43:773-75.

Morton, Joan. 1976. "Women Offenders: Fictions and Facts." *American Journal of Corrections* 38:36-37.

Morton, Joan, and Judy Anderson. 1982. "Elderly Offenders: The Forgotten Minority." *Corrections Today* 44:14-16, 20.

Myers, M. A., and J. Hagan. 1979. "Private and Public Trouble: Prosecutors and the Allocation of Court Resources." *Social Problems* 26:439-51.

Nagel, S. S. 1982. "Discretion in the Criminal Justice System: Analyzing Channeling, Reducing, and Controlling It." *Emory Law Review* 31:603-33.

Newman, Donald J. 1956. "Pleading Guilty for Considerations: A Study of Bargain Justice." *Journal of Criminal Law, Criminology, and Police Science* 46:780-90.

Newman, Donald J., and Evelyn S. Newman. 1982. "Senior Citizen Crime." *Justice Reporter* 2:5-10.

Newman, Evelyn, Donald Newman, and Mindy Gewirtz. 1984. *Elderly Criminals.* Cambridge: Oelgeschlager, Gunn and Hain.

Nye, F. Ivan. 1958. *Family Relationships and Delinquent Behavior.* New York: John Wiley and Sons.

Pandiani, John A. 1978. "Crime Time TV: If All We Knew Is What We Saw." *Contemporary Crisis* 2:437-58.

Panton, J. 1976-1977. "Personality Characteristics of Aged Inmates Within a State Prison Population." *Offender Rehabilitation* 1:203-8.

Parisi, N. 1982. "The Prisoner's Pressures and Responses." In *Coping with Imprisonment,* edited by N. Parisi, pp. 9-26. Beverly Hills: Sage Publications.

Parker, Robert Nash, and M. Dwayne Smith. 1979. "Deterrence, Poverty, and Type of Homicide." *American Journal of Sociology* 35, 3:614-24.

Perkinson, M. 1980. "Alternative Roles for the Elderly: An Example From a Midwestern Retirement Community." *Human Organization* 39:219-26.

Peterson, R. D., and J. Hagan. 1984. "Changing Conceptions of Race: Toward an Account of Anomalous Findings in Sentencing Research." *American Sociological Review* 46:56-70.

Phillips, Lorne, A. 1976. "An Application of Anomy Theory to the Study of Alcoholism." *Journal of Studies on Alcohol* 37:78-84.

Phillips, L., H. L. Votey, Jr., and D. Maxwell. 1972. "Crime, Youth and the Labor Market." *Journal of Political Economy* 80:491-504.

Pollak, O. 1941. "The Criminality of Old Age." *Psychiatry Digest.* 3:213.

Poole, Eric, and Robert Regoli. 1979. "Parental Support, Delinquent Friends, and Delinquency: A Test of Interaction Effects." *Journal of Criminal Law and Criminology* 70:188-98.

Pope, Hallowell, and Miller D. Ferguson. 1982-83. "Age and Anomia in Middle and Later Life: A Multivariate Analysis of a National Sample of White Men." *International Journal of Aging and Human Development* 15:51-74.

President's Commission on Law Enforcement and Administration of Justice. 1967. *Task Force Report: Science and Technology.* Washington, D.C.: U.S. Government Printing Office, pp. 55-64.

Radosevich, Marcia J., Lonn Lanza-Kaduce, Ronald L. Akers, and Marvin D. Krohn. 1980. "The Sociology of Adolescent Drug and Drinking Behavior: A Review of the State of the Field: Part II." *Deviant Behavior* 1:145-69.

Rains, Prue. 1984. "Juvenile Justice and the Boys' Farm: Surviving a Court-Created Population Crisis, 1909-1948." *Social Problems* 31:500-13.

Raskin-White, Helene, Valerie Johnson, and Allan Horwitz. 1982. "An Application of Three Deviance Theories to Adolescent Substance Use." Paper presented at the Society for the Study of Social Problems, San Francisco, CA, September 4.

Reckless, Walter C. 1967. *The Crime Problem.* 4th ed. New York: Appleton-Century-Crofts.

Reed, Monika, and Francis Glamser. 1979. "Aging in a Total Institution: The Case of Older Prisoners." *The Gerontologist* 19:354-60.

Reiss, Albert J., Jr. 1951. "Delinquency as the Failure of Personal and Social Controls." *American Sociological Review* 16:196-207.

______. 1971. *The Police and the Public.* New Haven, CT: Yale University Press.

Rhodes, W. M. 1978. *Plea Bargaining: Who Gains? Who Loses?* Washington, D.C.: Institute for Law and Social Research.

______. 1979. "Plea Bargaining: Its Effect on Sentencing and Convictions in the District of Columbia." *Journal of Criminal Law and Criminology* 70:360-75.

Roberg, R., and V. Webb. 1981. *Critical Issues in Corrections.* St. Paul, MN: West Publishing.

Rodstein, Manual. 1975. "Crime and the Aged." *Journal of the American Medical Association* 234:639.

Rosenthal, Douglas. 1974. *Lawyer and Client: Who's In Charge?* New York: Russell Sage.

Rosow, I. 1974. *Socialization to Old Age.* Berkeley: University of California Press.

Rowe, Alan R., and Charles R. Tittle. 1977. "Life Cycle Changes and Criminal Propensity." *The Sociological Quarterly* 18:223-36.

Rubenstein, D. 1984. "The Elderly in Prison: A Review of the Literature." In *Elderly Criminals,* edited by E. Newman, D. Newman, and M. Gewirtz, pp. 153-68. Cambridge: Oelgeschlager, Gunn and Hain.

Rubenstein, Michael, and Theresa White. 1979. "Alaska's Ban on Plea Bargaining." *Law and Society Review* 13:367-83.

Ryan, John P., Marcia Lipetz, Mary Luskin, and David Neubauer. 1981. "Analyzing Court Delay-Reduction Programs: Why Do Some Succeed?" *Judicature* 65:58-75.

Ryan, John P., and James Alfini. 1978. "Trial Judges' Participation in Plea Bargaining: An Empirical Perspective." *Law and Society Review* 13:486-95.

Salzmann, D. 1963. "Delinquency in Later Years." *Medical Trial Technique Quarterly* 9:54.

Schmidt, Peter, and Ann D. Witte. 1984. *An Economic Analysis of Crime and Justice: Theory, Methods, and Applications.* New York: Academic Press.

Schroeder, P. L. 1936. "Criminal Behavior in the Latter Period of Life." *American Journal of Psychiatry* 92:915-24.

Seeman, M. 1959. "On the Meaning of Alienation." *American Sociological Review* 24:783-91.

Seeman, Melvin, and Carolyn Anderson. 1983. "Alienation and Alcohol." *American Sociological Review* 48:60-77.

Sheley, Joseph F., and Cindy D. Ashkins. 1981. "Crime, Crime News, and Crime Views." *Public Opinion Quarterly* 45:492-506.

Sherman, L. 1980. "Causes of Police Behavior: The Current State of Quantitative Research." *Journal of Research in Crime and Delinquency* 17:69-100.

Shichor, David. 1984a. "The Extent and the Nature of Lawbreaking by the Elderly: A Review of Arrest Statistics." In *Elderly Criminals,* edited by E. Newman, D. Newman, and M. Gewirtz, pp. 17-32. Cambridge: Oelgeschlager, Gunn and Hain.

______. 1984b. "Patterns of Elderly Lawbreaking in Urban, Suburban and Rural Areas: What Do Arrest Statistics Tell Us?" In *Elderly Criminals,* edited by W. Wilbanks and P. K. H. Kim, pp. 53-63. New York: University Press of America.

Shichor, David. 1985. "Male-Female Differences in Elderly Arrests: An Exploratory Analysis." *Justice Quarterly* 2:399-414.

Shichor, David, and Solomon Kobrin. 1978. "Note: Criminal Behavior Among the Elderly." *The Gerontologist* 18:213-18.

Short, James F. 1964. "Gang Delinquency and Anomie." In *Anomie and Deviant Behavior,* edited by M. D. Clinard, pp. 98-127. New York: Free Press.

Short, James F., and Roman Riveria. 1965. "Perceived Opportunities, Gang Membership, and Delinquency." *American Sociological Review* 30:56-67.

Silfen, Peter. 1977. "The Adaptation of the Older Prisoner in Israel." *International Journal of Offender Therapy and Comparative Criminology* 21:57-65.

Simmons, Ronald L., Martin G. Miller, and Stephen M. Aigner. 1980. "Contemporary Theories of Deviance and Female Delinquency: An Empirical Test." *Journal of Research in Crime and Delinquency* 17:42-57.

Simon, A., and L. Epstein. 1968. "The Elderly Offender." *Gerontologist* 8:23.

Simon, Carl P., and Ann D. Witte. 1979. "The Underground Economy: Estimates of Size, Structure and Trends." Prepared for the Special Study on Economic Change conducted by the Joint Committee of the U.S. Congress.

Smith, D. 1986. "The Neighborhood Context of Police Behavior." In *Communities and Crime*, edited by A. Reiss, Jr., and M. Torry, pp. 313-41. Chicago: University of Chicago Press.

Smith, D., and C. Visher. 1981. "Street Level Justice: Situational Determinants of Police Arrest Decisions." *Social Problems* 29:167-77.

Spector, Malcolm, and John Kitsuse. 1977. *Constructing Social Problems*. Menlo Park: Cummings.

Spohn, C., J. Gruhl, and S. Welch. 1981. "The Effect of Race on Sentencing: A Re-Examination of an Unsettled Question." *Law and Society Review* 16:71-88.

Srole, L. 1956. "Social Integration and Certain Corollaries: An Exploratory Study." *American Sociological Review* 21:709-16.

Stack, Steven. 1982. "Suicide: A Decade Review of the Sociological Literature." *Deviant Behavior* 4:41-66.

Stitt, B. Grant, and Sheldon Siegel. 1986. "The Ethics of Plea Bargaining." Paper presented at the Annual Meeting of the Academy of Criminal Justice Sciences, Orlando, FL.

Straus, A., and R. Sherwin. 1975. "Inmate Rioters and Nonrioters: A Comparative Analysis." *American Journal of Corrections* 37:34-35.

Sunderland, George. 1982. "Geriatric Crime Wave: The Great Debate." *The Police Chief* 49:40, 42, 44.

Sutherland, E. H. 1947. *Principles of Criminology*. 4th ed. Philadelphia: J. B. Lippincott.

Sutton, L. P. 1978a. *Variations in Federal Criminal Sentences: A Statistical Analysis at the National Level.* Albany, NY: Criminal Justice Research Center.

______. 1978b. *Federal Sentencing Patterns: A Study of Geographical Variations.* Albany, NY: Criminal Justice Research Center.

Swimmer, Eugene. 1974a. "Measurement of the Effectiveness of Urban Law Enforcement—A Simultaneous Approach." *Southern Economic Journal* 40, 4:618-30.

______. 1974b. "The Relationship of Police and Crime: Some Methodological and Empirical Results." *Criminology* 12, 3:293-314.

Sykes, R., J. Fox, and J. Clark. 1976. "A Socio-Legal Theory of Police Discretion." In *The Ambivalent Force: Perspectives on the Police*, 2nd ed., edited by A. Niederhoffer and A. Blumberg, pp. 171-83. Hinsville, IL: Dryden Press.

Szasz, Thomas. 1970. *The Manufacture of Madness*. New York: Delta.

Tardiff, K., and A. Sweillam. 1979. "The Relation of Age to Assaultive Behavior in Mental Patients." *Hospital and Community Psychiatry* 30:709-11.

Teller, G., and R. Howell. 1979. "Criminal and Psychological Characteristics of the Older Prisoner." Salt Lake City: Utah Division of Corrections.

Teller, F. E., and R. J. Howell. 1981. "The Older Prisoner: Criminal and Psychological Characteristics." *Criminology* 18:549-55.

Thomson, R., and M. Zingraff. 1981. "Detecting Sentence Disparity." *American Journal of Sociology* 86:869-80.

Tiffany, L., Y. Avichai, and G. Peters. 1975. "A Statistical Analysis of Sentencing in Federal Courts." *Journal of Legal Studies* 4:369-90.

Time. 1982. "Old Enough to Know Better." September 20, p. 77.

Toch, H. 1977a. *Living in Prison: The Ecology of Survival.* London: Collier Macmillan Publishers.

______. 1977b. *Living in Prison*. New York: The Free Press.

Uhlman, T., and D. Walker. 1979. "A Plea is No Bargain." *Social Science Quarterly* 60:218-34.

Unnever, J. D., C. E. Frazier, and J. C. Henretta. 1980. "Race Differences in Criminal Sentencing." *Sociological Quarterly* 21:197-206.

Ursprung, A. W., and P. Hayman. 1983. "Measurement of Adaptive Behavior in Prison Environments." *Rehabilitation Psychology* 28(4):217-29.

U.S. Bureau of the Census. 1966-1985. *Statistical Abstract of the United States.* Washington, D.C.: U.S. Government Printing Office.

U.S. Code Annotated. 1986. *Title 18, Federal Rules of Criminal Procedure*. St. Paul: West Publishing.

U.S. Department of Justice, FBI. 1986. *Age-Specific Arrest Rates and Race-Specific Arrest Rates for Selected Offenses: 1965-1984.* Uniform Crime Reporting Program, FBI (6/86). Washington, D.C.: U.S. Government Printing Office.

______. 1964-1984. *Uniform Crime Reports: 1964-1984.* Washington, D.C.: GPO.

U.S. Department of the Treasury, IRS. 1979. *Estimates of Income Unreported on Individual Income Tax Returns.* Washington, D.C.: U.S. Department of the Treasury, Publication 1104 (9-79).

U.S. News and World Report. 1982. "New Police Worry: Old Lawbreakers." March 29, p. 10.

Utz, P. J. 1978. *Settling the Facts: Discretion and Negotiation in Criminal Court.* Lexington: Lexington Books.

Uviller, Richard H. 1977. "Pleading Guilty: A Critique of Four Models." *Law and Contemporary Problems* 41:102-31.

Visher, C. 1983. "Gender, Police Arrest Decisions, and Notions of Chivalry." *Criminology* 21:5-28.

Weigand, Douglas, and Jane Burger. 1979. "The Elderly Offender and Parole." *The Prison Journal* 59:48-57.

Weis, Joseph. 1976. "Liberation and Crime: The Invention of the New Female Criminal." *Crime and Social Justice* 7:17-27.

Welch, Susan, John Gruhl, and Cassia Spohn. 1984. "Sentencing." *Criminology* 22:215-27.

Weller, D. C., M. K. Block, and F. C. Nold. 1978. "Unemployment and the Allocation of Time by Criminals." Technical report CERDCR-3-78, Center for Econometric Studies of Crime and the Criminal Justice System, Hoover Institution, Stanford University.

Wheatley, John. 1974. "Plea Bargaining—A Case for Its Continuance." *Massachusetts Law Quarterly* 59:31-40.

Wheeler, S., D. Weisburd, and N. Bode. 1982. "Sentencing the White Collar Offender: Rhetoric and Reality." *American Sociological Review* 47:641-59.

White House Conference on Aging. 1982. Vol. 2, Department of Health and Human Services. Washington, D.C.: U.S. Government Printing Office.

Whiskin, F. 1968. "Delinquency in the Aged." *Journal of Geriatric Psychiatry* 1:243.

Wiatrowski, Michael, David Griswold, and Mary Roberts. 1981. "Social Control Theory and Delinquency." *American Sociological Review* 46:525-41.

Wilbanks, W. 1984a. "The Elderly Offender: Placing the Problem in Perspective." *In Elderly Criminals*, edited by W. Wilbanks and P. K. H. Kim, pp. 1-15. New York: University Press of America.

______. 1984b. "The Elderly Offender: Sex and Race Variations in Frequency and Pattern." In *Elderly Criminals,* edited by W. Wilbanks and P. K. H. Kim, p. 41. New York: University Press of America.

Wilbanks, W. 1984-85. "The Elderly Offender: Relative Frequency and Pattern of Offenses." *International Journal of Aging and Human Development* 20(4):269-81.

Wilbanks, W. 1985. "Are Elderly Felons Treated More Leniently by the Criminal Justice System?" Paper presented at the Third National Conference on Elderly Offenders, Kansas City, MO, April 25-26.

Wilbanks, William, and Paul Kim. 1984. *Elderly Criminals*. New York; University Press of America.

Wilbanks, W., and D. D. Murphy. 1984. "The Elderly Homicide Offender." In *Elderly Criminals,* edited by E. Newman, D. Newman, and M. Gewirtz, pp. 79-91. Cambridge: Oelgeschlager, Gunn and Hain.

Williams, T. A., G. Calhoun, and R. L. Ackoff. 1982. "Stress, Alcoholism, and Personality." *Human Relations* 35:491-510.

Wilsnack, R. W., A. A. Klassen, and S. C. Wilsnack. 1984. "Retrospective Analysis of Lifetime Changes in Women's Drinking Behavior." Presented at the International Society for Biomedical Research on Alcoholism and Research Society on Alcoholism, Santa Fe, NM.

Winslow, Robert. 1967. "Anomie and Its Alternatives: A Self-Reported Study of Delinquency." *Sociological Quarterly* 8:468-80.

Wooden, W., and J. Parker. 1980. "Age Adjustment and the Treatment Process of Criminal Behavior Strategies." Paper presented at the National Gerontological Society Meeting, San Diego, CA.

Woolgar, Steve, and Dorothy Pawluch. 1985. "Ontological Gerrymandering: The Anatomy of Social Problems Explanations." *Social Problems* 32:214-27.

Zatz, M. S. 1984. "Race, Ethnicity, and Determinate Sentencing." *Criminology* 22:147-71.

Zatz, M. S., and A. J. Lizotte. 1982. "Benign Neglect, Constitutional Cruising, and Normal Crimes: Racial and Ethnic Plea Bargaining." Paper presented at the American Sociological Association Meetings, San Francisco, CA.

Zeegers, M. 1966. "*Dementie Verbana met het Delict Ontucht.*" *Tijdschrift Voor Strafecht* 75:265.

Zellner, A. 1962. "An Efficient Method of Estimating Seemingly Unrelated Regressions and Tests for Aggregation Bias." *Journal of the American Statistical Association* 57:348-68.

Author Index

Subject Index

About the Contributors

RONALD L. AKERS, Ph.D., is professor of sociology and senior research associate of the Center for Studies in Criminology and Law. He is also affiliated with the Alcohol Research Center and the Center for Gerontological Studies. Professor Akers is a Fellow and former president of the American Society of Criminology. His scholarly work has been in crime, delinquency, alcohol and drug abuse, and law. He is author of *Deviant Behavior: A Social Learning Approach.*

DONALD J. BACHAND is associate professor of criminal justice at Saginaw Valley State College in University Center, Michigan. He received his Ph.D. in adult and continuing education from the University of Michigan at Ann Arbor. With ten years of law enforcement experience with the Detroit Police Department, he is currently engaged in professional consulting for area police departments in mid-Michigan and research on the elderly offender in the criminal justice system.

DEAN J. CHAMPION is professor of sociology at the University of Tennessee, Knoxville. He received his Ph.D. from Purdue University. He has authored *Basic Statistics for Social Research, Methods and Issues in Social Research, Sociology of Organizations, Sociology,* and numerous articles in his specialty areas. His current work, *Criminal Justice,* will be published in 1988.

GEORGE A. CHRESSANTHIS is an assistant professor and graduate faculty member of the Economics Department at Mississippi State University. He received his Ph.D. in economics from Purdue University. His writing and research efforts involve issues concerning public finance, applied microeconomics, microeconomic theory, the economics of crime and law enforcement, and mathematical economics and quantitative methods. Previous works have appeared in *Growth and Change, Economics of Education Review, Journal of Education Finance,* and the *Midsouth Journal of Economics & Finance.*

ERNEST L. COWLES received his doctorate in criminology from the School of Criminology at Florida State University. He is presently the director of the Division of Classification and Treatment for the Missouri Department of Corrections and Human Resources. His current research interests include long-term incarceration, prisoner adaptation strategies, and offender classification.

GARY FEINBERG, M.A., is assistant professor, sociology, St. Thomas University, Miami, Florida. His contributions to the field of elderly criminality include numerous empirical studies of elderly shoplifters, the behavior of elderly defendants, and sanctions imposed upon elderly criminal law violators. He has introduced the subject of crime by the elderly at the International Sociological Association meetings in San Jose, Costa Rica (1984) and at Aix-en-Provence, France (1985).

CRAIG J. FORSYTH is an assistant professor of sociology at the University of Southwestern Louisiana. His other research interests are the maritime industry, deviant life-styles, and the interrelationship between family and work. He has published in *Quantitative Sociology, Deviant Behavior, Free Inquiry in Creative Sociology, Work and Family, Maritime Policy and Management, The Journal of Ethnic Studies, Sociological Focus,* and *Sociological Forum.*

LINCOLN J. FRY received his Ph.D. in sociology and is presently on the faculty at Loma Linda University. Besides elderly offenders, his current research interests include prison overcrowding, the juvenile justice system, and Child Protective Services.

KENNETH E. GEWERTH is currently a staff associate in the Programs section of the American Judicature Society, where he is responsible for the review and analysis of a wide variety of policy issues in the criminal and civil justice systems. In addition, he is working on his doctoral dissertation, a study of prosecutorial decision making in cases involving elderly offenders.

ROBERT GRAMLING is an associate professor of sociology at the University of Southwestern Louisiana. His research interests lie in the areas of microscopic social theory, the family, and socioeconomic impacts, particularly of offshore oil and gas activities. He is co-editor of *Sociological Spectrum.*

ELMER H. JOHNSON, Ph.D. in sociology, University of Wisconsin (1950), is Distinguished Professor of SIUC, Center for the Study of Crime, Delinquency and Corrections, Southern Illinois University at Carbondale (1966 to date). Previously, he taught at North Carolina State University at Raleigh. While on academic leave, he served as Assistant Director of Prisons, North Carolina Department of Corrections (1958-60). Among his numerous publications in criminology are *Crime, Correction, and Society,* 4th ed. (1978), *International Handbook on Contemporary Developments in Criminology,* two volumes (1983), and *Handbook on Crime and Delinquency Prevention* (1987).

PETER C. KRATCOSKI is a professor of criminal justice studies and sociology at Kent State University and serves as the chairperson of the Department of Criminal Justice Studies. He received his Ph.D at Pennsylvania State University. He has taught at Pennsylvania State University and the College of St. Thomas. A co-author of several books, including *Criminal Justice: Process and Issues* and *Juvenile Delinquency,* he has also written numerous articles for journals specializing in criminal justice topics. He serves as the editor of the *Journal of Crime and Justice.* His current research interests center on violent crime among the elderly, child abuse, and international comparisons of policing.

ANTHONY J. LA GRECA, Ph.D., is associate professor of sociology at the University of Florida, Gainesville. He is also director of the Urban and Regional Research Center as well as the Institute for Community Studies. He is also an associate of the Alcohol Research Center and the Center for Gerontological Studies. His research interests include alcohol use/nonuse among older adults, stress and adaptation of older adults, retirement communities, and urban housing.

ROBERT LANGWORTHY is an assistant professor at the University of Cincinnati. He has published in the areas of police organization, police use of deadly force, police cynicism, and attitudes toward punishment. His articles have appeared in *Justice Quarterly, Criminology, Journal of Criminal Justice, American Journal of Police, Journal of Quantitative*

Criminology, and he is the author of *The Structure of Police Organizations.* Dr. Langworthy holds a Ph.D. in criminal justice from the School of Criminal Justice at the State University of New York at Albany.

BELINDA McCARTHY is associate professor of criminal justice and associate dean of the School of Social and Behavioral Sciences, University of Alabama at Birmingham. She received her Ph.D. from the State University of New York at Albany. Her research interests include sentencing, corrections, and juvenile justice; her most recent publication is *Intermediate Punishments: Intensive Supervision, Home Confinement and Electronic Surveillance.*

MICHAEL J. SABATH received his Ph.D. degree from the Graduate School of Public and International Affairs at the University of Pittsburgh. He is currently managing a National Institute of Justice grant for the Missouri Department of Corrections and Human Resources that focuses on ways of managing long-term inmates. Prior to this, he was an assistant professor of public administration at the University of Missouri-Columbia.

CHRISTINE SELLERS is an assistant professor of criminal justice at Louisiana State University. Her main areas of research center on testing theories of deviance, drug and alcohol behavior, and elderly offenders.

DONALD B. WALKER is an assistant professor in the Department of Criminal Justice Studies at Kent State University. He received his Ph.D. from Wayne State University and previously taught at the University of Michigan, Flint Campus. A co-author of *Criminal Justice: Process and Issues,* he has also contributed articles in *Police Studies, Journal of Crime and Justice, American Journal of Police,* and the *Criminal Justice Review.* His current research interests include violent crime, particularly juvenile and elderly homicide offenders as well as a study of Canadian police officers under a grant from the Canadian government.